Becoming imaginal

BECOMING
IMAGINAL

Seeing and Creating
the Future of Education

by

THOMAS R. RUDMIK

Geenius Publisher Inc.
Calgary

Thomas R. Rudmik is a visionary, author, educator, international speaker, and entrepreneur. He is the Founder of Master's Academy and College, an award-winning K-12 school in Calgary, Canada, and the Profound Learning Institute, which has developed an ecosystem of solutions for transforming education. He has created an innovative and powerful organizational transformation model on how to become an *Imaginal* Organization, and has additionally facilitated other organizations that are confronting issues of obsolescence and the need for transformation. Thomas is the creator and facilitator of the *Imaginal* Transformation workshop, which takes leaders through a process of Discovering, Defining, and Designing their future.

Geenius Publisher 4414 Crowchild Trail SW, Calgary, Alberta, T2T 5J4.

First Edition
Printed in the United States of America

ISBN: 978-1-881189-76-3
Library of Congress Cataloging-in-Publication Data
Rudmik, Tom,
        Becoming Imaginal: Seeing and Creating the Future of Education/
Tom Rudmik

Website:
www.becomingimaginal.com

Road Less Traveled by

The Road Not Taken

Two roads diverged in a yellow wood,
And sorry I could not travel both
And be one traveler, long I stood
And looked down one as far as I could
To where it bent in the undergrowth;

Then took the other, as just as fair,
And having perhaps the better claim,
Because it was grassy and wanted wear;
Though as for that the passing there
Had worn them really about the same,

And both that morning equally lay
In leaves no step had trodden black.
Oh, I kept the first for another day!
Yet knowing how way leads on to way,
I doubted if I should ever come back.

I shall be telling this with a sigh
Somewhere ages and ages hence:
Two roads diverged in a wood, and I—
I took the one less traveled by,
And that has made all the difference.

- Robert Frost

Table of Contents

Preface

"Dream big dreams son, nothing is impossible to them that believe."

These words of my father were indelibly printed into my very being as a young boy. Although he was a simple man, with only a high school education, he had learned a secret: *if you can see the invisible you can do the impossible.* Little did I know as a child that this secret would be transferred by him to me in such a profound way as it has.

The journey of Profound Learning over the past twenty years has been characterized by a pursuit of a vision—of a big dream. During the early years of our journey we chose the road less travelled—exploring areas such as innovation and creativity that at the time were on the fringe or non-existent for most educational initiatives. It was this exploration off the beaten path that led to some of the most important discoveries that today are at the core of our Profound Learning Model. Many reform initiatives are calling for a new system of education that prepares students to be more innovative and creative. Speakers are paid thousands of dollars to deliver this message, but few have actually created a system that can deliver these important capacities. We are seeing and creating such a system.

This book lays out philosophically, strategically, and tactically our vision for how the system of education can be transformed. It all begins with a narrative of how a visionary life was transferred to me by my father, and a series of snap-shots of how it has unfolded throughout my adult life.

My story

My father lived in Estonia, a small country just south of Finland. At the age of 16, he was conscripted by the Germans during World War II as the country was held under German occupation. He had survived five years of some of the worst conditions imaginable fighting on the Russian front. Only twelve in his unit of close to a thousand men survived.

It was Christmas Eve during the war in 1944 when my father, while on leave in Prague, met a lovely Estonian young lady, named Endla

Turk, at a party. That evening my father proposed to her; and needless to say she was taken aback by the offer of marriage from a man she had just met. He said he needed someone to send his officer's pay to, and, more importantly, a reason to endure the hardship of war. He asked her to give him an answer by the next morning, since he was going back to the front. The next morning Endla said yes and my father headed back to battle.

When the war ended everything was in disarray. My father was in Denmark, and he had no idea of the whereabouts of the young lady he had proposed to almost a year prior. He distributed a picture of Endla to his friends, who helped find his fiancee. It did not take long for one of his friends to find her in a refugee camp in Germany, and shortly thereafter they were united and married. As a wedding gift they received a pound of butter, which they traded for a bed sheet. My oldest brother, Andy, was born in the refugee camp, and it was quite a miracle that he survived given that our mother at the time was very ill.

Eventually, my father, mother, and their young son made their way to England where they worked on a farm for about three years while saving money to immigrate to Canada.

Starting a new life in Canada, my father was about to have an experience that would establish the Big WHY of his and Endla's life.

My father was a visionary, a history-maker, a man who influenced an entire nation. After WWII, Estonia became a part of the Soviet Union, which created some of the darkest years in this little country's history.

Shortly after arriving in Canada, my father, in response to a deep sense of calling to help his people, began a radio broadcast that was beamed back to Estonia. For thirty-five years, the Estonian people were able to tune-in to his short-wave radio broadcast twice a week to listen to a message of faith and hope. Countless thousands of people have testified to the life-giving power that these radio broadcasts brought them. At his funeral, my father was given the Medal of Honor from the president of Estonia in recognition of the impact he had made on his country.

How does a simple penniless man turn out to be such a giant of hope to a nation in the throes of despair? *He was able to see opportunities where others only saw dead-ends; he had an unprecedented determination, perseverance and steadfastness, because at the center of his being was an unquenchable passion that was ignited by a vision.*

This was my father's gift to me. No I did not inherit a multi-million dollar fortune, or a successful business—I inherited something of much greater value: faith that dreams do come true, that nothing is impossible to them that believe, and that there is a universe of unlimited possibilities waiting for us to enter.

Finding my Big WHY

At the age of twenty-one, I married my beautiful wife Silvia. Right from the beginning of our marriage we both knew that we were not to live ordinary mundane lives, but rather there was a destiny for the two of us, and it was only a matter of time when it would be revealed.

I began my teaching career in the late 1970s at the ripe-old age of twenty-three—a young, energetic idealist. It did not take long for me to see that the system of education was broken. After eight years of teaching in the public school sector, I decided to try private education thinking that the grass is greener on the other side of the fence. Private education has many advantages; however, I came to the same conclusion that as a system it was broken as well. Both systems were based on a factory model of education, and even though one system outperformed the other, I realized that something new needed to be created, but I had no idea of what it would be. All I had was a deep desire for something better.

It was in the early 1990's that my dissatisfaction with the system of education began to reach a boiling point. "Surely, there has to be something better out there somewhere," I thought. I began to research various education reform movements, attended Dr. Daggett's first model school conference, and connected with anyone who was looking to affect change. It was at Daggett's conference where I met David P. Langford for the first time, not realizing that this connection would forge a life-long relationship and friendship that would be instrumental in the formation of the Profound Learning model.

And then it happened: that epiphany moment, that encounter that changes your life forever—it was my 'burning bush' moment. My mind was being flooded with all kinds of possibilities of what could be, and at that moment a dream was given birth: to transform education, to build a prototype school for learning in the 21st century that would impact schools around the world. Immediately, I began to think, "Who am I? I don't have the power or ability to do all this. This is impossible." The voice of limitation, the voice of reason, the voice from the universe of measurement was shouting at me, *"Don't be a fool—you can't do this!"*

Then I heard my father's voice: "Son, dream big dreams, nothing is impossible to them that believe." I heard the voice from the universe of unlimited possibilities calling me to journey into the unknown. This voice wasn't shouting at me, rather it was gently wooing me, calling me to come—that my life will never be the same again.

In 1995, we moved as a family to Calgary, Alberta, and two years later launched Master's Academy and College: a K-12 research and development school; a field of dreams. Master's was founded on a vision to produce Profound Learning: a breakthrough 21st century learner-centric model elevating achievement for all students to heights not attainable in the traditional industrial age; a model whose signature is innovation and creativity.

Sir Isaac Newton once wrote to a colleague that we all stand on the shoulders of giants. Likewise, back in the summer of 1996, I had the chance to attend Dr. Jeannette Vos's Learning Revolution Summer Institute. Her training program in Accelerating Learning principles was essential in helping us establish some of the foundational principles upon which we would build our Profound Learning model. The importance of setting the right conditions for learning, incorporating music, the need for various state changes, activating one's imagination, mind-mapping, and giving students choice are just a few of the many strategies we have implemented at Master's.

By this time many people probably thought that I had lost my mind. "Tom this is no small dream you have taken on, why don't you scale back the rhetoric until you have something to show? All this talk about revolutionizing education is going to come back to bite you. This is very risky. What if you fail? No one has done this before." My problem was that I had seen the invisible. I knew in my heart that we would achieve this dream, but I just wasn't quite aware of how challenging it really would be. Over time the dream matured into a vision, which became actionable. Today, Master's Academy and College is an award-winning, internationally acclaimed school. Master's has become a prototype model for Profound Learning.

As I was advancing my vision for breakthroughs in learning, it was apparent that certain solutions needed to be invented and developed that did not exist. The development of these solutions was generally out of the norm for schools, so I had to consider an alternate route. There were no options other than to create these solutions ourselves.

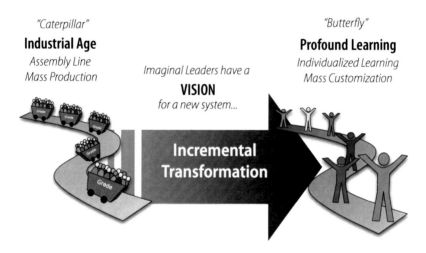

Figure P.1 - Vision for Profound Learning

In the year 2000, as *Imaginal* leaders ourselves, my brother Andy and I began working together in pursuit of developing breakthrough learning software. Andy is a visionary engineer with a PhD in computer science, and I was a passionate crusader for transforming education. And so we began our journey to make our "dent in the universe". I wish our dad could see us today!

In 2003, we obtained a US patent on our adaptive knowledge transfer technology that has been independently proven to boost learning effectiveness, as measured by retained knowledge, up to 800%. What this means is that we had developed a system through which one would be able to retain 90% of everything one learns. But there was more to come: if we were to break free from the traditional industrial age model of education, then we needed to design and develop a completely new way of delivering and managing learning.

Today, a whole ecosystem of solutions has been developed that empowers and supports schools, districts, and states to go through real transformation. This learning ecosystem uses the latest neurological and genetic research, combined with new emerging web and computer technologies. Essentially we invented a core structure that enables the shift from the factory model of education to a model that is personalized for every student. Teachers are able to design powerful brain compatible learning adventures that are delivered using the Profound Learning Orchestration System (PLOS). Students are able to track their own learning through self-reflection. Embedded in each learning experience are Future Ready skills (those relevant to the 21st Century) through which students can track their personal development in who they are uniquely becoming.

Master's Academy and College's vision has grown over the years to include the sharing of Profound Learning to schools around the world. The Big WHY driving the development of Profound Learning was now calling us to make a difference around the world. This was a much more challenging vision. To create a single Future Ready 21st century prototype school was quite challenging in itself, but to envision thousands of schools for Profound Learning around the world was an entirely different matter. I will share more on this in Appendix A.

Today, Profound Learning is not only a reality, but also being taken to countries around the world as we fulfill the vision that has been placed in our hearts. It is only a matter of time before Profound Learning will become a common household term.

Download

During my life I have experienced a number of epiphanies; those inexplicable moments when something is deposited into your spirit that ignites a passion and a vision. Most of these moments have led to the unfolding of events that have proven to be significant. One such moment occurred in June 1999. I was flying from London to Nairobi to conduct an educational symposium in the country of Uganda. It was two o'clock in the morning, and the airplane was quiet as most people were sleeping. Suddenly, I was awakened with a steady stream of ideas as if someone had pressed the download button for a large file over the internet. I grabbed a notepad and pen, and began writing and illustrating the four capacities of an *Imaginal* leader, which I called at that time the iCubed (I^3) Model.

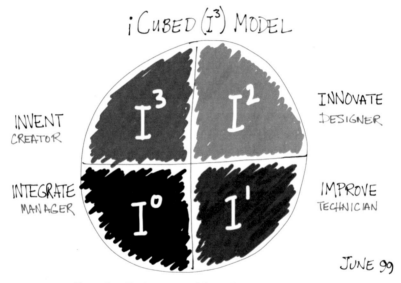

Figure P.2 - The Inception of the iCubed Model- June 1999

The most common capacity is I^0, which is the capacity to INTEGRATE —when we take on the role of a manager or system integrator. In mathematics any number to the power of 0 is equal to 1. Also any number multiplied by 1 remains unchanged. The manager identity is defined by researching what is already known, as well as finding best practices. This manager role maintains the status quo, keeps things in balance, and helps ensure that things run smoothly. As an Integrator identity, managing the system needs to be performed well, but not to the exclusion of experiencing and developing the other three capacities.

I^1 is the capacity to IMPROVE, and is represented by the role of the engineer and technician. This is when we take on the role of improving our situation or the system we are a part of. Improvement is always a good thing, but seldom leads to profound change or breakthroughs.

The top two quadrants are where life begins to get interesting and exciting. I^2 is the capacity to INNOVATE; the ability to push the boundaries of your life and organization, or "the box" as some people like to call it. The capacity to innovate is truly an earmark of some of the more successful companies, such as Apple, and the reason why, for instance, it was able to stage a remarkable comeback after near certain death in the late 1990s.

Finally, the fourth capacity is the rarest of all: I^3 is the capacity to IN-VENT—to be a visionary and entrepreneur. The visionary is someone who is willing to risk, go where no one has gone before, and explore the boundaries of what is possible.

These two capacities—to innovate and invent—introduce one to the role of being a creator, designer, futurist, and entrepreneur; one who can see the future and bring it into the HERE through the creation process.

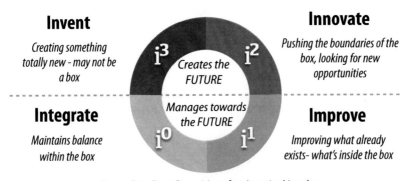

Figure P.3 - Four Capacities of an Imaginal Leader

Most people have never been trained to function effectively in the innovation and invention capacities, in spite of the fact that they are inherent in all of us. Consequently, these capacities have atrophied. In fact, the ability to imagine and to create is thwarted very early on in a person's life as he or she is consistently and increasingly exposed over many years to the Industrial Age system of education, which demands conformity, compliance, and having the 'correct' answer. The current system of education produces good managers—those who fit the system and manage towards the future through goal setting, and other such linear processes. People living in these two quadrants—namely management and improvement—experience the future by default, and are taught to cope as best as they can.

The upper two quadrants of the iCubed model represent the ability to see and create the future. Those who dwell in these two quadrants have learned how to rise above their current reality and create the future they want. The truth is, that while a manager operates solely in the bottom two quadrants, the *Imaginal* leader can function in all four iCubed capacities with a high level of proficiency. They know when a process or system needs to be managed, improved, or created either through innovation or invention. This makes an *Imaginal* leader truly future ready.

Stuck Patterns of Thinking and Behavior

In June 1999, on my way to Uganda to conduct an education symposium with educators and politicians, I was pondering how I would as a Canadian born educator be able to relate to the unique conditions in a culture vastly different than my own.

Uganda, at that time, was emerging from its tumultuous past with a brutal dictator. There was so much hurt, so much distrust, so much poverty, and yet so much opportunity. Wherever we traveled I was struck by the beauty and richness of the land. I watched children in their colorful uniforms walking to school, often barefoot. And as they laughed and played they seemed no different than children in North America. Yet when I looked into the faces of adults I saw something different: there was a worn, tired look—subsistence living was definitely taking its toll. Why in the midst of such richness of opportunity could poverty exist? For many people, meeting the daily needs of food and shelter was their all-consuming purpose. These were purpose-driven people with the main goal of survival. Yet there were some who had been able to break out of the trap of subsistence living, and were thriving with all of the new opportunities they were seeing around them on a daily basis. Why was it that some would thrive while others were seemingly trapped by their circumstances?

While conducting a leadership seminar in the town of Soroti, Uganda, I came across a scene that both fascinated and astounded me. There were eight men sitting under the shade of a very large tree, each with a bag of charcoal tied to the backs of their bicycles. Their mission for the day was to sell their one bag of charcoal to anyone who would pass by. Charcoal was an essential source of energy used to cook food, so the prospect of making a sale was very good. What I found interesting was why it took eight men to sell eight bags of charcoal. Why not have one person sell the eight bags while the other seven do something more productive? The potential to leverage time and effort seemed obvious to me. But why didn't the men see what I saw? I was an outside observer clearly ignorant of the cultural patterns of thinking that would explain this kind of behavior in the minds of these men.

Figure P.4 - Uganda, why do this?

And then it hit me: we in North America do much the same thing, only the context is different, namely, for one thing, our standard of living is much higher. Instead of sitting under a tree, we sit in offices enslaved to unfulfilling jobs; instead of bicycles, we drive comfortable cars; and instead of selling a bag of charcoal, we transact our lives for a wage that seems merely fair to us. Are we not doing much of the same thing as those eight men sitting under the tree? Are we not prisoners of our own system of beliefs and assumptions that define meaningful work and life? Like the eight men, what are the opportunities for us that go unnoticed?

Principle of Transference

Education is one of the most powerful cultural structures that influences the future direction of society. How does this happen? It is called the Principle of Transference: the ability of leaders to transfer values, beliefs, and behaviors to other people.

Harriet Zuckerman, a sociologist from Columbia University, studied Nobel laureates in the United States.[1] She found that many of the students of these super elite Noble laureate scientists became Noble laureates themselves. For example, six students of Enrico Fermi, four students each of Ernest Lawrence and Niels Bohr, and seventeen students of John Thomson and Ernest Rutherford went on to win Nobel Prizes. These students clearly had the advantage of being mentored by the elite of the scientific world, which included better funded projects, and greater exposure to the larger scientific community. Zuckerman thinks that it is the socialization into the culture of elite scientists that was the main factor for why these students went on to attain the success they did. For instance, she shows that elite scientists helped their students choose the right problems to solve, as well as understand how to recognize elegant solutions.

There is a principle of life that like produces like, in other words, elephants produce elephants, lions produce lions and so on. People who have an orientation toward taking on immense and seemingly impossible challenges live their lives differently than most people. They have different priorities, a drive that comes from a different source, the ability to see differently, and a unique capacity to see the impossible become possible. And they are able to transfer or impart that same orientation to those who are closest to them.

A study by sociologist Richard Dugdale in 1874 showed the principle of transference at work not only with those who had experienced positive outcomes, but also those who had experienced negative ones. Max Juke was a famous criminal in the mid 1700s, and of his 540 descendants, 310 died as paupers, 150 were criminals, 7 were murderers, 100 were drunkards, and more than half of the women were prostitutes. His 540 descendants cost the state one and a quarter million dollars.

Conversely, an investigation was made of the descendants of Jonathan Edwards, a well known preacher from the same era as Max Juke. Of the 1,394 known descendants, 13 became college presidents, 65 college professors, 3 United States senators, 30 judges, 100 lawyers, 60 physicians, 75 army and navy officers, 100 preachers and missionaries, 60 authors of prominence, 80 public officials in various capacities, 295 college graduates, among whom were governors of states and ministers to foreign countries, not to mention one vice-president of the United States. Incidentally, his descendants did not cost the state a single penny.

In my own life, I have experienced and received the benefit of being raised in an environment where taking on challenges—and even seemingly impossible ones—was the norm. Not only did my parents teach me the principles of living by faith, with the fundamental belief that nothing is impossible, but they also lived it out. I did not sit at the feet of a great mentor/teacher, but I lived in an environment where the principles found in this book were being lived out and modeled daily. These underlying principles formed our family dynamic; and only years later have I been able to unpack these hidden secrets and make them explicit.

Education and Transference

What is the fundamental role of schools in our society? What basic orientation toward being successful is being transferred in our education system? For most people, schools are places in which one receives knowledge, and develops basic academic and thinking skills. Success is measured by academic test scores and the ability to conform to and comply with the system. It is no wonder that some of the more successful entrepreneurs of our time dropped out of school, such as Richard Branson, Steve Jobs, Bill Gates, Mark Zuckerberg, David Karp, Mike Hudack, Quentin Tarantino, Francois Pinault, George Foreman, James Cameron, and Tom Hanks, to name a few. In no way am I suggesting that these highly successful high school or college dropouts represent the norm for dropouts. Without question, the vast majority of dropouts do not attain the level of success of those I have mentioned. However, these nonconformist entrepreneurs and artists did not fit the system of education, hence had to drop out to follow their passion and vision. With this in mind, let's look at the other end of the spectrum, namely at those who excelled in the system.

In Chapter 9, I will present research from Karen Arnold (Associate Professor of the Educational Leadership and Higher Education Department at Boston College's Lynch School of Education) that shows that success in a test-oriented academic environment does not necessarily translate to success in life or the workplace.

It is my belief that the role of schools is to prepare students to pursue their own personal vision without limitation. However, preparing students with an orientation to become designers and creators of their future is as massive of a change as moving education from the assembly line mass-production approach to customized, personalized learning.

Our vision for Profound Learning goes beyond shifting the overall academic performance of students. It is also about preparing students for the world of massive change; it is who the students are becoming that matters most in life. To accomplish this vision, we must integrate Future Ready skills in such a way that they can be tracked and measured. The old adage that you only measure those things that are important, and you can only manage what you can measure, must be considered as we create the future model of education, especially since behavior is driven so strongly by these measurement structures of the system.

As mentioned previously, a principle of life is "like produces like"; therefore, we need *Imaginal* teachers, and, more importantly, to establish schools, cultures, and programs that will propagate this desired outcome. For years I have heard politicians and educational experts tell the public that we need schools to be more innovative and creative, and yet programs specifically designed to do this are by and large absent. How do we inculcate innovative and creative mindsets and skills without an intentional strategy to do so? This is a perfect example of the gap that exists between the rhetoric of politicians and reality. Our vision is to close that gap.

The main point of this book is that if we want our students to become *Imaginal* people—meaning that they can envision and create the future they want—then we need to have educators and a system that can transfer and develop this capacity to their students.

They need teachers who, like my father, can both live out and transfer their own most visionary life.

They need *Imaginal* leaders who can say to them, "Dream big dreams. Nothing is impossible to them that believe."

Acknowledgements

To my beloved wife, Silvia, whose undivided support, faith, and encouragement have given me the strength to pursue my dream.

To my four children, Luke, Ben, Bethany, and Karin: thank you for your love and belief in me. I love you all.

To my parents, who gave me the greatest gift any son can receive: the gift of faith that nothing is impossible to them that believe.

To my brother, Andy, who, along with his wife Norma, has demonstrated an unwavering commitment to a vision we share and love.

To Doreen Grey, without whom the realization of the dream for Profound Learning would not have been possible.

To my Master's community who has found its Big WHY, and responded to the call of developing Profound Learning and sharing it with the world.

To Jeff Graham, my editor and colleague, who helped me find my authentic swing for this book.

I stand on all of your shoulders and say thanks!

Introduction

"It is a clear consensus that the future now emerging will be extremely different from anything we have ever known in the past…. There is no prior period of change that remotely resembles what humanity is about to experience. We have gone through revolutionary periods of change before, but none as powerful or as pregnant with…peril and opportunity as the ones that are beginning to unfold".

- Al Gore

World of Massive Change

We are living in a world of "massive change," to borrow a term from Canadian designer Bruce Mau and his compelling exhibition of the same name. In such a world, the rate of change and complexity is surging exponentially and our ability to manage this phenomenon is becoming increasingly more difficult. Education is one of the most complex systems to change, and most, if not all, of the proposed reforms over the past number of decades have addressed only the symptoms of the system, but not the real problem. It is no wonder that there is so much discouragement and disillusionment that exists in the system. The woes of the system have been well documented—there is enough finger-pointing and blame to last a lifetime.

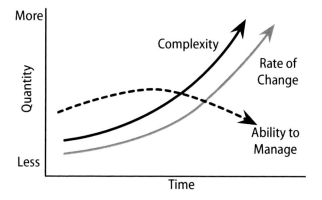

Figure I.1 - Our Ability to Handle Today's Complexity

Why So Many Failed Attempts?

Why have so many reform initiatives, such as No Child Left Behind, fallen short of transforming education? The focus on teacher performance or raising test scores, although on the surface sounds like a good thing to do, does not address the real problem with education. The current system is doing exactly what it was designed to do: produce workers for the industrial age who will conform, comply and meet industrial age standards. A question is, if we could elevate the test scores of all students, would that system prepare students for the world of *tomorrow* or the world of yesterday? No amount of improving an obsolete system will produce the changes we so desperately need. Invariably what happens is we end up in a blame game, with fingers pointed at teachers, unions, students, parents or politicians. It is time to stop the blame game. The *real* problem is about system *transformation*. Therefore, a bold vision for a *completely new* system of education is needed.

The Factory Model of Education

The existing assembly line approach to education exists because it was the only way we knew how to manage large groups of students back in the early 1900s. Students were put into classes, and the teacher taught to the middle of the class. Those who could learn quickly became bored or were classified as gifted, and those that required more time were labeled as slow learners and fell behind or dropped out of school. In this factory model of education the time to learn was *rigid*, meaning that all students were expected to learn at the same speed. In addition, the quality of learning was *flexible*, meaning that it was acceptable if only a small number of students excelled with their learning. This system has been the norm for so many decades that people actually believe that the learning performance output is due to the abilities of children. Years ago, Edwards Deming proclaimed that the variation of performance of the system is primarily caused by the system itself and not the people. We have proven, in hundreds of schools over the years, that by changing the system we can dramatically improve the performance of the system. Deming was right!

Deming's System of Profound Knowledge

Not recognizing that the system itself is the primary cause of the system performance, we try to improve the system by pushing the existing system harder. We do this by expanding the homework load, increasing the length of the school day or year, adding more standardized testing, hiring private corporations to run public schools, initiating a voucher system, paying teachers for performance, and implementing programs like "No Child Left Behind."

Deming taught that real change and transformation start with transformed individuals at all levels of the system. It is impossible to rely on past results for change. Real transformation can only be found by looking forward, and for this we need *Imaginal* leaders.

Instead of increasing the cost per student, we should be evaluating the *quality* per student. But here lies the fundamental conflict: the factory assembly line approach to education is such that *the time to learn* is rigid and the *quality of learning* is flexible. It has been this way for over 100 years, so educators have created their own interpretation of the performance variation of students simply by labeling students by their ability to learn within the system. Once that was the accepted norm, the system was no longer viewed as the primary cause of the variation, it was rather the abilities of students. We created categories for students that were labelled "gifted", or, on the bottom end, "slow" learners. For the academically challenged, special intervention programs were created with the intention of integrating the students back into the assembly line. I will not deny that there are some physiological reasons why students may need special programs; however these are not the students I am talking about, rather those that fit the wide range of the normal spectrum of learning.

Outdated Educational Theory

One reason why we continue to rely on outdated educational theory in the 21st century is based on an underlying false belief that the brain can either consciously or unconsciously encode *everything* that is presented to it. The misconception that the brain is like a tape recorder that somehow remembers most everything presented to it has helped us maintain learning systems that have become little more than memorization factories.

In fact, the mind is not an empty vessel in which memory is created simply by pouring in words, as John Locke and the behaviorists who came centuries later maintained. Instead, the brain is a biological instrument which must be stimulated in very specific ways before learning and long-term memory can be created. Without understanding that there is a biological and cognitive process by which we gather new information, we will continue to build learning systems that continue to fall short of what is demanded.

We have developed and proven that we can shift from a time is rigid and quality is flexible paradigm to a system in which *time is flexible and quality is rigid.* This is a monumental shift in the system, which required us to invent new system structures that would change the behavior of the system itself. I will share more on this in later chapters, but we have proven Deming right: that it is the system that is the primary cause of the variation and *not* the people. It is possible to increase the quality of education through a completely new system in which the costs per student will decrease. The bottom line is that the more we spend on our education without total transformation, the more our educational costs increase on an individual basis without any added benefit. This cycle of events has been happening for over 50 years.

The Current Condition is *not* the Problem!

Many people are dissatisfied with the output of the current system and will ascribe that as the problem itself, when in fact it is merely a symptom of the existing system. By taking more of a systems view, one will soon see that most reform attempts focus merely on tweaking an obsolete system, hence the desired outcomes are seldom realized.

Consider the past number of years when over $100 Billion was spent on programs like No Child Left Behind, which yielded very little improvement, and, in many cases quite frankly, made things even worse. The travesty is not only the waste of money, but also the loss of time to effect real change.

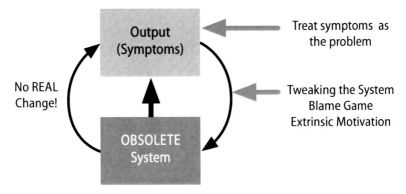

Figure I.2 - Why Reform Attempts Fail

The Gates Foundation over the past 10 years has poured billions of dollars into its school initiatives with very little improvement. Why? Because these programs, and many others like them, are not addressing the real problem with education. We cannot continue to pour money into an outdated, antiquated system and expect different results. Someone once defined this as insanity.

The theory behind why we have not changed from the factory model is called "The Fallacy of the Familiar," which states that how we learn today is virtually the same as those generations before us.[2] Under this fallacy, to transform how we educate is simply unimaginable. Accepting the current methodology is easier to understand, because that is the way we have always done it. The world was once believed to be flat—a long accepted fact, because to consider the world as a sphere was simply not comprehensible.

About a decade ago, the Gates Foundation set out to see what could be done. In an interesting interview in the Wall Street Journal, Bill Gates talked about what his foundation had learned after investing some $5 Billion in education philanthropy. "The experience had been sobering," Gates reflected, stating further that, "It's hard to improve public education." He went on to admit to some missteps:

- More funding isn't the answer: Efforts by the Ford, Carnegie, and Rockefeller foundations, among others, increased investments in some regions, but the efforts made little difference in closing the achievement gap.

- Smaller schools are not the answer: One of the foundation's main initial interests was schools with fewer students. Improvement was small—about 10% more kids went on to college.

The United States has become the richest and most powerful country in the history of the world, yet its education system ranks 30th in the world among developed countries. Among these countries, the US education cost per student is one of the highest in the world.

We need a Better "Driver"

I have often used a car and driver metaphor to describe the current approach to addressing the woes in education. After years of focusing on raising test scores with no real improvement the focus has now shifted to teacher performance, the "driver" of the vehicle. If the "car" representing the system is broken, then no amount of "driver training" or incentives will change that fact. Actually, the situation is worse: the notion of the system being broken means that it can be repaired, like fixing a flat tire; however if the system is both broken and obsolete, no amount of reward and punishment of the "drivers" will produce the results desired.

So why do we engage in system improvement in the first place? The answer to this question would take a rather lengthy discourse, which is not the intent of this book. In very simple terms, as one looks at the larger system of education, at the top of the "food chain" is a political system that by design is self-serving. Policies for reforming education must appeal to an electorate that doesn't understand the real problem of education, but can easily be swayed by propagandistic sound bites. Policies that focus on treating symptoms will get you elected, but will not transform the system. Recently, several US states have introduced 'pay for performance' incentives, which may sound good on the surface and may garner general public support, but are ultimately based on a failed theory, as Daniel Pink in his book *Drive* so aptly explains. You will find this virtually in every country that is looking to reform education. The focus is on test scores, OECD world rankings, or trying to improve teacher practice. Usually these reform attempts end up being highly manipulative by introducing reward and punishment into the system—after all, one must have consequences for non-compliance—and hence the industrial age system continues to be perpetuated.

What Is The REAL Problem?

Often when people have asked me, "What is the problem with education?" I like to respond with, "Nothing," followed by a pause, and then I would finish by saying, "—if you were living in the 1950s. The system is doing exactly what it was designed to do, and that is to produce workers for the industrial age who will conform and comply to industrial age standards." The vast majority of people would agree with this perspective; however, the difference lies in trying to identify, then, what the *real* problem is. If you can understand what the *real* problem is, then you can apply your attention and resources to "solving" it.

The *real* problem only emerges when you have a compelling vision or a future state that is significantly different than your current reality. The *real* problem or 'Probletunity', as we will describe it later, is generated by the creative tension between your vision and your current reality. It is about closing this gap, which requires *system transformation*.

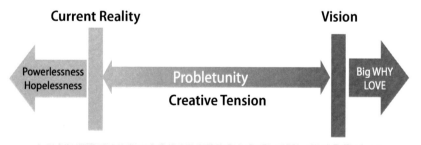

CREATIVE TENSION is generated, when you decide to resolve the probletunity, which is the interplay between your vision and current reality.

Figure I.3 - Creative Tension

The creative tension can be resolved in one of two ways: either by moving your current reality toward your vision, or by moving your vision toward your current reality. There are opposing forces at work; for many educators have a deep sense of powerlessness and hopelessness which over time converts into an automatic response of cynicism and judgment anytime someone suggests that there may be a better way to deliver education.

We have learned how to identify these voices and overcome them while engaging in the creation process. The other forces at play include your overarching Big WHY and the love you have for your creation. These forces are foundational to *Imaginal* leadership.

For profound change or transformation to occur we need *Imaginal* leaders in all sectors of our society. We need *Imaginal* politicians, educators, administrators, school board members, parents, business leaders, and students.

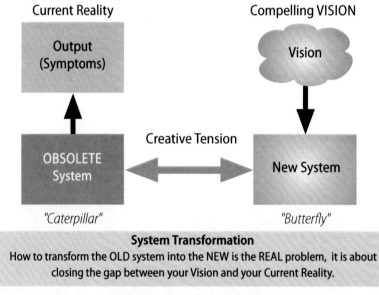

Figure I.4 - What's the REAL Problem

Transformation Process

Having worked with a large number of educators in various parts of the world, I have found that most have a difficult time envisioning the future of education. Educators are so strongly entrenched into the thinking that supports the existing system that it is very difficult to envision anything different. Sure we can add more technology and better resources, and even modernize the look of a school and call it the school of the future, but the fundamental nature of education really hasn't changed in a hundred years. There are always exceptions; there are those outlier schools that truly have taken a step into the future, but unfortunately they are few and far between.

A main point of this book is that even if a group of educators came up with a vision for the future, it would have great difficulty in creating that vision since most educators are not trained to be designers of complex systems, rather their expertise lies in the design of learning programs for students. Michael Fullan, a Canadian thought leader in education reform maintains,

> [That] we have been fighting an ultimately fruitless uphill battle. The solution is not how to climb the hill of getting more innovations or reforms into the educational system. We need a different formulation to get at the heart of the problem, a different hill, so to speak. We need, in short, a new mindset about educational change.[3] … Yet, education far from being a hotbed of teaching people to deal with change in basic ways, is just the opposite. To break through this impasse, educators must see themselves and be seen as experts in the dynamics of change. To become an expert in the dynamics of change, educators, administrators, and teachers alike must become skilled change agents.[4]

Fullan's point is a good one: for the system to change, educators must be educated and trained to be change agents, or, more poignantly, *become Imaginal*. But how?

As we were developing Master's culture and vision for Future Ready Education it was very apparent that living with one foot in the future and one foot in the present was a very challenging orientation for many of our teachers. Although we created a culture that embraced risk-taking by offering soft landings, there still was a lack of understanding by many about what it actually means to walk into the future by faith and not by sight alone. The patterns of thinking that drove the behaviors of educators were so strongly entrenched in the old paradigm that it was difficult to gain the kind of momentum we needed to create and ultimately break free from the gravitational pull of traditional education. We needed more; we needed to understand how we could shift the fundamental orientation of a person to becoming *Imaginal*—a person who can see and create the future he or she wants. This was no easy endeavor since we are all so different. Were there some universal laws or keys that we could discover that would unlock the "coding" for becoming *Imaginal*?

Download - Five Keys

Late December 2005, a few short years after my visit to Uganda in 1999, I had another epiphany moment, in which the Five Keys to Becoming *Imaginal* were downloaded. These keys are essential if you want to function in the I^2 and I^3 capacities of an innovator and inventor.

The first of the five keys is *finding your Big WHY*. The Big WHY defines your primary purpose that enables you to not only dream big, but also engage with the universe of unlimited possibilities, and have a compelling vision to make a difference in your world. The Big WHY is expressed through the vision you carry and have been called to. The Big WHY is the foundation which gives rise to vision and from which an *Imaginal* leader draws the courage and strength to make choices. The Big WHY enables you to live above the circumstances of life.

The second key is *activating your personal drive*. This is your commitment to pursue your Big WHY by discovering and activating your unique breakthrough drivers, and demonstrating courage, passion, initiative, and perseverance.

The third key is *seeing the invisible*. This is the ability to activate your imagination, to have insight (the ability to see what is) and foresight (the ability to see what could be). Using this key you will begin to discover why life is the way it is, and how to free yourself from the prison of your past.

The fourth key is the *ability to create your future*. This is making visible the invisible. When using this key you will begin to move from wishful thinking to intentionally creating your future.

The final key, Grow, is *doing the impossible*, or at least what seems to be impossible given your track record. Once you have taken the limits off your thinking it is time to grow your vision beyond anything you have imagined. As your faith grows, so will your vision.

These five keys can be simplified to one or two word each as follows:

- Finding my Big WHY is BIG WHY.

- Activating Personal Drive is DRIVE.

- Seeing the Invisible is VISION.

- Making Visible the Invisible is CREATE.

- Doing the Impossible is GROW.

Becoming Imaginal

Recently, while sharing in Nigeria to hundreds of leaders, I heard myself saying that we must equip educators to become *Imaginal* leaders so they can transfer this ability to their students. Specifically I said, "You can't give what you don't have." Immediately, I was convicted to finish this book—I needed to put in writing the secrets I have learned to help educators, parents, and leaders become *Imaginal*.

Becoming *Imaginal* is derived from one of the wonders of nature: when a caterpillar transforms into a butterfly through the process of metamorphosis. This miracle of metamorphosis is found within special imaginal cells embedded in the caterpillar itself, which have the capacity to see and create the butterfly. Imaginal cells have both the vision to become a butterfly and the ability to execute this amazing transformation. Analogously, *Imaginal* leaders have the capacity to see the future and pull it into the now; they have the capacity to see beyond what most people can see, and the courage, commitment, and know-how to lead the transformation process.

The world needs more *Imaginal* leaders, and organizations that can see a better future and have the courage and the know-how to create it. Throughout this book I will share with you the secrets I have learned along my journey that I believe are universal secrets, or keys, for unlocking the *Imaginal* way of living and leading.

I have had the opportunity to lead transformation in education, an industry that is highly resistant to any kind of change, let alone disruptive transformational change. Most everyone is in agreement that traditional education is both a broken and obsolete system. By broken I mean a system that simply is underperforming; and by obsolete, I mean that even if the system where performing optimally it still falls short of meeting the needs of today's rapidly changing world.

Broken   **Fixed**

Figure I.5 - Fixing a System that is Broken

This book introduces the *incremental transformation process* in Part III which is significantly different than incremental improvement. Incremental improvement focuses on improving processes within an existing system; it assumes that the overall system is fine. Incremental transformation sees an entirely new system, the THERE, and begins pulling new structures of the future model into the present, the HERE. Over a period of time a new system will emerge representing a significant leap into the FUTURE. You will learn, as an *Imaginal* leader, how to lead the transformation process even when the system begins to push back, which it will. You will learn how to set conditions for powerful transformation to occur in a way that is embraced by your key stakeholders. In essence, you will be implementing disruptive change in your organization in a way that causes the least amount of disruption.

Obsolete   New System

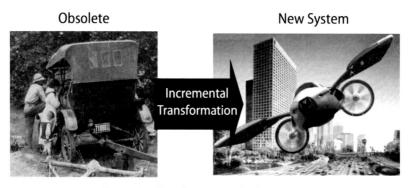

Figure - I.6 - Transforming an Obsolete System

We have discovered that it is possible to transform education from a voracious "caterpillar" into an elegant beautiful "butterfly" symbolic of students being able to pursue their destiny without limitation. Becoming *Imaginal* is intended to inspire and create hope for the millions of parents, educators, students, politicians, and business owners who may have a sense of powerlessness and hopelessness regarding the future state of education. Throughout this book I will share our journey of becoming *Imaginal* in the context of our vision for transforming education. The same keys, however, are applicable to anyone who wants to create the future he or she wants.

An *Imaginal* leader is one who has the passion, courage, and vision to engage in the creation process of seeing the invisible and doing the impossible. Steve Jobs was an *Imaginal* leader; he was able to live in the tension of his "reality distortion field" to create one of the greatest technology companies against insurmountable odds.

This book is divided into 5 parts, summarized in what follows.

Part 1: Becoming Imaginal

Metamorphosis is one of the most beautiful and inspiring events in nature—when a caterpillar transforms into a butterfly—and stands as a foundational metaphor for how I envisage education being transformed. Chapter 1, *Becoming Imaginal*, elaborates on this metaphor drawing an analogy between the role of imaginal cells in the process of metamorphosis and the role of imagination and vision in the process of transforming education. But having a vision requires *Finding Your Big WHY*—that thing that you have uniquely been placed on this earth to do—which is the title and topic of Chapter 2. Digging deeper into your Big WHY leads to finding what is at the center of your life. Or, to put it another way, finding what is at the center of your life will lead you to your Big WHY. This process is the topic of Chapter 3, *What is at Your Center?* And part of finding what is at your center, and in turn discovering your Big WHY, is figuring out what drives you to do the thing you do; hence the topic of *Activating Drive* in Chapter 4, and the further elaboration of *Breakthrough Drivers*, namely what has driven history makers to do extraordinary things, in Chapter 5.

Part 2: Seeing

Seeing is fundamental for creating the future and becoming *Imaginal*. Part 2 introduces the concept of *Vision* in Chapter 6 as it is situated within two very different worlds: The Universe of Measurement and the Universe of Unlimited Possibility. Understanding how to live in the tension of those two worlds is critical for becoming *Imaginal*. And there are two aspects to Vision: *Insight* and *Foresight*, which form, respectively, Chapters 7 and 8. To create the future requires the ability to see into the very heart of what is going on around you (Insight), and where the present is going as it pushes out into the future (Foresight).

Part 3: Creating

Creation is that which is endowed to all of us—not just the elite few. However, many people do not actualize their own creative potential. An important part of becoming *Imaginal* is actualizing the creative potential that lies uniquely inside of you, which is the topic of Part 3. Chapter 9, *Creation*, lays out the creative orientation as a way to realize your vision and live as a creator. And to be a creator means that you love that which you create, which is the subject of Chapter 10, *Built on Love*. Design is defined as the application of creativity to the world we live in—as opposed to that which merely makes things look cool, or that which creates widgets or websites. Design is fundamental to actualizing your vision for transforming education, and thus the subject of Chapter 11—*Your Future...by Design.*

Part 4: Growing

Imaginal leaders not only see and create the future, but also grow their vision, which is how I see education being transformed around the world. The focus of Part 4 shifts becoming *Imaginal* from the individual to the organization—that is, from becoming an *Imaginal* leader to becoming an *Imaginal* organization. What does it mean to grow? When a vision is first created, it requires great care, not unlike a seedling. It has to be nurtured. But how do you nurture that vision, and how do you create the conditions for it to grow around you? That is the main theme of Chapter 12. Additionally, many people are afraid to create because they think they need to get it right the first time—but that is simply not so. In response to this misconception, I lay out the Maturity Principle of growth, which presents the importance of iterations in the growth process. Chapter 13 looks at what an *Imaginal* educational organization looks like, from finding its Big WHY to the application of the 5 Keys, and finally to its visionary development. The school I founded, Master's Academy and College in Calgary, Alberta, was created as an *Imaginal* prototype school, which is the subject of Chapter 14: Our journey to becoming *Imaginal*, and where we are heading in the future. The purpose is to provide insight and ideas to fellow *Imaginal* leaders and organizations.

Epilogue: I Have A Dream

The Epilogue is a special place for me, for it is where I share my dream for education and the vision as it has unfolded over almost two decades. It is written to edify and inspire present and future *Imaginal* leaders.

Appendixes

Appendixes provide a more in depth overview of the following:

Appendix A: Profound Learning
Appendix B: 24 Elements of the Learning Code
Appendix C: Profound Learning Orchestration System
Appendix D: Imaginal Transformation Workshop
Appendix E: 10 Characteristics of an iCubed Organization
Appendix F: Teacher Anxiety Audit

Part 1. Becoming Imaginal

1.

Becoming Imaginal

"I saw the angel in the marble, and carved until I set it free."

- Michelangelo

The system of education needs to be transformed from the inside out, which requires educators to become *Imaginal* leaders. But how does one become *Imaginal*? Isn't such a destiny only endowed to those with special potential or pre-natal giftedness? Perhaps being an *Imaginal* leader is purely a result of nature rather than nurture. Is this not what we are led to believe when we witness extraordinary people all around us doing such seemingly amazing things?

Metamorphosis

Metamorphosis, in which a caterpillar transforms itself into a butterfly, is one of the most amazing processes found in nature. The caterpillar is a slow, voracious consumer, and extremely vulnerable to external predators. The caterpillar skin, or exoskeleton, does not grow by stretching, but rather by molting (shedding the outgrown skin) several times. Metaphorically speaking, some consultants are experts in helping organizations through this molting process; unfortunately, however, this is not transformational even though some may make that claim—it is simply enabling the organization to grow bigger. But it's still a caterpillar.

The incredible transformation of a caterpillar into a butterfly occurs in the pupa, or chrysalis. The caterpillar begins to excrete enzymes that literally destroy the caterpillar. However, within the caterpillar are these special imaginal cells that have the "vision" and "know-how" to become the butterfly. During this "rebirth" moment these imaginal cells begin to form the various parts of the butterfly.

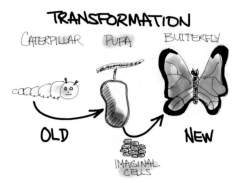

Figure 1.1 - Transformation: a major change in form, nature and function of an entity

Over time a mature butterfly is formed and is ready to emerge out of the chrysalis. As you watch the butterfly exiting, it faces a considerable amount of resistance—it is literally trying to squeeze itself out of the protective shell that has held it captive during the transformation process. This struggle is essential to the survival of the butterfly, since fluid necessary to inflate the wings is pushed to the extremities of the wings themselves. Organizations will experience similar kinds of moments as the "butterfly" begins to emerge. There will be a struggle, but it will not last forever. In Part III of this book you will learn strategies to help you navigate through such times of stretching.

Transformation Defined

For the purposes of clarity, I will define transformation as a major change in form, nature, and function analogous to a caterpillar becoming a butterfly. I can change the color of my hair, but that would hardly be deemed transformational since the essence of who I am has not changed.

In today's world, many people are using the term transformation very loosely to mean "change." You will find the term "transformation" plastered all over websites that are providing consulting services to organizations. Recently, I read one website that claimed to be transforming education by improving professional practices of teachers, which was in alignment with the latest US government's reform attempt, Race to the Top.

Transforming Education is an immensely challenging task; the system is very complex and resistant to change. The mental models that support the current education system are so strongly entrenched and have been accepted for so long, that it is difficult for most educators to envision a different future. Many school reform initiatives, such as No Child Left Behind or Race to the Top in the USA, have focused on improving test scores or improving teacher performance. These initiatives invariably end in failure, because they are treating symptoms of an obsolete system. A question is if we could elevate the test scores of all students, would that system prepare students for the world of tomorrow or the world of yesterday?

If the system of education is obsolete, then no amount of teacher training within that system is going to change the overall condition of obsolescence. What is needed is a new system of education; and the training of teachers needs to be focused on developing the skills needed to support the new structures of that new system. We need teachers, administrators, students, parents and politicians to become *Imaginal* leaders—those who can see and create the future they see, need and want. We need *Imaginal* leaders that can lead the transformation process of the caterpillar becoming a butterfly.

Imaginal Leaders – Born or Developed?

Are *Imaginal* leaders born with special endowments or can ordinary people develop their innate *Imaginal* abilities? A few years ago I was in dialogue with a friend who was building a successful network marketing business. He had noticed that only a handful of the many people he had sponsored would eventual go on to build successful businesses which was the norm for the industry. His question to me was, "How do I find more of these diamonds?" to which I responded, "Yes you can try and build your business with these proven high performers, but chances are they are already committed to and doing many other things. Why not create conditions in which one could develop *Imaginal* leaders out of the large pool of people caught in the middle living ordinary mundane lives?" I call these latent *Imaginal* leaders. Is this possible?

A main premise of this book is that each and every one of us has the fundamental "wiring" of becoming *Imaginal*. For most people, however, having been under the influence of an industrial age model of education, this basic ability remains under-developed, just as muscles atrophy when not used.

Over my life time, I have observed that people fit into one of three categories: Quitters, Ordinary People, and *Imaginal* leaders. Quitters are a small group of people who have fundamentally quit on life, they carry a strong victim mentality and really are quite miserable. On the other end of the spectrum is another small group of *Imaginal* leaders, namely those who have learned how to create the future they want; they have found their Big WHY, and thus can rise above their current circumstances. The vast majority of Ordinary People live ordinary mundane lives caught in the "rat race" of life. These are what I consider to be *Latent Imaginal Leaders*, who, as such, function primarily in a reactive/responsive manner. Most have not discovered their Big WHY, but once they do, they can become *Imaginal* leaders.

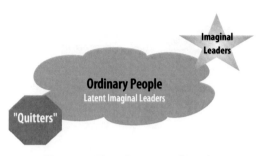

Figure 1.2 - Three Groupings of People

Is it possible to elevate Quitters and Ordinary People types into *Imaginal* leaders? The answer is YES, and this is the intent of this book. Reading a book seldom changes anyone's life—if it were the case our world would be a vastly different place—but it does minimally provide some hope along with some powerful keys

Figure 1.3 - Becoming an Imaginal Leader

that, when implemented, provide a pathway for you to become an *Imaginal* leader.

Becoming an *Imaginal* leader is all about learning how to create the future you see, need, and want. It is foundational to our "formulation" for transforming education or any other obsolete system.

Imaginal leaders are truly made not born. Indeed, if you are living a life less ordinary, but have a desire to make a difference in this world, *then you can become Imaginal.* However, to embark on this journey of transforming from a caterpillar to a butterfly will first take some effort and intent—not unlike the caterpillar's pupa stage. You will have to delve deeply inside yourself, for to become *Imaginal* you first have to find your BIG WHY—that very purpose for which you are on this earth.

2.

Finding Your Big Why

"There is more in a human life than our theories of it allow. Sooner or later something seems to call us onto a particular path. You may remember this 'something' as a signal moment in childhood when an urge out of nowhere, a fascination, a peculiar turn of events struck like an annunciation: This is what I must do, this is what I've got to have. This is who I am."

- James Hillman

To become *Imaginal* you need to find your BIG WHY in life. But what is a BIG WHY? Why is it essential for becoming *Imaginal*? And how do you find it?

The Big WHY is that force that keeps you going when all others would have quit. The Big Why calls you to be creative, to take a risk, to do something that you have never done before, to begin experiencing the richness of a vision-led life, and what it means to be vision-driven and not just purpose-driven.

The Big WHY model (Figure 2.1) will help you answer the following five questions in the pursuit of your own Big WHY:

- Who am I? (My identity)

- Why am I here? (My purpose)

- What will define my life mission? (My cause)

- What am I inspired to create that advances my cause? (My dream)

- What will be my commitment to the vision? (My calling)

These five elements of your Big WHY are all influenced by your worldview, beliefs, values, and assumptions.

Identity

Who am I?

Calling

What will be my commitment to the vision?

Purpose

Why am I here?

Dream

What am I inspired to create that advances my cause and purpose?

Cause

What will define my life mission?

VALUES IDENTITY BELIEFS

CALLING **Big** PURPOSE

WHY

DREAM CAUSE

WORLDVIEW

Figure 2.1 - Five Dimensions of your Big WHY

1. Identity

My identity is all about how I view my self, and how I interpret others' view of me. My sense of identity is the sum total of all my experiences interpreted through a filter of my worldview—the beliefs, values, and assumptions I hold about life and myself.

So much of my behavior is derived from my sense of who I am. There are numerous personality tests and gift inventories that are designed to help you better understand who you are, such as the Myers-Briggs Personality Identifier (MBPI), the DISC Assessment, and the Winslow Personality Profile. Rachel Redfern recently wrote in her blog,

Since the 1960s, personality tests have been a commonly accepted process in corporate hiring procedures, despite their vague and generally unscientific foundation. Consider the MBPI test, a test developed by two women in the 1940s who had no scientific background, and which enjoys widespread popularity even outside of human resources departments. While people who take the test outside of job requirements don't follow the test religiously, it is common to use it as a self-identifier.[5]

Despite widespread use of these tests, the scientific validity is still somewhat suspect. Since our personality is very much an expression of our neurological wiring of billions of neurons, it goes without saying that we should avoid the categorization or labeling of people based on a few questions. I have heard my friend JW Wilson (neuroscience researcher and author of *Cracking the Learning Code*) often claim that there are 7 Billion geniuses walking on this planet earth, each one being uniquely gifted. We need to avoid the tendency to look for things that fit our profile instead of stretching ourselves into new opportunities. As humans we tend to seek comfort, so it is natural that we will gravitate to those situations that we feel most comfortable in.

The formation of my identity or who I am has two main contributors: my genetics and my environment. We have very little or no control over our genetics, or even our environment—our life is what it is. Our thinking about our identity, how we view ourselves, establishes everything, from our behaviors to our sense of purpose. The formation of this identity is the cumulative result of our experiences whether good or bad.

Killer phrases (such as, "You'll never amount to anything!" "You can't do that!" "No one I know has ever succeeded at doing that.") can place limits on a person's life and may be a source of hinderance over many years. Some people carry with them a shame-based identity, in which they have been shamed into performing for someone else.

There is a big difference between feeling guilt and feeling shame. Guilt is our conscience responding when we know that we have done something wrong. For example, just look at a child's face when his or hands have been caught in the cookie jar. Conscience, which leads to our moral understanding and knowing that there are right and wrong behaviors, is what helps keep our world from self-destructing. Shame, however, is the belief or mindset that something is wrong with *me*. This can have a devastating effect on people, which often results in becoming a prisoner of one's past. We cannot escape this prison until we understand why we think the way we think, and why we do what we do. Prison break from our past is possible. Our future is not solely determined by our past—we can make choices, and become designers of our future, those *Imaginal* leaders who escape the mundane and experience the extraordinary.

Two clear indicators of people who carry a shame-based identity are chronic over-achievers, or the opposite, namely under-achievers. Over-achievers are constantly over-reaching to gain approval, and even when it comes they really don't accept it, so they keep on trying harder. We all know of people with tremendous talents and gifts, but seemingly have underachieved all their lives. These people somewhere along life's journey have quit trying because of all the negative messaging that has come their way. Often these people quit on the verge of success, since they do not know how to handle success even if it came.

Over Achievers

Under Achievers

Shame Based Identity

Figure 2.2 - Shame Based Identity

In trying to understand who I am, it is equally important to contemplate who I am *becoming*. This book is about becoming an *Imaginal* leader; it is about equipping you to engage with your future by design and not default.

2. Purpose

Purpose answers life's biggest question: Why am I here? Purpose defines in general terms my life's mission—what I want to accomplish with my life. Purpose is often expressed through goal-setting, such as "I want to retire at the age of 55," or "I want my children to get the best possible education." Most people act as though life has a purpose, which is usually characterized as the pursuit of happiness. Purpose is directly linked to both my identity, the way I view myself, and my worldview, which shapes the lens through which I view life.

Approximately 85% of the world's population has some kind of religious belief in a "God" or a "Source" that has established a moral code by which we live our lives, and provides a sense of higher purpose. These values and beliefs are the foundation from which both our understanding of purpose is derived and our Big WHY will emerge.

Purpose provides a general framework for my life's mission or aim. However, being purpose-driven is not the same as being vision-driven.

Vision-driven people are those *Imaginal* leaders who go out and change the world and become history-makers. You can be purpose-driven and not have a compelling vision, but you cannot be vision driven without a clear understanding of purpose.

3. Cause

Cause moves our focus away from ourselves to some endeavor that has a greater good attached to it and is generally much bigger than any one individual. Discovering the cause or causes that will elevate our lives is at the core of helping us define our Big WHY.

There are innumerable causes that people have committed their lives to, such as animal rights, humanitarian projects, saving the environment, and religious causes. The website *Causes* was created in 2007 as an advocacy fundraising application within Facebook, and has become one of the world's largest online platforms for activism with 100 million installed users, and has raised millions of dollars for nonprofits.

Why do people start causes, and why do causes attract others to join? There seems to be an impulse within the human psyche that is seeking to be a part of something bigger than oneself, and that advances a noble cause. Not all causes are noble, for example terrorists are recruited and brainwashed into doing unthinkable acts; however, the vast majority of causes are motivated by acts of kindness or advancing the betterment of our world. In our next chapter, we will explore the nature of what drives people to be causal in their orientation toward life by looking at history-makers who have shaped the world we live in.

It is *cause* that elevates the human experience, for it is what compels us to escape the world of self absorption, to flee the entrapment of materialism and consumerism. Victor Frankl observed that survivors of the holocaust often were those who had a strong sense that they still had something significant to contribute to their world, which thus enabled them to endure unthinkable suffering.

4. Dream

Dream can be defined very loosely as a picture one carries of an ideal future. Dream is the early stage development of a vision, and tends to be big and lacking in details. Dreams are designed to inspire and ignite the passion within people; and truly compelling dreams are those tied to a cause that is bigger than the dreamer.

Dreams over time become more specific and ultimately mature into a vision. For an *Imaginal* leader, and for the purposes of this book, vision is defined as *the specific expression of what I am inspired to create that advances my cause and purpose.* A true and authentic vision can be one of the most powerful forces in our life. It keeps pulling us forward to live an extraordinary life. Visionary people seldom, if ever, lose focus or quit. A vision once formed will bring greater focus to your Big WHY. You can see that vision goes beyond purpose; it requires the ability to design and create the future through innovation and invention.

For example, the vision that drives much of what I do is attached to the cause of transforming education around the world with Profound Learning. To accomplish this vision I needed to specifically start an R&D school in 1997, hire faculty to a vision, establish a vision community, begin the process of developing Profound Learning, launch a software company, and continually refine Profound Learning to the point where it has become a powerful system of education that can be shared with schools around the world. This process has taken almost two decades, and at its core has been an unwavering commitment to a vision that is attached to the cause of advancing education.

5. Calling

Calling defines my role within a vision, as well as my commitment. Everyone can have a vision for their life, which often means being a part of a larger vision-community. Calling is applying my gifts and talents appropriately to the vision. Not everyone is called to lead a vision, but everyone can be a contributor to the advancement of a vision. This is when personal vision melds with community vision—they become one and the same.

Calling is a very important step that helps to solidify your Big WHY. Many people can carry dreams and aspirations for a number of things, but *calling* takes it beyond a wish list item to something far more tangible and observable.

Big WHY

Human beings have a unique endowment of living life with a deep sense of purpose and vision. Finding your Big WHY, or having your Big WHY find you, and living it out is your ultimate destiny.

Your Big WHY becomes your primary reason for being; it becomes the lens through which you view the world, and your primary driver that activates all other drivers in your life. Your Big WHY is the soil from which vision is sprouted and nourished. Your Big WHY becomes the primary choice that renders all other choices its servant.

Your Big WHY works in a synergy with the vision you have for your life, for those closest to you, and the cause you are inspired to advance. The blend of these three begin to form the vision for your Big WHY.

Self-Centered vs Big WHY Creation

Why is it that a person who is ego-centric or self centered finds it difficult to nurture and develop a true compelling vision for life? An ego-centric person is playing to a self-serving agenda with the goal of advancing personal comfort and control. Vision is limited to what is both achievable and possible—there is no attempt to try the seeming impossible. The notion of calling and cause are all secondary to preservation and promotion of self.

A vision, which is inspired deep within the human spirit, is able to soar when there is something bigger than self to draw its life from.

Below is an outline of the difference between a vision created from a self-centered person and a vision created from one motivated by one's own Big WHY.

Table 2.1- Self versus Big WHY Creation

Self-Centered Creation	Big WHY Centered Creation
Worth is gained through acquisitions and accomplishments	Worth is gained by advancing your Big WHY
Judged by our failures	No judgment
Self doubt is a constant battle	Faith that nothing is impossible
Limited resources	Access to unlimited resources

Self-Centered Creation	Big WHY Centered Creation
Scarcity mindset	Abundance mindset
Win/lose mindset	Win/win mindset
Intent is often self-serving	Intent is giving and serving
Proud	Humble
Fear of failure	Hope and faith inspire action
Competition	Co-operation
Greed	Generosity
Sole creator	Co-creation with others
Operates by- envy, strife, jealousy, over-bearing, fear, domination	Operates by- love, joy, peace, kindness, gentleness, faith

Path of Least Resistance

Robert Fritz, in his book the *Path of Least Resistance,* lays out the premise that energy within structures will take the path of least resistance. The most powerful structures in our lives are the beliefs, values, and assumptions we carry about ourselves and about life in general. Fritz presents three insights:

You go through life taking the path of least resistance.

The underlying structure of your life determines the path of least resistance.

You can change the fundamental structures of your life. [6]

If you want to understand a person's belief system, just observe his or her behavior. One's dominant belief structures provide a path of least resistance for one's behavior. Deep rooted values and beliefs are what we live out everyday. It's not our declared values that determine our behaviors, it's what we live out that illustrates what we really believe.

J.W. Wilson, author of *Cracking the Learning Code* (See Appendix B), states that if you want to have a behavioral change you must first have a neurological change. The changes that he is talking about are structural neurological networks within the brain. This notion is substantiated not only by neuroscience, but also by ancient scripture as found in the Bible in Romans 12:2,

Do not conform to the pattern of this world, but be transformed by the renewing of your mind.

It is possible to change the "programming" of your mind, to create new structures that will change the path of least resistance in the direction of your Big WHY. This is what happens when you become vision-driven and not just purpose-driven. In Chapter 10-11, I introduce the creation process that an *Imaginal* leader uses to bring a vision into fulfillment. The vision-fulfillment structure becomes the path of least resistance for an *Imaginal* leader.

Vision Formation Model

Vision typically starts with a burning desire or deep rooted need—something that needs to change or needs to be invented that will solve a problem. This first stage is the place where a vision is conceived. In my own case I became dissatisfied with the way education was being delivered, and this dissatisfaction ignited a desire to do something about it. However, in spite of this desire I really did not have a clue what that something would be.

A burning desire ignites the passion within us that begins to shape our dreams and aspirations. I began to incubate a dream, a generalized picture of the future—some may even call it a "pipe dream." Dreams emerge when we allow our imagination to play in the universe of unlimited possibilities. These are big images of what could be. They tend to inspire people, because the dream projects a future that is more utopian than a real possibility. Dreaming is a good and essential step in the whole process, but if it stops there then all you will have become is a dreamer, and we all know that wishful thinking about the future will not cause that future to come into being. We must move beyond the dream stage.

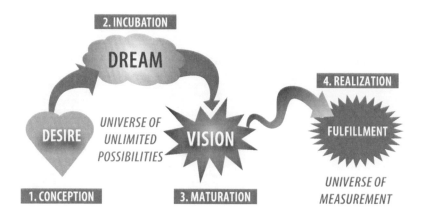

Figure 2.3 - Vision Formation

For dreams to come true they must mature into a vision. A vision is a more specific articulation of the dream that has a context of time and space. In my case, a vision arose which resulted in the launch of Master's Academy and College in Calgary, Alberta, in 1997. As I saw it, this school would pursue breakthroughs in learning as characterized by the following vision statement—written sometime later—of producing Profound Learning:

Profound Learning is a 21st century learner-centric model of education elevating achievement for all students to heights not attainable in the traditional industrial age model of education, with the signature being innovation and creativity.

This vision calls for us to move from a mass production factory model of education to mass customization, where the learning is customized to meet the needs of the individual student. To do this we would need to invent new models of assessment and management of learning, different delivery systems that would pace the learning in a way that is optimal to the student; and a model that would deliver both rigor and relevance. As you can see, a vision becomes much more of a specific expression of the preferred future. When vision is communicated it begins to draw people into it, and soon forms into a vision community.

The final stage is the realization or fulfillment of the vision itself. You move from vision to fulfillment by intentional design, rather than by default, hence future by design and not default (a fuller elucidation of which will be provided in Chapter 11).

During the incubation stage, your dream tends to be rather fragile. There are many dream killers who, whether intentionally or unintentionally, will try to crush your dream—sometimes even out of the desire to protect you.

The biggest dream killer will be yourself. Many people simply do not allow themselves to dream; they are prisoners of their past. When a dream is being incubated it is important that you are able to float your dream. You can only build that which you see working through the eyes of faith. When you see your dream working, then all the barriers you face become mere obstacles to overcome. While floating your dream, there are two voices to be mindful of: the affirmative voice will say that it is possible, while the negative voice will tell you that it can't be done. You sink your dream if you can't see it working. Vision cannot be formed when you are filled with self-doubt.

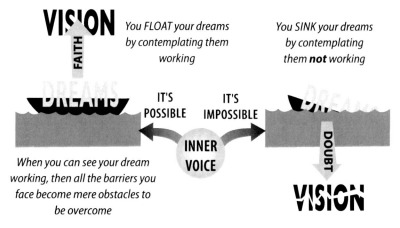

Figure 2.4 - Floating your DREAM

Martin Luther King Jr. had a dream; a dream of an America that would be free from racial prejudice. Many picked up on this dream, which was translated into a personal vision of something specific they were to accomplish with their lives. This collective vision of many people resulted in the election of the first African-American president, Barak

Obama—something that was inconceivable back in the 1950s and 1960s.

The *Imaginal* visionary spirit within each of us wants to be released; it is wooing us; it is saying, "Astonish me. Build something great—make it immortal, insanely great."

Passion versus Knowledge

A few years ago I had a conversation with a friend regarding a major issue we faced as a society, a problem that seemingly could not be solved. We engaged with deep passionate discussion for quite a while when it dawned on me that neither of us really knew what we were talking about; nevertheless, we were deeply passionate about our opinions on this subject. As I began to reflect on that discourse, a question arose: How can passion and ignorance both coincide? Then it hit me: passion is often fueled by ignorance. I call it "ignorance on fire."

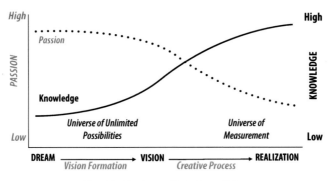

Fig. 2.5 - Passion as Early Stage Driver

Vision starts with a dream—a big audacious view of the future. A dream may initially strike us as being intellectually outrageous, which is not only its appeal, but also a necessity. The more knowledge you possess, the more open to criticism and analysis your dream becomes. The dream is still a fragile flower and cannot stand the scrutiny of a deep intellectual discourse. Martin Luther King Jr., Mahatma Gandhi, John Kennedy, to name a few, all inspired their nation with their dream. There were no detailed plans—simply a bold vision of a future that people wanted. Over time a dream matures into a vision which becomes actionable. The transition from dream to vision occurs as greater knowledge and clarity become evident.

The BIG WHY is what you are uniquely born with to fulfill in this life. In fact, as we saw with neuroscience, even if we have ventured away from it, we can literally re-direct our thinking toward it. This is vital for becoming *Imaginal*, because if the self is at the center of your life, rather than the BIG WHY, then you will not be able to take the necessary risks to achieve it.

But to find your BIG WHY requires you to move beyond this point and engage in more inward searching, that is to find what's at the center of your life—or, what I like to call your *authentic swing*.

3.

What's at Your Center?

"Look in your own heart. Unless I'm crazy, right now a still small voice is piping up, telling you as it has ten thousand times, that calling that is yours and yours alone. You know it. No one has to tell you."

- Steven Pressfield, author of The Legend of Bagger Vance

Is it possible to change the destination of my life, to find my BIG WHY, what's authentic to me, to the life I have been given here on Earth? Or am I determined to live a life of mediocrity, below my deeply held aspirations and the fulfillment of my dreams?

Each one of us has an authentic swing, something we are uniquely born with, a destiny that is ours and ours alone. Finding our authentic swing is key to finding our Big Why. To find our authentic swing requires first coming to know and understand what is at the center of our life.

According to Steven Covey, whatever is at the center will be your source of security, guidance, wisdom, and power. It's what gives you your sense of worth, your direction, your ability to make decisions and your capacity to act. It is thus critical to becoming *Imaginal*.

Finding your Swing

In the year 2000, the movie *The Legend of Bagger Vance* was released. It is a metaphor about finding your life and your authentic swing. The setting takes place in Savannah, Georgia during the Great Depression.

Junuh, played by Matt Damon, is the best golfer in Savannah. He's living well and has a girl, Adele, who's the daughter of a wealthy landowner.

It's the beginning of World War I, and Junuh goes to Europe to fight. The only survivor of a dangerous mission, Junuh doesn't return to Savannah for 15 years.

In 1930, he returns, and Adele's father has committed suicide during the Depression. Pressured by tax collectors to sell the golf course her father built to pay off debts, Adele, now older, vows to bring to Savannah the greatest match ever played on the greatest golf course—her late father's. She's able to round up the two greatest golfers of their time, Bobby Jones and Walter Hagen, to play for $10,000. The townspeople insist on having "one of their own" compete also, and Junuh is rounded up.

Two people enter Junuh's life, one is a young boy named Hardy, and the other is Bagger Vance, played by Will Smith. Bagger is more than a golf caddy: he is somewhat of a mystical figure who has come to rescue Junuh from his self-pity and self-destructive behaviors. Hardy has an unusual belief in Junuh, as he goes to encourage him to play in the golf tournament.

Junuh by now is an alcoholic, hangs out with bums, and has lost his authentic swing from 15 years ago. At first he turns down the offer. One night, he gets out his old set of golf clubs and balls and starts practicing, only to find that he has lost his swing. Startlingly, Bagger Vance shows up from the shadows into which Junuh had been teeing off. He strangely offers to be Junuh's caddy and help him regain his authentic swing, which Junuh agrees to, and, eventually, to play in the big match itself.

The night before the tournament, Bagger and Hardy go out to measure the golf course, during which Bagger reveals to Hardy his philosophy on life,

Inside each and everyone of us is one true authentic swing, something we were born with, something that is ours and ours alone, something that can't be taught or learnt; it is something to be remembered. Over time the world can rob us of that swing, and we are left with all of would haves or could haves.

The Extraordinary Life

How do we live a life that is extraordinary, that is fulfilling in the truest and deepest sense of the word? Fulfillment is not defined by how much money you earn, or by the size of your house or bank account, it is about significance—the impact that you are making in your world. Steve Jobs when he was recruiting a new CEO for Apple challenged John Scully from Pepsi Cola, "Do you want to sell sugar water the rest of your life or do you want to join Apple and make a dent in the universe?"

A recent Gallup poll in the US found that 52% of all full-time workers in America are not involved in, enthusiastic about or committed to their work. Another 18% are "actively disengaged," meaning they've gone beyond just checking out mentally and could even be undermining their colleagues' accomplishments. That leaves just 30% of American workers who feel excited about their jobs. What a travesty!

So many people have settled for a life that is mundane and unfulfilling. They work in jobs they do not like, and their life is not filled with passion and joy, but rather feels like drudgery. Many people are living some form of subsistence life: working simply to provide food and shelter for themselves and the people they love. In countries with higher standards of living, consumerism has become a major driver. People are pursuing happiness by buying more "things" or having more leisure time, none of which can satisfy us or create a sense of fulfillment.

Authentic Swing

Each of us has a true authentic swing. It is our destiny, what we were born to do. How do we, like Junuh in the Legend of Bagger Vance, find it?

There are four components to your authentic swing:
1. Setup
2. Backswing
3. Forward swing
4. Impact and follow through

Your authentic swing begins with beliefs and values that guide and direct your life. This is the setup for our authentic swing, which consists of unspoken values, but are evident in everything we do: our language, our behavior, our thought life. They include things like honesty, integrity, justice, servanthood, love, and our spirituality. In golf, if your setup is wrong, everything else falls apart. You must grip the club just the right way, your feet need to be pointing in the right direction, and your body relaxed, since muscle tension will weaken your swing. All of these are essential when you are preparing to swing the golf club.

The backswing represent me. The authentic swing recognizes my unique talents and gifts, the way I am wired. You will notice that on the professional golf tour many pros have unique backswings. Jim Furyk, for instance, has a backswing that simple is unique. The point here is that not everyone has a back swing like Tiger Woods—we are uniquely gifted and this is what makes life so rich, the diversity we all bring to the game of life.

The forward swing is our relationship with others, for we are created as social beings to build and sustain healthy relationships with people. We are to honor and respect one another; we are to consider those who are less fortunate than we are, to show kindness and love.

All of this is for one purpose: to hit the ball. It is all about the impact. What will be the impact of your life? How will you seize the day? The impact is the cause that you attach your life to; and it is this cause that enables us to transcend ourselves. The most courageous people are those who are cause-centered, like Mother Teresa, Martin Luther, David Livingstone, Martin Luther King Jr., Gandhi, and Jesus Christ to name a few. Your authentic swing is when all four come together as a cohesive whole. When you begin to understand your authentic swing, discovering your Big WHY becomes a very natural process. To find your authentic swing you need to understand what is at the center of your life.

What's at Your Center?

There are many possible centers, but they all can be distilled into three. What is at the center will also be your source of comfort, security, success and recognition. These three centers are:

- Self
- Others
- Cause

These centers are wrapped up in our values and beliefs, which frame how we behave and view the world.

Self-centeredness is arguably the most common center—certainly with children as well as many adults. People who are self-centered often find their sense of identity in what they do, namely work, a particular role in life, or various awards and achievements. Self will dominate those caught in the trap of materialism by its insatiable appetite for more things, more holidays, a bigger house, etc. This kind of person often takes on a victim mentality when life doesn't go as planned, and when failure comes it's always someone else's fault. The real downside when self is at the center is one never really takes a risk. This self protectionism leads people to sterile, boring, and unproductive lives. A person with an extreme case of self-centeredness is called a narcissist, around whom everything revolves. Such people often becoming extremely controlling since self needs to have control over all aspects of life.

Being other-centered sounds on the surface like a good idea, after all should we not think of others instead of ourselves? Yes, we are to experience healthy and vibrant relationships with other people, but this isn't what is meant when others are at the center. If others become your source of approval, wisdom, guidance, and power then you have turned a positive virtue into an unhealthy co-dependency in which a relationship determines your worth. Often other-centered people end up being people pleasers and manipulators.

Cause-centered people, in contrast, have found something bigger than themselves that drives their behavior. History has shown that such people demonstrate great courage, and are willing to take risks that others would not consider. Think of explorers, pioneers, humanitarians, missionaries, scientists, and social activists who have taken on a cause the benefits of which we all enjoy today.

To find our authentic swing, we need to find an equilibrium of all three centers. We need to have a healthy sense of who we are as individuals; we need to be caring of others, and have something bigger than ourselves that will create a deep sense of significance. Over time what will happen is that our cause center will begin to grow. You will find that you do not have to sacrifice relationships or even some of your own personal aspirations to become more cause-centered. You will begin to try new things, take bigger risks, failure will not be viewed negatively, and life will become a real adventure filled with significance and meaning.

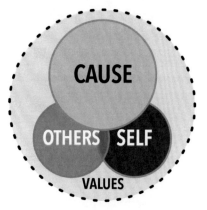

Figure 3.1 - A Balanced View

Facing Your Fears

Coming back to the Legend of Bagger Vance, Junuh finds his swing, and begins to experience success which over time plays on his mind. He starts to get a little cocky, and his game begins to fall apart—his short lived success quickly evaporates into thin air.

He slices his ball badly into the woods. As he approaches it he finds himself reliving his experience from the war. Fear grips his heart as he faces the situation in which he finds himself. He doesn't know what to do. Just as he is ready to pick up his ball as an unplayable lie, Bagger stops him by asking if he needs another club. Here is the dialogue between Junuh and Bagger, perhaps the most powerful moment in the whole movie:

Junuh: *I can't do this.*

Bagger: *Sure you can, just loosen your grip.*

Junuh: *That's not what I am talking about.*

Bagger: *I know.*

Junuh: *What I am talking about is a game that can't be won, it can only be played. You don't understand.*

Bagger: *I don't need to understand. You are not the only person that is carrying a burden. It is time for you to lay down your burden, stop hugging your pain, and move on with your life.*

Junuh: *I don't know how.*

Bagger: *You've got a choice: you can stop or you can start. Start walking to where you were,*

Junuh: *it was too long ago.*

Bagger: *No—it was only a moment ago. It is time for you to come out of the shadows.*

Junuh: *I can't.*

Bagger: *You are not alone, I am right here with you. Now play your game—your game. The one that only you can play. Are you ready? Now strike that ball like you have never struck it before—now is the time.*

Many people have lost their authentic swing; they have become prisoners of their past. It is time to stop hugging your pain and to start playing the game like it was meant to be played.

Prison Break

Take some time to reflect on your past that may have formed the "prison" you are in today. Prison break is possible, it is a question of how badly you want to be set free. Some people may be able to break free from the prison of their past with deep reflective thinking, others may require the help of a friend or a counsellor.

- What were some of the events or killer phrases that have formed your prison?
- What keeps you in your prison?
- Is prison break something you want?
- Design a plan for your prison break and share it with someone you trust.

David Shapiro, in his book *Repacking your Bags,* explains:
We've discovered that many people are laboring through their lives, weighed down by attachments that no longer serve them. Patterns of behavior that have helped them get where they are, aren't helping them get where they want to be. As a result, many people feel desperate. They are grieving over the loss of life—their own.... Many people are worn down with trying so hard, while the oasis of life that was promised is still tantalizing inches beyond the reach of their dry and thirsty souls.[7]

To help unlock the visionary, *Imaginal* spirit within you, you first need to ask the following questions:

- What am I carrying in my backpack that is weighing me down? What's my baggage?
- How do I overcome my fear of failure?
- What's the Big Why of my life?
- Is it time to repack my bags?

Is it possible to change the direction of my life or am I destined to fulfill a life of mediocrity? As previously stated, I have observed that there is a small percentage of high performers who have this innate ability to strive for greatness and achieve it. I define greatness as living life to the fullest, being all that I am destined to be. There is also a small percentage of people who have quit on life and just simply don't care anymore—there is no notion of purpose or destiny. I believe that most people are latent high performers. Greatness resides in them, but it has been bottled up or suppressed and not allowed to be expressed. This book is about releasing this greatness that resides in everybody to live an exciting adventuresome life; to be not only purpose driven, but also VISION-driven.

You *can* live a life of vision. You *can* find your BIG WHY, unlock the visionary spirit inside you, and become *Imaginal*. You *can* break out of the prison of your past and regain your authentic swing—that unique calling that is yours and yours alone. Joining your life to a vision centered around a cause that's greater than you will enable you to venture out further, and not feel as averse to taking risks. Failure will not be viewed negatively, and your life of being *Imaginal* will be that of adventure and meaning.

But risk and failure, even in the pursuit of your BIG WHY, are not easy to deal with. That's why to pursue your calling and become *Imaginal* takes something else—something that separates those who fulfill their dreams from those who don't.

4.

Activating Drive

"Take care of your dreams, and your dreams will take care of you."

-Paulo Coelho

Why is it that some people have tremendous courage to pursue their dreams, yet others quit when the going gets tough? Why are there those who succeed beyond measure in their giftings, while others remain stagnant and unfulfilled?

Activating personal drive is the second of the Five Keys to Becoming an *Imaginal* Leader, and truly separates those who fulfill their dreams from those who don't. Drive is like high-octane fuel—what gets you moving towards the fulfillment of your BIG WHY. And, like fuel, drive is made up of some pretty hefty core ingredients:

- Courage is at the heart of personal drive. Courage is an artifact of our humanity, it is the ability to make choices in the face of adversity.

- Passion is the quality, intensity and depth of our commitment, often expressed through emotion.

- Initiative is taking action, which is fueled by courage and passion. Initiative is turning the key in the ignition and starting to drive the vehicle.

- Persistence and perseverance are directly related to the quality and depth of courage and passion.

I have found that courage is linked to your center and Big WHY. Self-centered people do not take risks, since these kinds of people are consumed with self-preservation, protection, and promotion.

As you study history, you will find that the most courageous people were those who were caused-centered. These people were often willing to lay down their lives for the cause since the cause came before self and comfort. Since your personal vision is a specific expression of what you are inspired to do to advance a cause and purpose, as vision grows, so does courage. Cause-centered people have a much bigger vision from which courage can grow.

Someone once said, "Afflict the comfortable rather than comfort the afflicted; make comfort zones into discomfort zones". This is what it means to become a cause-driven visionary.

Figure 4.1- Courage & Commitment

Figure 4.2 - Big WHY vs Self-Centered Courage

Courage is expressed in four realms. The first is physical courage, which is the traditional view of courage held by Socrates, Plato, Aristotle, and many others. This is when you place your life at physical risk, whether at war or when trying to save someone's life

Moral courage is when you stand up for what is right; it is the preservation of virtue. It took moral courage for Gandhi and Martin Luther King Jr. to take a stand for social justice.

It takes courage to create. Creation seldom matches what is imagined. It can be rejected, and sometimes involves destruction of something first before the new can be built. It will take courage for you to design your future as opposed to engage it by default.

Finally there is the courage to live to pursue your dream, to become all that you can become, to live the authentic life, to be an entrepreneur, innovator and inventor, living fully in all four I^3 capacities.

Figure 4.3 - Four Realms of Courage

Courage is the motivation to step outside the traditional boundary and comfort zone, to take risks, take the lead, take a stand, and be willing to error and in so doing learn and grow.

Courage Self Assessment

You can use the following self assessment tool to reflect on your courage. There is no right or wrong score—this is simply an exercise to help you reflect on your courage and your Big WHY. Shade in your score starting from zero and ending on the number you choose:

0. Not at all
1. Seldom- only if I have to
2. Occasionally when I think of it
3. Occasionally without having to think of it
4. Consistently by intentional effort
5. Consistently without thinking

Type of Courage	Score					
Physical - Courage to place your life at physical risk	0	1	2	3	4	5
Moral - Courage to stand up for what is right	0	1	2	3	4	5
Create - Courage to create what you desire and envision	0	1	2	3	4	5
Live - Courage to live and pursue your dream without restraint	0	1	2	3	4	5

Back to Egypt Syndrome

The Back to Egypt Syndrome is a metaphor taken from the Jewish exodus story with Moses. Egypt represents the status quo; it's the place of captivity where you are a prisoner of your past, and held captive to maintaining the status quo. In the exodus story, the Israelites have left Egypt with great expectations and excitement of seeing the promised land. Along comes the Red Sea with Pharaoh's army in pursuit.

We all have Red Sea moments when we have enrolled into a program that is promoting a better life to the participants. Up to this point you have enrolled into a program with a promise of a better life, the vision, because it intrigued you. But now you must make a decision: do I turn around and go back to Egypt, or do I find a way through the Red Sea? The Red Sea is the place of disclosure, which is where you find out what is motivating you to pursue the vision. You have probably exhibited some degree of commitment and exerted some effort to get to this point, but now your resolve is put to the test.

In life, when you face your Red Sea moments you will soon find out where your real commitment lies. You can very readily enroll into a vision

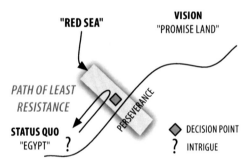

Figure 4.4 - Back to Egypt Syndrome

that holds out the prospect of something better, the "promised land"—a land flowing with milk and honey—but your true commitment is revealed when the journey becomes difficult. Dissatisfaction with being in "Egypt" may cause you to enroll into a vision or program that promises a better life, but seldom will it provide the energy to accomplish the vision itself.

Imaginal leaders create not to attain satisfaction or avoid dissatisfaction, but rather because they want to—they have been called to create, they love the cause and vision they serve, and they have a Big WHY that becomes their true north star. (more on this in Chapter 10.)

For an *Imaginal* leader, the structural tension that is created between the vision and the current reality creates a dominant structure in which the path of least resistance is toward the fulfillment of the vision and not toward going back to Egypt. For those who are just enrolled into a vision their

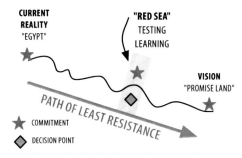

Figure 4.5 - Path of Least Resistance for an Imaginal Leader

path of least resistance will lead them back to Egypt. The Red Sea moment for an *Imaginal* leader is not just a time of testing, but also a time of learning to better understand the dynamics that are at play in the system they are living in.

The *Imaginal* leader is creating the future envisioned out of love, which arguably is the most powerful motivating force in the universe. The reason why a true *Imaginal* leader's commitment can seldom be questioned is because love and commitment go together, they are inseparable. A husband and wife who truly love each other are also committed to each other; and parents' love for their children means that they are committed to their children's success in life.

When I was 11 years old my parents decided that it would be a good idea that I learn how to play the piano. Something happened very early on as I started with my piano lessons: I had a vision to become a concert pianist. I was no child prodigy, but under the tutelage of an amazing piano teacher by the name of Hilda Capp, I rapidly progressed with my piano playing. In three short years, I had completed my grade 9 Royal Conservatory piano exam, as well as my grade two theory. I never became a concert pianist, but during those three years of my young life, having a long-term vision caused an acceleration in my musical abilities.

In 1997, Gary McPherson, a leading researcher in music development with children from Melbourne, Australia, undertook a study with 157 randomly chosen children to determine why certain ones progressed quickly at music lessons while others did not. Was the difference due to

IQ, mathematical skills, genetics, socio-economic level, motor skill development or some special gift? None of these turned out to be factors. He was stunned by what he discovered. At the beginning of the study he asked all the children, "How long do you think you will play your instrument?" the answer to which became a prime indicator of future success. McPherson condensed the answers into three categories:

- Short-term commitment

- Medium-term commitment

- Long-term commitment

Those children that expressed long-term commitment outperformed the short-term commitment group by 400 percent. The long-term commitment group, with a mere twenty minutes of weekly practice, progressed faster that the short-termers who practiced four times as much per week. When long-term commitment was combined with high levels of practice the skill skyrocketed. What McPherson found was that the vision the child brought to the first lesson, coupled with a commitment to learning an instrument, were far more important factors than anything the teacher said or the amount of practice.

The path of least resistance for these young children was toward their vision to become a musician as exemplified by their long-term commitment. People who truly have a vision for the future create a structural tension that causes life to flow toward its fulfillment.

Joseph Effect

Over the years I have discovered a principle or phenomenon which I call the Joseph Effect—which I could have very easily called the Steve Jobs Effect. According to ancient Hebrew scriptures, Joseph was the youngest of twelve sons and his father's favorite. Joseph had dreams that his life was to make a big difference and that he would be elevated above his brothers. Out of jealousy, his brothers sold Joseph into slavery, and he eventually ended up in Egypt. Joseph rapidly rose in stature as a servant only to be falsely accused of a crime and thrown into prison. Eventually, after many years of obscurity, Joseph rose to prominence in leadership in

Egypt and was instrumental in saving not only Egypt itself, but also his own family from a drought.

The Joseph Effect postulates that the height to which you aspire to make a difference in this world will correspond to the depth of testing, pain and suffering you will experience before you attain your vision. Of course this is only a generalized hypothesis and one could find many exceptions to the rule. Steve Jobs carried a huge vision for Apple in its early years, only to be fired from his own company in 1985. In 1997, Jobs returned to Apple as interim CEO, and had what seemed to be an insurmountable job of trying to save the very company he had founded from near bankruptcy. From 1997 until his death in 2011, Apple rose to become the number one recognizable brand in the world with one of the highest market capitalization.

I always tell people that if you aspire to make a big difference in the world, then be prepared to experience a lot of pain. The Joseph Effect modifies the popular saying, "No pain, no glory" to "*More glory, more pain.*"

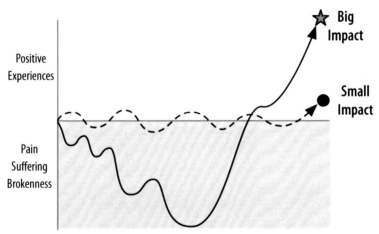

Figure 4.6 - The Joseph Effect

The reason why the Joseph Effect is an observable phenomenon is that those *Imaginal* leaders who carry a vision to make a big impact are sold out to their vision—they so love their vision that they are willing to endure whatever hardship comes their way to attain it. And at some point in their lives *Imaginal* leaders have had to make the firm decision not to go back to Egypt when the destination seemed completely out of view—the drive toward their BIG WHY was too strong, even in the face of those forces that wanted them to recede into mediocrity and oblivion.

Integrated Model

What drives people to do extraordinary things? There are many who seem content living ordinary lives, which are marked by a pursuit of comfort rather than significance. And there are those who live from an entirely different orientation to their lives, willing even to sacrifice comfort for the significance of a vision pursued, and eventually fulfilled.

I have introduced you to three models: the I³ model, the Big WHY model and the Centers model. It is time now to merge these three models into one.

Most people live their lives in the bottom two quadrants—they exhibit the managerial spirit and walk by sight. The managerial identity seeks balance, consistency, comfort, and security; their limited vision is determined by what they can see in the "real" world as determined by the five senses and measurement. People living in this mode can be quite purposeful. They generally set goals, which are in their power to achieve, and attain a level of satisfaction by accomplishing them. But where is the adventure, and where is the significance that goes with a life that is vision driven?

The top half of the I³ model is where vision is incubated and matured. This is where the *Imaginal* spirit is released to see the invisible—to walk by faith and not just by sight. *Imaginal*, visionary people have learned to activate their imagination, to accept mystery, to give up control, to take a risk, to create and challenge doing the impossible. These people go beyond being purpose-driven—they are vision-driven; and as such they hold to a vision that is rooted in a cause that is bigger than they are.

Vision Driven	**Entrepreneurial Spirit**	**Walk by Faith**
	Finds great **JOY** in creating what they **LOVE**. Willing to take risks and endure hardships for their **Big WHY**.	Enters the **Universe of Unlimited Possibilities** with their imagination, accepts mystery, gives up control, is challenged with doing the impossible.
Purpose Driven	**Managerial Spirit**	**Walk by Sight**
	Seeks **BALANCE**, consistency comfort, and security. Great enjoyment in seeing things running smoothly.	Lives in the **Universe of Measurement**, what is real, measurable, predictable, safe, controllable and goal oriented.

Figure 4.7 - Vision Driven Life

The personal drive of the *Imaginal* leader toward the fulfillment of a vision *is* the path of least resistance. And it is a drive that is personal—it is inside you as it is inside me, and activated when we serve a cause bigger than ourselves.

But now that we've taken a hard look at the fuel that gets us moving, we need to consider the various vehicles, for as we are unique, so we have unique drivers. Finding what drives you is absolutely critical to finding your BIG WHY and becoming *Imaginal*.

5.

Breakthrough Drivers

"In and through the personal re-discovery of the great, we find that we need not be passive victims of what we deterministically call 'circumstances'.…But that by linking ourselves…with the great we can become freer—freer to be ourselves, to be what we most want and value."

- W.J. Bate, The Burden of the Past.

"Not everyone is like you," a good friend once rather boldly declared to me. I was in conversation with him about the various levels of commitment I was sensing in the faculty of the school I had founded. And at first I was taken aback by his comment, but the more I began to think about it the more I realized that in that comment was a profound truth: *we are all wired so differently.* I had staff members that were so marinated with compassion, you would swear that every other sentence was about Mother Teresa. Others felt the call to equip teachers, and their sense of fulfillment came from seeing others rising to their potential. There were those that had a deep curiosity about how students learned best and how to activate creativity within them. Out of this reflection on the words of my friend came a revelation: *not everyone is like me.*

Seven Breakthrough Drivers

I began thinking about what drives people to do extraordinary feats, which in turn led me to think about great history-makers—people who have profoundly shaped the world we live in. I found that there are basically seven drivers that motivate people to accomplish various kinds of breakthroughs.

Figure 5.1 - Seven Breakthrough Drivers

The seven breakthrough drivers (all starting with the letter "c") are the following:

- Curiosity: the drive to know something.

- Compassion: the drive to help others less fortunate.

- Conscience: the drive to right a wrong.

- Creation: the drive to build and create.

- Cause: the drive to advance a noble cause or ideology.

- Crazy: the drive to be the first; to take extraordinary risks.

- Capital: the drive to create wealth and to give it away.

I have found that these drivers generally come in clusters of two or three. Think about what drives you to do what you do as we look at each of these drivers.

Curiosity

Many of the great scientific breakthroughs over the centuries have been made by people with an intense need to know something. These are people that are driven by curiosity. We all know that the seat of all learning with young children is their insatiable curiosity. For most, this sense of curiosity is lost early in a child's life while attending traditional schools that are over emphasizing convergent thinking. Even in good inquiry or problem-based learning, students are not asked to create new knowledge, rather they are directed to discover what is already known, even though it may be new to them.

People who are driven by curiosity have developed a heightened sense of wanting to find answers to what is *not* known. Human curiosity drives most of today's scientific discoveries. We have built the Hubble space telescope to view the universe in a way not possible on earth. We have spent $6.5 billion to build the Large Haldron Collider, a 27 km circular underground tunnel with all kinds of sophisticated equipment, to observe particles colliding. Recently, scientists were able to confirm the existence of an elementary particle, the Higgs Boson, or the 'God particle' as others have called it, originally postulated in 1964 by Peter Higgs and several other scientists. Why all this expense to discover this obscure particle? Because at the heart of human exploration is the need to find answers to mysteries, in this case how our universe came into existence.

Throughout history, people have been driven to solve the mysteries of the universe.

Nicolaus Copernicus (1473-1543) started what is called the Copernican Revolution. He proposed a huge paradigm shift from an earth-centric model of the universe, to a heliocentric model, meaning that the earth actually rotated around the sun. This was a huge shift not only scientifically, but also philosophically, since the prevailing paradigm was that earth and man were at the center of the universe.

Galileo (1564-1642), who has been called the "father of modern observational astronomy," was able to prove Copernicus's theories as well as advance many others of his own. His quest for scientific discoveries and truth about our solar system were not embraced by the political and religious powers of the day. Galileo was tried in the Roman Inquisition, which began in 1615, was found "vehemently suspect of heresy," forced to recant, and spent the rest of his life under house arrest. Galileo paid a heavy price for his curiosity and pursuit of scientific discoveries.

Isaac Newton (1642-1727) was an English physicist, mathematician, astronomer, natural philosopher, alchemist, and theologian, and one of the most influential men in human history. In his work, Newton described universal gravitation and the three laws of motion, which laid the groundwork for classical mechanics, which dominated the scientific view of the physical universe for the next three centuries, and is the basis for modern engineering. In mechanics, Newton enunciated the principles of conservation of momentum and angular momentum. In optics, he built the first "practical" reflecting telescope, and developed a theory of color based on the observation that a prism decomposes white light into a visible spectrum. He also formulated an empirical law of cooling and studied the speed of sound.

Albert Einstein (1879-1955) was a German-born theoretical physicist. He is best known for his theory of relativity and specifically mass–energy equivalence, expressed by the equation $E = mc^2$. His theory of relativity has a wide range of consequences, which have been experimentally verified, including those considered counter-intuitive, such as length contraction, time dilation and relativity of simultaneity, contradicting the classical notion that the duration of the time interval between two events is equal for all observers. Many of Einstein's revolutionary theories, which recently have been proven to be true, were created as a result of thought experiments. He would imagine himself flying on a beam of light and would ask thought provoking questions from various vantage points.

Compassion

The next driver is compassion. I mentioned at the beginning that these drivers come in clusters, an example of which is *Louis Pasteur (1822-1895)*. As a French chemist and microbiologist he is best known for his remarkable breakthroughs in the causes and prevention of disease. His experiments supported the germ theory of disease, also reducing mortality from puerperal fever (childbed), and he created the first vaccine for rabies. He was best known to the general public for inventing a method to stop milk and wine from causing sickness—this process came to be called Pasteurization. Pasteur was driven by compassion to prevent un-wanted death, as well as curiosity to find the answer.

Saint Mother Teresa (1910-1997) was an Albanian Roman Catholic nun with Indian citizenship who founded the Missionaries of Charity in Calcutta, India in 1950. For over 45 years she ministered to the poor, sick, orphaned, and dying, while guiding the Missionaries of Charity's expansion, first throughout India and then in other countries. She won the Nobel Peace Prize in 1979 and India's highest civilian honor, the Bharat Ratna, in 1980 for her humanitarian work. Mother Teresa's Missionaries of Charity continued to expand; and at the time of her death it was operating 610 missions in 123 countries, with services including hospices and homes for people with HIV/AIDS, leprosy and tuberculosis, soup kitchens, children's and family counseling programs, orphanages, and schools. Her philosophy was simple, "Do not think that love, in order to be genuine, has to be extraordinary. What we need is to love without getting tired."

Conscience

The next driver is conscience, which is about justice, about doing the right thing and making things right. History is full of people who have impacted our world by doing the right thing, even those who started out with less laudable motivations.

Oscar Schindler (1908-1974), although initially motivated by greed, soon found that he was consumed with trying to save Jewish prisoners from the concentration camps. Schindler has been credited with saving over 1,200 Jews during the holocaust by employing them in his enamel-ware and ammunitions factories. The 1993 Steven Spielberg movie, *Schindler's List*, highlights the contradictory trajectory of an opportunistic and amoral man initially motivated by profit, who came to show extraordinary initiative, tenacity and dedication in order to save the lives of his Jewish employees, subsequently ending his life in poverty.

Mahatma Gandhi (1869-1948) was the preeminent leader of the Indian independence movement who, by employing non-violent civil disobedience, led India to independence. His actions have inspired movements for non-violence and civil rights around the world.

Martin Luther King, Jr. (1929-1968) was an American clergyman, activist and prominent leader in the African-American civil rights movement. His main legacy was to secure progress on civil rights in the United States, and he is frequently referenced as a human rights icon today. King's efforts led to the 1963 March on Washington, where he delivered his *I Have a Dream* speech. There, he raised public consciousness of the civil rights movement and established himself as one of the greatest orators in U.S. history. In 1964, King became the youngest person to receive the Nobel Peace Prize for his work to end racial segregation and racial discrimination through civil disobedience and other non-violent means.

Creation

Creation is a drive to invent or create something new. Creators must be driven by vision; they must have the ability to envision something with imagination first before it can be realized in the real world.

Filippo Brunelleschi (1377-1446) was one of the foremost architects and engineers of the Italian Renaissance. All of his principle works are in Florence, Italy.

In 1296, work began on the construction of Santa Maria del Fiore in Florence, Italy. It was an enormous undertaking, particularly when it came to the design and construction of the dome. The original planners of the cathedral had no idea how the dome could be built, for no one had ever built a dome over the vast chasm of 140 feet. They merely expressed the faith that sometime in the future God might provide a solution, for at the time it was deemed impossible.

In 1419 there arose a competition to design a dome and cupola for the cathedral with a large prize of 200 gold florins to the winning design. Brunelleschi's winning solution was ingenious and unprecedented: the distinctive octagonal design of the double-walled dome, resting on a drum and not on the roof itself, allowed for the entire dome to be built without the need for scaffolding from the ground. It was the first large dome ever to be built without centering.

This enormous construction weighs 37,000 tons and contains over 4 million bricks. He made several models and drawings of details during the construction. Brunelleschi had to invent special hoisting machines and lewissons for hoisting large stones. These specially designed machines and brilliant masonry techniques were Brunelleschi's spectacular contribution to architecture. Brunelleschi literally turned the impossible into the possible by engaging with the innovation and invention identities—he was driven by his vision to create and do the impossible.

Cause

Cause is generally connected to an ideology, or a large scale transformation of our society or its institutions. For instance, I am personally driven to affect real change in education and participate in the reformation of education as a system. Freedom fighters tend to be driven by a cause to the point that they would be willing to lay down their lives for it. Cause often has a religious underpinning as well.

Martin Luther (1483-1546) was a seminal figure in the reformation of the church in the 1500s. He strongly disputed the claim that freedom from God's punishment for sin could be purchased with money—called indulgences. Luther taught that salvation is earned not by good works, but by grace through faith in Jesus Christ. In 1517, Pope Leo X announced a new round of indulgences to help build St. Peter's Basilica. On October 31, 1517, an angry Martin Luther nailed a sheet of paper with ninety-five theses on the university's chapel door. Martin Luther is one of the most influential and controversial figures in the Reformation movement. His actions fractured the Roman Catholic Church, and set into motion the rise of Protestantism.

Karl Marx (1818-1883) was a German philosopher, economist, sociologist, historian and revolutionary socialist. Marx's theories about society, economics and politics—collectively known as Marxism—hold that human societies progress through class struggle: a conflict between an ownership class that controls production and a proletariat that provides the labour for production. He called capitalism the "dictatorship of the bourgeoisie" believing it to be run by the wealthy classes for their own benefit; and he predicted that, like previous socioeconomic systems, capitalism produced internal tensions which would lead to its self-destruction and replacement by a new system: socialism and ultimately a classless society called communism. This led to the rise of communism that at one point in modern history had one fifth of the world population under its influence. Ultimately, communism failed not only as an economic system, but as a social and political system.

Crazy

History is full of examples of people taking extraordinary risks, to discover new lands, or to scale the highest mountain. Why do this? These people have what I call the crazy driver. They are driven by adventure, by the goal of being the first, and are willing to take extraordinary risks to accomplish their dream. The people I place into the crazy category are not taking foolish risks, such as a drunk driver, rather they are extremely methodical and spend a lot of time in planning and preparation for their adventure. By no means am I suggesting that these people had a death wish—quite the opposite—but they were uniquely wired to push the boundaries of what was possible. Modern neurobiologists explain this motivation as being driven by the dopamine system. Dopamine helps to elicit a sense of satisfaction when we accomplish a task; therefore, the riskier the task the bigger the dopamine hit. I will not deny that much of our behavior can be explained biologically, but if this were purely a biological phenomenon then why are there so few explorers and risk takers? Something else is at play that comes from deep within the human soul.

Shackleton's (1874-1922) 1914 Imperial Trans-Antarctic Expedition, was one of the greatest tales of survival in naval expedition history.

The following ad was placed in the newspaper:

MEN WANTED: FOR HAZARDOUS JOURNEY. SMALL WAGES, BITTER COLD, LONG MONTHS OF COMPLETE DARKNESS, CONSTANT DANGER, SAFE RETURN DOUBTFUL. HONOR AND RECOGNITION IN CASE OF SUCCESS.

It has been reported that 5,000 people responded to the ad of which 27 men were selected. Although this piece of the Shackleton story is in dispute, it does not diminish its heroic nature.

Just one day's sail from the continent of Antarctica, the ship Endurance became trapped in sea ice. Frozen fast for ten months, the ship was crushed and destroyed by ice pressure, and the crew was forced to abandon ship.

After camping on the ice for five months, Shackleton made two open boat journeys, one of which—a treacherous 800-mile ocean crossing to South Georgia Island under hurricane conditions—is now considered one of the greatest boat journeys in history. Finally reaching land on the unoccupied side of South Georgia, Shackleton and his two companions decided to trek 32 miles across the mountains and reached the island's remote whaling station 36 hours later. Soon after, Shackleton organized a rescue team, and saved all of the men he had left behind.

What would motivate *Edmund Hillary (1919-2008)* a New Zealand mountaineer, explorer and philanthropist, to become the first to summit Mount Everest and return alive? Many attempts to summit Mt. Everest were either met with failure or with death. Following his ascent of Everest, he devoted much of his life to helping the Sherpa people of Nepal through the Himalayan Trust, which he founded. Through his efforts many schools and hospitals were built in this remote region of the Himalayas.

Capital

The final driver is Capital, represented by people who are driven to create wealth. People that come to mind are Bill Gates, Warren Buffett and Mary Kay.

Creating enormous wealth is usually accompanied by the willingness to explore the boundaries of what is possible, take a risk on an unproven idea, and persevere until the dream has been realized. Wealth is primarily created in business; and the great wealth creators over time have usually been pioneers with new technologies or solutions.

Bill Gates (1955-Present) in 1975, before graduation, left Harvard to form Microsoft with his childhood friend, Paul Allen. The pair planned to develop software for the newly emerging personal computer market. Bill Gates's company, Microsoft, became famous for its computer operating systems and killer business deals. For example, Bill Gates talked IBM into letting Microsoft retain the licensing rights to MS-DOS, an operating system that IBM needed for its new personal computer. Gates proceeded to make a fortune from the licensing of MS-DOS

Now, in the later stages of his career, Gates has pursued a number of philanthropic endeavors, donating large amounts of money to various charitable organizations and scientific research programs through the Bill & Melinda Gates Foundation, established in 2000. In June 2010 Bill Gates and Warren Buffett launched "The Giving Pledge" that challenges the wealthiest billionaires in the world to give half their wealth to charity. By April 2013 over 100 billionaires have signed the pledge.

Many wealth creators have turned to philanthropy. Having "been there and done that," philanthropists have found the joy of giving back and making a difference, particularly in those parts of the world that face hardships and great suffering.

Driver Clusters

Just like in personality types, these drivers tend to form clusters. There could be one main driver with two or three subservient drivers that provide the context for the main driver itself. A person with a dominant capital driver could also be driven to create as well as take a lot of risks thus also falling under the driver "crazy".

Someone like me may have a strong visionary drive for creation that is connected to a cause like transforming education thus requiring a good dose of the crazy drive or the willingness to take risks.

As you can see, these drivers can be combined in many different ways. Take a few minutes to reflect on your dominant driver and a couple of supportive drivers. Understanding what drives you will help you understand your role within a vision community and the world at large. It will also help you as an *Imaginal* leader show greater empathy to the people you lead.

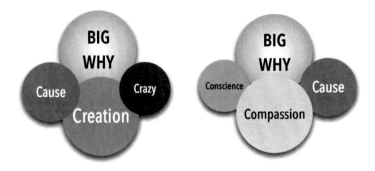

Figure 5.2 - Examples of Driver Clusters

Driver Assessment

You can use the following simple assessment tool to find your dominant drivers. There is no right or wrong score. This is simply an exercise to help you reflect on what drives you to do what you do. Shade in your score starting from zero and ending on the number you choose.

0. Not at all
1. Seldom: only if I have to
2. Occasionally: when I think of it
3. Occasionally: without having to think of it
4. Consistently: by intentional effort
5. Consistently: without thinking

Your Driver	Score					
Curiosity - the drive to know something	0	1	2	3	4	5
Compassion - the drive to help others less fortunate	0	1	2	3	4	5
Conscience - the drive to right a wrong	0	1	2	3	4	5
Creation - the drive to build and create	0	1	2	3	4	5
Cause - the drive to advance a noble cause or ideology	0	1	2	3	4	5
Crazy - the drive to be the first - to take extraordinary risks	0	1	2	3	4	5
Capital - the drive to create wealth and to give it away	0	1	2	3	4	5

We've looked at the main ingredients for becoming *Imaginal*: The pursuit of your BIG WHY by understanding what's at your center and ultimately what drives and motivates you. These ingredients make up the *internal* components of becoming *Imaginal*.

And while they are absolutely fundamental, there is more to this metamorphosis. For as *Imaginal* leaders all know and will tell you, they have developed over time a profound way of seeing reality in ways that others have not.

They have cultivated the skill of seeing into the future.

Part II: Seeing

6.

Vision: Seeing the Invisible

"Vision is the art of seeing what is invisible to others."

- Jonathan Swift

What would you do if you were not afraid? What a profound question. I think if we were honest many would say our lives would be different. Ben and Roz Zander made the comment *that much more is possible than people ordinarily think.*[8] Many would agree with this statement, but why is it so?

As we'll see, the frame through which we view the world is an invention that usually filters through one of two lenses: that of limitation and scarcity, which I call the Universe of Measurement, and that of Unlimited Possibility. The *Imaginal* leader has a unique ability to see both the future and the current reality, and allow the tension of these two worlds to drive the creation process: that of pulling the future into the now. This unique ability comes from living in these two worlds.

Universe of Measurement

How our Brain Works?

The human brain is comprised of roughly 85 to 100 billion neurons, each connected to, on average, 7000 other neurons making some 600 trillion connections. If we were to connect all the neurons of a single brain end to end it would run about 165,000 km or four times the circumference of our earth. Simply put, the human brain is the most amazing complex mechanism known to humanity.

At its core, the brain is a pattern-producing mechanism. It is designed to store information in neural networks. For instance, we have a concept network for a chair, and over time we have added details that expand the concept network to include recliners, soft and hard chairs, ergonomic, and utilitarian chairs—there are literally hundreds of variation of this one concept. The same would apply to facial recognition. The retina found in the back of the eye, contains 5 million cones and 120 million rods as sensors of light, so every image that enters the eye stimulates 125 million neural signals that together represents the image. This image is sent to the visual cortex, which is processed from a general overall image to specific details of the image. Now put this in the context of watching a movie, in which you are receiving 24 images per second along with audio that also has to be processed. Needless to say, it is quite a marvel the way we are able to process inputs from all five senses out of which we can create meaning. For all of this to occur, the brain processes raw data through established networks.

I cannot do justice to the marvels of how the brain works—not only does it process data from all the five senses, it also creates outputs or responses to data being received. Neural outputs are also patterns embedded into the neural networks. When you combine these two phenomena of input patterns, as well as the output patterns, you will begin to understand the notion of habituation and biases.

Another way of looking at the same concept, but more from a behavioral viewpoint, is the ladder of inference found in Peter Senge's book *The Fifth Discipline*. The following six steps help to explain human behavior and how biases are formed:

1. I have observable "data" experiences.
2. I select "data" from what I observe.
3. I make assumptions based on the meanings I have added.
4. I draw conclusions.
5. I adopt beliefs about the world.
6. I take action based on my beliefs.

Suppose I am walking down the hallway consumed in my thoughts about the meeting I am going to. I walk by a person without acknowledging him, not on purpose, simply because I was thinking about the meeting coming up. The person I pass by thinks, "Tom walked by, but didn't say 'hello,' I wonder why he didn't say 'hi'?" Suppose it happens again the next day. Now the person begins to add meaning to this data, "Tom is intentionally not acknowledging me. Perhaps he doesn't like me, or perhaps he simply is a snob." Now the person remembers from a past situation that his previous boss had done the same thing, so now he begins to develop a belief that people in authority tend to be snobs. In the future when he interacts with people in leadership he will only select data that support his belief. A leader could be talking in a room to a lot of people, but because the leader did not talk to him, that leader must be a snob. You will find, as well, these kinds of inferences strongly entrenched within political perspectives: "That person is a liberal, he can't be trusted," or, "That person is a conservative, she must not really have compassion for the poor." When these patterns form into beliefs they become powerful mental models or structures that begin to dictate how we view the world and ultimately live in it.

Paradigm

Understanding that our brain interprets the world through patterns, it goes even one step further: it actually looks for data that fit patterns that already exist. In other words, the brain biases the information by accepting the input that fits pre-existing networks or patterns. Thomas Kuhn called this pattern of thinking a *paradigm*, which is defined as a set of assumptions, concepts, values, and practices that constitutes a way of viewing reality for the community that shares them, especially in an intellectual discipline. The following passage from Wikipedia summarizes what Thomas Kuhn wrote in *The Structure of Scientific Revolutions*:

> *For well-integrated members of a particular discipline, its paradigm is so convincing that it normally renders even the possibility of alternatives unconvincing and counter-intuitive. Such a paradigm is opaque, appearing to be a direct view of the bedrock of reality itself, and obscuring the possibility that there might be other, alternative imageries hidden behind it. The conviction that the current paradigm is reality tends to disqualify evidence that might undermine the paradigm itself."* [9]

Kuhn argued that 'normal' science is all about clearing up the accepted paradigm, and tends to discover what it expects to discover. Discovery happens when somethings goes wrong with the experiment; when an unexpected anomaly occurs. Even then, it takes a long time for anomalies to be seen as those which are contrary to the accepted paradigm. Scientists have a difficult time even seeing data that do not fit the expected paradigm, thus making it even more difficult to discover anomalies that may eventually lead to a crisis and ultimately a new paradigm.

The shifting of one's paradigm does not occur easily. Thomas Kuhn observed that,

The decision to reject one paradigm is always simultaneously the decision to accept another, and the judgment leading to that decision involves the comparison of both paradigms with nature and with each other. [10]

Mental Models and Limiting Mindsets

Mental models are the images, assumptions, and stories we carry in our minds about ourselves, other people, institutions, and every aspect of the world. Like a pair of glasses framing and subtly distorting our vision, mental models determine what we see.

Mental models explain why two people can observe the same event and describe it differently. A prime example was back in 1995 during the infamous O.J. Simpson trial. If you were to ask African Americans if O.J. was guilty or innocent the vast majority would have said he is innocent; but ask the same question of 'white America' and you would have received the opposite answer. Why would that be? Everyone has access to the same information from the news media. The difference was the mental models that were applied to the information about the case itself.

Mental models powerfully shape how we act. Our mental image of ourselves drives our behaviors. Mental models are usually tacit, which means they exist below the level of our awareness. Our mental models often remain untested and unexamined, and most people become very defensive when trying to examine their mindsets.

All mindsets, by definition, are limiting; they are merely patterns of thinking formed over time. Let's look at some classic examples:

- "The government should close the patent office because everything that could be invented had been invented." *Charles Duell, 1899, the director of the US Patent Office.*

- *1997—Action at US Patent Office:*

  237,000 applications received at US Patent office. A 15% in crease from previous year.

  124,127 patents were granted. A 16% increase from previous high.

  IBM alone had 2,657 patents granted.

- "Television won't be able to hold on to any market it captures after the first six months. People will soon get tired of staring at a ply-wood box every night." *Darryl Zanuck, Head of 20th Century Fox, 1946.*

- "There is no reason for any individual to have a computer in their home." *Kenneth Olson, President and Founder of Digital Equipment Corp., 1977.*

Our thinking is what holds us as prisoners of our past. These limiting mindsets are the lens through which we interpret life. Unfortunately our vision has been impaired. We cannot escape this prison until we understand why we think the way we think and do the things we do. We need to question the validity of our fundamental assumptions and unconscious beliefs that power our thinking and drive our actions.

Albert Einstein once observed that the present problems cannot be solved at the level of thinking at which they were created. Working with mental models means that you are working at the highest leverage point for change—the transformation of your thinking.

Lens that Frame Scarcity or Abundance

● ● ●

● ● ●

● ● ●

Join all nine dots with four straight lines without lifting your pen from the paper

We all know that the glasses we wear help us see better, but in some instances the lens actually hinders our ability to see.

Take a moment and try this assignment here on the left. Were you able to do it?

It is impossible to do this assignment by staying within the boundary of the 9 dots. However, the moment you go outside the boundary of the box new possibilities arise— what was impossible, becomes *possible*.

Every problem, every dilemma, every dead end we find ourselves facing in life, only appears unsolvable inside a particular frame or point of view.

Enlarge the box, or create another frame around the data, and problems vanish, while new opportunities appear.

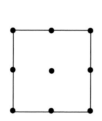

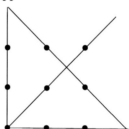

In nearly everyone, the context of instructions lie within the square formed by the outer dots.

What if we went outside the box and used the whole page?

A shoe factory sends two marketing scouts to a region of Africa to study the prospects for expanding its business. Each scout sent back a telegram:

Scout 1:

SITUATION HOPELESS. NO ONE WEARS SHOES.

Scout 2:

GLORIOUS BUSINESS OPPORTUNITY. THEY HAVE NO SHOES.

What's at play here? Why is it that two different people facing the same circumstances respond in two vastly different ways? The answer is quite obvious—it's the lens they wear.

The lens that basically sets our orientation toward life is called our worldview. There are many things that go into this frame, but basically there are two orientations: one is *scarcity*, and the other is *abundance*.

We live in the natural world, the world of measurement. We engage in the world of measurement with our five senses. Our senses are wired to give us warning of real or imagined dangers. It is the framework of fear and scarcity that often causes us to go into a downward spiral with our thinking.

In the world of measurement we get to know things by measuring, comparing, and contrasting them. The underlying assumption is that life is about the struggle to survive and get ahead in a world of limited resources—there are only so many pieces to the pie.

I grew up in a family with three brothers. Whenever our mother would bake something we had a rule, that the person who slices the cake gets last choice of a piece. We knew that there was only so much of a cake available—and God forbid if I was stuck getting the smallest piece!

Modern day economics is based on the theory of scarcity. It is the management of limited resources. Economist Paul Zane Pilzer has proven that there is unlimited wealth-creation potential, and in fact we do not live in a limited economic pie at all. The pie can grow and will continue to grow bigger. The scarcity mindset is so prevalent in many people's lives—after all, I face limitation everyday of my life.

Universe of Unlimited Possibilities

There is another way! You don't have to live in scarcity and complacency. You can live in the Universe of Unlimited Possibilities, where nothing is impossible—what I call the land of dreams. Dreams are the language of the human spirit that calls upon our passions and not our fears.

We can invent and sustain a framework that brings forth possibilities of what could be instead of feelings of despair and hopelessness. In this realm of Unlimited Possibilities there is no division between ideas and action; no division between the spirit, soul, and body; no division between dreams and reality. Leaders are able to exhibit unusual courage, because they become their vision; they begin to live out their future as if it were already accomplished. This may sound rather fluffy or fantastical, but I can attest to the fact that one can live in both universes without any conflict. You can have your feet firmly planted in the real world, yet have your sight on something that is invisible, and experience everyday the invisible becoming more visible.

The universe of unlimited possibilities stretches beyond the world of measurement to include all worlds—it is infinite, generative, and abundant. In this universe you are free from the generalized assumption of scarcity. There are no limits to what can be done with an unfettered imagination.

Not only is the pie enormous, if you take a slice the pie is whole again. When you are oriented to abundance, you care less about being in control and you take more risks.

In the world of measurement, you set a goal and strive for it. In the universe of unlimited possibility, you set the context of a vision and let it unfold. What a different way of living. I can attest to the fact that this kind of thinking, although somewhat counterintuitive, actually works and is quite liberating.

As a child it is easy to engage the universe of unlimited possibilities with our imagination. But through school and other influences we have been taught that we need to engage in the real world of measurement, for this is how we will get ahead in life. "Forget about dreaming—just be realistic about life." How sad to have the fountain of imagination stifled so early in life.

Faith to Create the Impossible

The world's best selling book states that faith is the substance of things hoped for and the evidence of things unseen. Faith is an emergent property that occurs when one imagines a future and applies hope to its unfolding. Faith enables *Imaginal* leaders to boldly declare a future, since they already see it as a reality. An *Imaginal* leader has the ability to exercise this very powerful currency of faith. Faith goes well beyond wishful thinking to an absolute certainty that the future being imagined will come to past. Steve Jobs unashamedly declared a future by faith, and was able to elevate and motivate an entire company toward it through his compelling sense of vision.

Imagination and hope are the elements from which faith is generated. I like to think of imagination as the eye of the human spirit. Imagination is that unique capability that separates us from the rest of the animal kingdom. It is not only one of the key elements for faith but also the key element for creativity. Human beings, unlike any other animal, have a unique endowment of being able to create that which is made possible by imagination. Human beings build dog houses and not dogs; human beings design laptops and not monkeys; human beings will send a man to the moon or build elaborate machines, like the CERN particle accelerator, with the hope of discovering the mysteries of the universe.

In my own life, learning to walk by faith has been the single most important aspect of my journey. Faith gives you the courage and the strength to persevere, to continue when most people have given up. Often when we hear the term faith we immediately think of a religious context, since faith is foundational to most religions. One must exercise faith to believe in an unseen God or higher power; however the faith I am referring to is intrinsic to the human spirit—that part of our existence that transcends the biochemical and neurological makeup of our bodies, and makes us uniquely human and God-like.

Evolutionary science studies the capability of organisms to adapt to changing environments, and through processes of mutations and natural selection organisms *learn* to adapt by embedding this learning into their DNA. The human being, however, through the power of creativity is able to reshape the environment it lives in for its own benefit. In many ways this has resulted in some bad environmental outcomes, but that is not the point I am making. There are unlimited possibilities of what human ingenuity can produce, if only we can find a way to live harmoniously with each other.

Some Imaginal History Makers

Let's revisit the Universe of Unlimited Possibilities and the Universe of Measurement. The Universe of Measurement can be thought of as the natural world, the world that we perceive through our five senses. This universe is understood by various scientific laws which define its limitations. In the natural world, if I were to jump off a tall building the law of gravity would dictate what the result would be. However, if I would engage in the Universe of Unlimited Possibilities with my imagination I could begin imaging how I might safely land after jumping from it. Perhaps I see myself like a bird descending toward the earth or a leaf gently gliding downwards using the resistance of the air to dampen its descent. I could invent a hang glider or a parachute, and all of a sudden an event that would result in certain death now brings pleasure and exhilaration. The Universe of Measurement is all about limitations; the Universe of Unlimited Possibility is that place we go to with our imagination, where there are no limits and no boundaries. The great science fiction writers of the past were able to imagine seemingly impossible scenarios of the future, only to see many of them coming true today.

The great artists, innovators, and inventors of history were able to engage with the Universe of Unlimited Possibilities with their imagination. Let's examine a couple of these *Imaginal* innovators and inventors.

James Watt and the Steam Engine

Less than a couple of hundred years ago, the chief source of power for production was hand power, animal power, and wind or water mill power. In the 1700s, coal mining was an important industry in Great Britain—as important to the economy as oil is today. The problem with the coal mines was that as they got deeper they would fill up with water, and the technology of the day was unable to remove the water fast enough, hence they were no longer viable.

Some early technological solutions, such as the Newcomen engine first built in 1705, were inadequate, highly inefficient, and very expensive to run. Watt began to think of how he might overcome the massive inefficiencies of the current technologies of his day.

James Watt (1736-1819) spent much time and money trying to invent a better and more efficient steam engine, but to no avail. He has been quoted as saying, "Nature has a weak side, if only we can find it out." He toiled over days, months, and years trying to design a truly functional engine and pump that the world was needing.

One Sunday afternoon in 1765, while on a walk, a flash of brilliance came to him: he saw with his imagination a solution to the problem he had been struggling over for many years. It took another couple of days for him to complete the invention in his mind. All things are created twice: the first creation is in the mind of the inventor who engages in the Universe of Unlimited Possibilities, and the second creation is when what is seen is made visible in the Universe of Measurement through design and build (keys four and five).

It took eight month for Watt to build his new engine. Designing was the easy part, but building the engine was most challenging, since none of the machining tools existed that would build the various parts to the level of tolerance required. As a result, the early model failed; but there was enough indication that he was on the right track.

Buoyed up with faith that he was getting closer to a solution, he went out and found an investor partner to whom he sold two thirds of the rights to his invention. In 1767, he began building another trial engine. After many sleepless nights and a constant battle with anxiety, Watt finished his trial engine, only again to have its performance fall well short of what he was envisioning. Watt called this trial engine 'Beelzebub', and after months of tweaking it was abandoned to a junk heap. A despondent Watt wrote,

Of all things in life, there is nothing more foolish than inventing. I am resolved... if I can resist it, to invent no more. To-day I enter the thirty-fifth year of my life, and think I have hardly yet done thirty-four pence worth of good in the world.

In 1774, Watt—with a new funding partner, Matthew Boulton—began designing and building a new engine to be completed three years later. Right on schedule, it was completed in 1777, and, to the surprise of many skeptics, the engine proved to be a great success, and within a few days the mine was pumped dry. Within a few years all the mines in England and Scotland were using the Watt Steam engine pump.

In 1782, as orders for the new pump began to fall off, Watt and Boulton turned their attention toward building a steam engine for factories.

Their first factory engine was for a corn mill, but an unforeseen challenge arose. The factory workers viewed Watt's new mill as a threat to their livelihood, and thus publicly opposed this new technological advancement. As attention grew, so did the opposition to such a height that one evening the mill was burned to the ground. In spite of the tragedy, the factory workers' attempt was to no avail; for word had spread throughout Europe and the United Sates, and orders were being placed for Watt's technological breakthrough. By 1785, Watts ran into a series of issues that challenged the viability of his business: mine owners refused to pay, other companies were violating his patent, and rumors that a better engine was in the works. Eventually, however, the business began to turn around, and Watt was able to retire doing what he enjoyed doing the most: tinkering in his workshop as an inventor.

Steve Jobs the Innovator

Steve Jobs (1955-2011) was an American inventor, best known as cofounder and CEO of Apple Inc and Pixar Animation Studios. Through Apple, he was widely recognized both as a charismatic pioneer of the personal computer revolution, and for his influential career in the computer and consumer electronics fields—transforming one industry after another, from computers and smartphones to music and movies. As a master of innovation, and as some would describe the "Father of the Digital Revolution," Steve Jobs, when asked what was his greatest accomplishment, answered that it was the creation of Apple—not a product, but a company, an assemblage of brilliant minds within a culture of innovation that changed our world. He recruited John Scully from Pepsi Cola with the challenge of making a "dent in the universe."

In Walter Isaacson's biography of Steve Jobs, he writes about Jobs's unique ability to stretch what was possible. For those who worked closely with him at Apple, it was called "Steve Jobs's reality distortion field." The following quotes from Isaacson's book describes how some viewed his reality distortion field:

> Jobs's reality distortion field] came from willfully defying reality, not only to others but to himself. "He can deceive himself," said Bill Atkinson, "it allowed him to con people into believing his vision, because he has personally embraced and internalized it."[11]

Like Wozniak, [Debi Coleman] believed that his reality distortion was empowering: it enabled Jobs to inspire his team to change the course of computer history with a fraction of the resources of Xerox and IBM. "It was a self-fulfilling distortion, you did the impossible, because you didn't realize it was impossible."[12]

Steve Jobs was passionate about making a difference. He believed that great work can only be done as acts of love. This combined with his perfectionism and micro managing most every project made working for Jobs a real test of one's commitment and calling to work at Apple. Arthur Levitt, former chairman of he Security Exchange Commission, said this of Steve jobs: "He was one of these CEOs who ran the company like he wanted to. He believed he knew more about it than anyone else, and he probably did. He's among the best CEOs I've ever known, in spite of his irreverence, irascibility, and ego." It was ultimately that unrelenting single mindedness that ended Jobs's career at Apple in 1985.

Apple went through a real wilderness experience, and eventually, on the verge of bankruptcy, asked Steve Jobs to come back to Apple as interim CEO in 1997.

As an *Imaginal* leader, Jobs was able to see the future in ways that few of his contemporaries were able to see. He did not rely on market research to direct his product development. Instead, using his intuition he built products he believed people would want. He created new market segments with his revolutionary products like the iPod, which was not only a revolutionary consumer product, but also a re-creation of how the music industry distributed its music. The genius of Steve Jobs was that he was able to see the whole ecosystem. He knew that it's not good enough to have a ground breaking technology, rather it's the whole experience that matters, for example how easily a person could purchase and download music, and how easily that music could be organized into the playlists.

Steve Jobs was a seer of the future and an expert of bringing that future into the now—he was an *Imaginal* leader.

And this is where we arrive at the third key of Vision, which is at the heart of *Imaginal* leadership and living: it is seeing the invisible, it is having sight. This is the ability to activate your imagination, having both insight (the ability to see what is) and foresight (the ability to see what could be).

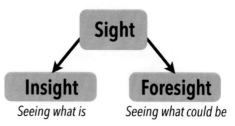

Figure 6.1- Two Kinds of Sight

These two ways of seeing—called Vision—are the outworking of the *Imaginal* leader, and open to all who are willing to enter the imagination and explore the Universe of Unlimited Possibility. In fact, the effectiveness by which you can function in both realms of Sight (Vision) will greatly determine your effectiveness as an *Imaginal* leader. It may seem foreign, or even frightening, but it *can* be learned.

7.

Having Insight

"One must forget many clichés in order to behold a single image. Insight is the beginning of perceptions to come rather than the extension of perceptions gone by. . . . Insight is knowledge at first sight."

- Rabbi Abraham Joshua Heschel

Insight vs Speculation

Speculation is rampant in today's 24 hour cable news networks. Seldom do we have the reporting of the news, rather the news is being interpreted, meaning that people are speculating as to why something happened. Often news networks bring people on as "experts" with opposing views, to give the impression of impartiality, but the truth is none of these experts really have much of a clue as to why things happened. You don't go on television as an expert to answer a question by saying, "I really don't know," or, "There are at least a dozen different answers depending on numerous factors, and because I do not know what the factors are, I really can't give a valid explanation." Rather these experts quickly provide their expert opinion as if they really *know* what happened. Now we are left with a choice of whom to believe; but actually what we do is add someone else's speculation that aligns with our speculation which most often leads us to the false conclusion that we actually know what is going on.

I have often been known to say in jest such profound statements as, "Things are the way they are because they got that way." If the truth be told, we actually seldom really know why things are the way they are. Perhaps another way of stating this point is that our understanding of reality is really quite distorted by the lens we wear to interpret it, which we have already touched on. Another factor that influences our ability to see is our natural tendency to resolve the tension of not knowing through speculation.

We have been raised in a world where knowing answers is rewarded. The education system rewards students for knowing the right answers and penalizes for not knowing. Unfortunately, this flawed model has far reaching ramifications on people's sense of identity and resultant behaviors.

When confronted with challenging circumstances that contain unknown factors, our natural tendency is to invent an explanation that relieves us of the tension of not knowing. For instance, your family may be in a crisis that may have been triggered by some kind of event that you were a part of. To make sense of the crisis you begin to speculate as to what just transpired. You begin to ascribe motives to people's behaviors based on inferences you have made about them—in essence you become an amateur psychologists. Even worse, you most likely will have a distorted view of your causality in the crisis. Your understanding of what is happening is only speculation, its an invention that seldom gets challenged.

Having insight into what *really* is going on around us is not as simple as we perceive it to be. We invent all kinds of meaning to explain events which creates the notion that we understand what's going on when in fact we don't. Just ask someone to tell you the story of his or her life. You will notice that the factual narrative will be sprinkled with a healthy dose of interpretation as to why things happened the way they did. In essence, we have created a well-rehearsed myth about our lives which seems entirely plausible and true. So true, in fact, that if you were to take a polygraph test you would pass it with flying colors.

Imaginal leaders need to understand what is going on around them—they need to see into the states of affairs that impact them and their world. This way of *seeing into* is called Insight—the opposite of mere speculation. But how do you gain insight? How do you amplify your ability to see into the nature of things?

The following are just a few strategies and tools that will help you to gain better insight:

- Reflective thinking

- Systems thinking
- Seeing at various levels of recursion
- Modeling
- Knowing the problem

Reflective Thinking

Imaginal leaders need to become reflective practitioners. Reflective thinking is the process of making a judgment about what is happening. Reflective thinking not only seeks to understand what is happening, but also to understand *why* something is happening.

For instance, you and your spouse just finished having an argument regarding the kind of disciplinary action that should be given to your child. You argue that your child's behavior was rather normal for his age, and we really don't need to make a big deal of it; whereas your wife argues that the child is learning that she can get away with anything, and by not addressing the situation seriously now, we are setting her up for bigger problems in the future. After several minutes of arguing you both decide it is best to leave the discussion to another time.

Argryis and Shön, pioneered in 1978 the concept of single and double loop learning, which can be applied when error or fault has been detected. Single loop learning will correct the error, but continues to rely on the same strategies or processes as before. Double loop learning goes much deeper to try to understand why an error occurred and what system or process modification can be made to prevent it from occurring again. A good reflective thinker will look for double loop learning whenever applicable.

Back to our argument scenario above, as a reflective thinker you go away and begin to ask yourself a number of questions:

- What just happened?
- Five Whys: Ask yourself, "Why did it happen?", then write down your answer and ask "Why?" again of the answer you just wrote. Now do this five times, then continue to ask these questions below.

- What was my wife trying to say, and what were the assumptions she was making for her position? Under what conditions would she be right, and under what conditions would she be wrong?

- What assumptions was I making? Under what conditions would I be right and under what conditions would I be wrong?

- Does she possess information that I do not have, such as seeing ongoing patterns that I do not see?

- What was I feeling? Why was I feeling this way?

- Why did I react the way I did? Is there a pattern to the way I react? Why does this pattern exist? Do I need to change this pattern?

- How do I go about cultivating a new pattern of behavior if needed?

- What can I learn from what just transpired?

- What actions should I take now that I am more aware of what just transpired?

Reflective thinking goes beyond dealing with situations involving conflict. Journalling is a great tool to open up one's self reflection,

- Why do I do the things I do?

- What are some of my goals and aspirations?

- What is keeping me from reaching my goals?

- Are my excuses valid? What make my excuses invalid?

- How might I better serve the ones I love?

- What's at the center of my life? Do the patterns align with what I am saying?

Systems Thinking

Systems thinking is a way of understanding and seeing reality that emphasizes the relationships of parts within a system. A system can be viewed as a cohesive whole made up of many parts that are essential to its functioning. If you have a bunch of parts that are not related, then you have a heap of parts; but once they become related you have a system. A system is perceived as a whole whose elements hang together, because they continually affect each other over time and operate toward a common purpose. The word 'system' comes from the Greek word '*sunistanai*,' which means, "to cause to stand together." Peter Senge explains this in the following from his book, *The Fifth Discipline*:

> *Systems thinking is a discipline for seeing wholes. It is a framework for seeing interrelationships rather than things, for seeing patterns of change rather than static 'snapshots'....Today systems thinking is needed more than ever because we are becoming overwhelmed by complexity. Perhaps for the first time in history, humankind has the capacity to create far more information than anyone can absorb, to foster far greater interdependency than anyone can manage, and to accelerate change far faster than anyone's ability to keep pace.*[13]

Systems are everywhere. There are natural systems, such as physical environments, organic or living systems, human-made systems, organizations, etc. Systems can vary in degrees of complexity, and the more complex a system becomes the more separate cause and effect become.

As an *Imaginal* leader you are interacting with systems every day. Your ability to see and understand what is happening will enable you to design better system solutions.

Here are some aspects of systems thinking that will help you gain greater insight:

- By its nature, systems thinking points out interdependencies and the need for collaboration.

- Don't look for leverage near the symptoms of your problem. Cause and effect will not be closely related in time and space.

- Beware of the easiest and fastest solution. Most people prefer to intervene in a system at the level of rules, physical structures, work processes, rewards systems, and control mechanism. But as you move toward the more intangible elements, such as people's deep-seated attitudes and beliefs, your leverage for effective change increases. You come closer to looking at the underlying reasons why the rules, structures and work processes take their current form.

- Behavior may grow worse before it grows better. As systems thinking makes underlying structures clearer, members of the group may have moments of despair because it points out the vulnerabilities, limited understandings, and fallibilities of the past, and the assurance that today's thinking will be the source of tomorrow's problems. Formerly "untouchable" problems and issues are now allowed to surface, which creates a new sense of hope.

System Levels Model

Systems thinking is the ability to see how a system works and where the leverage points are. It is a core competency of *Imaginal* leaders, for at some point one will need to implement changes to the system.

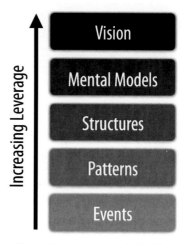

Figure 7.1 - System Levels Model

The Systems Levels Model provides insight to why certain patterns of behaviors exist for all kinds of situations, whether in your personal life, or in a broader organizational context. This model presents five levels of recursion, as shown in Figure 7.1. The model will help you see how system structures drive behaviors and the thinking that supports those system structures.

First let's define some terms:

System: A system is a collection of parts or elements that are all connected and together act as a whole. The human body is a system that is made up of many parts, or subsystems, that work together to produce an emergent property called life. No single part or subsystem—such as the nervous, endocrine, skeletal, vascular, and so on—can produce life, but all the parts working together in harmony produce life.

Vision: There are two kinds of vision, the vision in use and the vision declared. The vision in use is deduced from one's actual behavior. One might declare that his or her life's vision is to be a kind and caring person, and even may say with full sincerity that it is a desire to help needy people, yet act in a way completely contrary to those ideals. In Chapter 3 we introduced the Centers model and the concept that whatever is at your center will become your source of security, guidance, wisdom, and power. If self is at the center of one's life, then the vision in use may be stated more accurately, "I will help the needy only when I can afford the time and it doesn't risk personal security and comfort." Many corporations declare a powerful vision that includes a social agenda, yet at the end of the day the vision of making a difference may only be window dressing or a marketing ploy to the real vision in use which is to turn as large of a corporate profit as possible. There are companies that truly carry a powerful social agenda, and everyone in the company knows it and the vision in use aligns beautifully with the declared vision of the company.

Mental models represent the thinking and assumptions that underlie or are embedded into a system.

Structures are elements within a system that are related to one another, and designed to support and generate certain kinds of behavior. Structures can be physical and non-physical. The physical skeletal structure of a human being is designed to support and protect all of the other structures and organs, and when coupled with other structures enable us to move. If we changed the skeletal structure of humans it would vastly change our behaviors. Buildings have structures, there are hallways, rooms, furnishings and other physical elements that will architecturally determine our behavior. Organizations have many non-physical structures, such as policies, regulations, schedules, compensation plans, performance review processes, etc that drive to a large degree the behaviors of the people woking in it. One will see a large number of people eating in restaurants during lunch hour because the structure allows this behavior to occur. In education the assessment structure—how students, teachers, and schools are evaluated—will drive the behaviors of all the key stakeholders.

Perhaps the most powerful structures are those we don't see—our beliefs, our desires, our thinking, and the mental models we carry. These mental structures strongly generate human behavior, but rarely are they challenge or examined.

In 2011, over 30 educators in Atlanta Public Schools in the USA were arrested for falsifying standardized tests scores. This unethical behavior, while not excusable, is in part a response to a system that rewarded those schools and districts who did well on standardized test scores and punished those that did poorly. This is a classic example of unintended consequences of a system of extrinsic rewards and punishments that in fact is generating the wrong behaviors. I am sure that those educators that were involved in the falsification of scores had found a way to justify their wrong behavior by thinking that they are in, and responding to, an unjust system; that their students may have come from disadvantaged home environments, and thus by falsifying the test scores, they would receive the increased government funding that these students desperately needed. After all, we all enjoy the folk lore around Robin Hood who took money from the unjust sheriff of Nottingham and gave it back to the peasants.

Patterns of behavior are those events that repeat themselves over time, thus becoming a pattern; and when a pattern is discovered one can assume that there is some system structure that is generating this behavior. If your newspaper is consistently being delivered late on Mondays there is a strong likelihood that there is a system structure behind this pattern. Perhaps the newspaper delivery person has a situation at home that only occurs on Mondays and affects the delivering of newspapers on that day.

Events are simply those experiences that we observe on a daily basis. Every day when we drive our automobiles we experience traffic. Early morning rush hour traffic, which occurs every week day morning is elevated from being an event to a pattern which is generated by the city's start times for the workplace.

When using the System Levels Model, one generally starts at the bottom with Events and work of the levels to Vision.

1. Experience certain events or problems, and over time you begin to suspect that there is a pattern to these problems.

2. Begin to collect data, to see if there is a pattern associated with the problem.

3. Once you have discovered a behavioral pattern, an investigation into the structures that may be generating the patterns begins to give insight into the causes of the problem.

4. Now it's time to look at the belief systems or the thinking that built the structures in the first place. Understanding the mental models, or the thinking behind them that led to the creation of these structures in the first place, will help you to understand where changes need to be made if needed.

5. Identify the vision in use and compare it to the declared vision or preferred future. The result will increase the leverage for changing the system.

Vision Deployment Matrix

The Vision Deployment Matrix takes the above five system levels and juxtaposes the current reality with the preferred future or vision. Now this becomes a powerful tool for system transformation and the deployment of vision on which we will go into greater detail in Chapter 10.

The Vision Deployment Matrix creates tension at all five system levels which is resolved by deploying different strategies. The regeneration of vision is a spiritual activity: to create a new vision requires you to utilize your imagination, the eye of your spirit, to see a new future and pull it into the here by faith. This becomes your vision of the future.

To resolve the tension at all the levels you will need to reframe your thinking, redesign system structures, and reengineer processes resulting in new reactions or system behaviors, as the model on the following page shows.

Edwards Deming reminds us that 80-90% of system problems are generated by the system itself and only 10-20% can actually be attributed to the people in the system. Often, the initial response is to blame people for the problems without really understanding how the system structures are generating the behaviors.

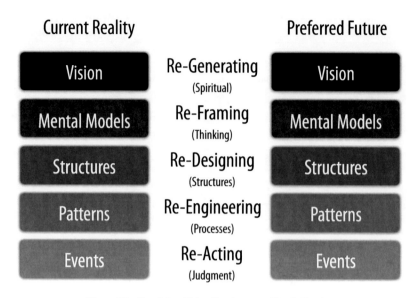

Figure 7.2 - Resolving Vision Deployment Matrix Tension

A Learning Experience

Many years ago, as a brand new private school administrator, I noticed a pattern of behavior in our school. Everyday immediately after school, the front foyer was jammed with students waiting for their parents to pick them up particularly during the winter when students did not want to wait outside. I also noticed that should visitors come to our school during this time, they would have to squeeze their way through this crowd of students. Surely, this is not how we should be welcoming visitors to our school. As a brilliant young administrator, I thought I could resolve this issue by making a rule: let's forbid students from exiting the front of the school, and instead make them leave via the back doors. So I issued the edict. This was back in the mid 1980s when there were no cell phones and parents could not text their students as they can today. Now, however, I had created a bigger problem. Once a rule or regulation has been established one needs to monitor compliance and determine punishment to the violators of the rule. It did not take long after the rule was established that the behavior pattern of exiting the front door returned. How could this be? Was there no respect for the school leadership that made such a wonderful rule? The problem was that the rule was counter intuitive: how would students know that their parents had arrived if they were not able to see through the front doors and windows? Since there was no parking for parents even a well intentioned parent with plenty of time to spare would not be able to park and come in to retrieve his or her student. "OK," I thought, "now we need some policing." So we created a teachers' supervision schedule to monitor the front hallway after school. The problem was inconsistency, for since teachers were not always able to make their supervision because of other priorities the school had set, we had conflicting goals. Fortunately, I did not go the punishment route, since what started as a minor irritation would have escalated to a full blown problem. Within a few weeks at a school assembly, I stood in front of the student body and faculty and shared what had transpired, namely the thinking that led to the creation of the rule in the first place, and ultimately why it was a dumb move on my part to fix the problem the way I had chosen. I apologized to the students and simply asked them to be respectful of visitors entering the school during the peak traffic hours—the problem was solved.

Levels of Recursion

Imaginal leaders will gain better insight into what is happening around them by examining their situation through various levels of recursion. Let's look at the following levels of recursion in education:

1. Student/Parent
2. Classroom/ Teacher
3. School/ Principal
4. District/ Superintendent
5. State/ State Minister
6. Country/ Federal Minister

The ability to view education at each level of recursion will help you have better insight into what is happening in the system. Any attempt to reform education has to be able to address changes at all levels of recursion in the system. If changes are being proposed at certain levels of the system without considering the whole, then one can end up with competing or conflicting goals.

Models and tools have been created to help gain better insight into what is happening in a particular situation or system.

One can also use the levels of recursion to look at a system in different ways. For instance you can look at an organization's culture by taking various vantage points:

- Behaviors
- Values and beliefs whether tacit or explicit
- Assumptions and underlying philosophies
- Policies and rules
- Strategies
- Logistics
- Tasks

Modeling

Everybody has heard stories of people drawing a breakthrough idea on a paper napkin over lunch. One famous story was with Herb Kelleher, a lawyer, and Rollin King, a banker and pilot who ran a small charter airline. In 1966, they had a drink at a San Antonio bar. Conversation led to an idea for an airline that would provide short intrastate flights at a low cost. They mapped out routes and a business strategy on a cocktail napkin. Looking at the notes on the napkin, Kelleher said, "Rollin, you're crazy, let's do it," and Southwest Airline was born.

As I shared in the Preface, I was flying from London to Nairobi when I received a download, an idea that would shape so many aspects of the rest of my life. I quickly drew a diagram of the iCubed (I^3) Model. This model became the inspiration for the following:

- iCubed Organization
- iCubed Leadership (morphed into *Imaginal* Leadership)
- iCubed Living (or the Vision Led Life)
- iCubed Profound Learning
- iCubed Transformation (morphed into *Imaginal* Transformation)
- iCubed Thinking

As an *Imaginal* leader, there is a tremendous power to visually illustrate or create visual models around key aspects of what you are envisioning. The power of building a visual model is that it allows you to look at relationships between various components of your system. It goes without saying that your visual model is a simplification and representation of reality, and not the reality in itself. So by definition any model is an imperfect representation, or one of many possible representations of a particular system, and should only be viewed as a slice of reality. In writing this book, I was constantly creating visual models of the concepts I wanted to write about. During this process, further insight was gained regarding the concept I was modeling. I even discovered certain discrepancies and conflicts that needed resolution while creating models.

Modeling can take many forms, such as a spreadsheet, where business people try and create economic projections of the future based on a certain set of assumptions. A business plan contains a financial pro-forma that attempts to predict the future of the business. What is important in this modeling process is to make explicit the assumptions you are making regarding your business. Modeling is a great way by which deeper insight is gained and subsequently communicated to others.

What's the Problem

What most people describe as "problems" really are not problems at all, but rather symptoms of underlying structures of the system. Problems such as failing schools, poor student performance, and unmotivated students are only symptoms of a system that is obsolete. In today's culture, we are inundated with politicians and pundits who are constantly identifying problems, creating the illusion that if you can identify a problem, then you know something about it and you have a way of fixing it. Unfortunately, most of the time people are only addressing *symptoms of systems* that have antiquated structures that are driving certain undesirable behaviors. Problem solving that lacks deep insight gives a sense of false hope that we are doing something important and that things will get better as a result of our actions.

With the increase in complexity in our world, the notion that one can identify problems in simple terms is rather naive. But this happens all the time, partly because if we can articulate a problem then somehow we are outside it, or even above it. "If others knew what I knew then we would not be in the mess we are in." Still others become really good at identifying "problems" that may not really exist (at least not to the degree that is being stated), but that merely create an opportunity for them to come and "save" the day.

In 2008, the USA and the rest of the world experienced a major financial crisis. Financial institutions collapsed or had to be rescued, unemployment skyrocketed, and the global markets were in disarray. To address "the problem," large sums of money were used to stimulate the economy, with marginal success. New business regulations were passed by the US congress to address the financial collapse, only to have created more regulations that made it more difficult for small businesses to borrow money and grow the economy. The symptoms of the system were being treated but not the real cause, namely *the underlying structures that created the "problem" in the first place.* For a politician to address the real problem, he or she would have to run on a platform that advocates tough decisions with short to mid-term pain for long-term prosperity. Unfortunately that would not get you elected. You have to sell the notion that you can fix the problem without pain, hence the real problems never get addressed or are pushed down the road for someone else to address.

More often than we would like to admit, the problem-solving approaches we use end up failing simply because they are not addressing the underlying structures of the system that are causing the symptoms we are calling problems. In today's world we have created a hero culture that rewards people for quick fixes, not realizing that long after they have been promoted someone else now has to deal with the "problems" that the last problem solver created. Whenever you have a number of fixes failing over time, such as in education, you will see a pattern of people addressing symptoms of the system and not the real problem.

Problem solving can give the illusion that you are doing something worthwhile—it could even distract you from fixing the real problem as I previously described. Problem solving remains, however, a useful skill that all *Imaginal* leaders should possess. Shackleton, an *Imaginal* leader, when faced with extreme adversity was able to show great courage, leadership and problem solving skills in saving his men. This book is about creating your future, hence the focus is chiefly on the creation process and not problem solving itself.

Problem solving can be of value when your are dealing with basic system cause and effect challenges, in which a continuous improvement philosophy may be useful; but problem solving can never replace the creative and creation process when one needs to create something new.

Great leaders, however, rise above being problem-solvers—they are visionary builders who are able to inspire people to follow their vision. John Kennedy, one of the great leaders of the 20th century, inspired a nation to put a man on the moon before the end of the decade—a vision which spurred on a cycle of innovation and invention that was unprecedented for his time. In his acceptance speech on July 15, 1960 Kennedy stated:

But I tell you the New Frontier is here, whether we seek it or not. Beyond that frontier are the uncharted areas of science and space, unsolved problems of peace and war, unconquered pockets of ignorance and prejudice, unanswered questions of poverty and surplus. It would be easier to shrink back from that frontier, to look to the safe mediocrity of the past, to be lulled by good intentions and high rhetoric—and those who prefer that course should not cast their votes for me, regardless of party. But I believe the times demand new invention, innovation, imagination, decision. I am asking each of you to be pioneers on that New Frontier. My call is to the young in heart, regardless of age—to all who respond to the Scriptural call: "Be strong and of good courage; be not afraid, neither be thou dismayed." For courage—not complacency—is our need today—leadership—not salesmanship. And the only valid test of leadership is the ability to lead, and lead vigorously.

Steve Jobs was a visionary builder of Apple. Known to take great risks, he was not a pragmatic problem-solver. If anything, Steve Jobs was constantly creating problems for his staff by insisting they accomplish the seemingly impossible. One of the things that made Steve Jobs great was his ability to dwell in the discomfort and disruption of the creation process—to see the future clearer than most, and bring what he saw into the present. In essence, *creating the future* by creating his own problem.

What then is the real problem? As an *Imaginal* leader you will have a vision of a future that is quite different than your current condition. Your problem, which we will later define as a *probletunity*, becomes how to close the gap between your THERE and your HERE. You will need to begin pulling the future into the HERE by creating new structures of the future "butterfly" that will replace existing structures.

But this requires being able to see the future, which is the ability to engage in *foresight*. Indeed, this is where the transformation shifts from the inside of you to outside of you; from being impacted and transformed, to, as an *Imaginal* leader, transforming the world around you in an impactful way. Not as easy as it may sound, however, since we are dealing with systems that will push back on any attempt to change it. Foresight, if well-honed, can help see you through.

8.

Having Foresight

*"Imagination is more important than knowledge. For while knowledge
defines all we currently know and understand, imagination points to
all we might yet discover and create".*

- Albert Einstein

At the center of the art of foresight is the imagination. *Imaginal* leaders
have developed their imaginations in such a way that enhances their ability to see the future, to have foresight, and to pull that future into their
current reality. Such *Imaginal* skill is not a pre-natal gift only for the few
and not the many, but rather it is placed in each and everyone of us, and
therefore *can be developed and released*.

The Nature of the Human Being

There are many models that attempt to describe the nature of human
beings. I like to think of humans as having a body, a soul and a spirit.
The body is our physical structure and sensing mechanism that connects
us to the Universe of Measurement. Our soul is comprised of our mind,
emotions and will. Our spirit is a place of intuition, and conscience with
our imagination being the eye of the spirit into the Universe of Unlimited Possibilities.

Imagination

Foresight is the ability to see the future, to see the invisible, and what
could be, and bring that back into the here. All of this is made possible
by our incredible ability to use our imagination. But can it be developed?

Neuroscience may try to explain how the brain can store a concept
such as a chair, and how the mind can retrieve those concepts. But where

does imagination come from? I believe that humans are fundamentally different from all of the animals, because we have a unique spiritual aspect that allows us to imagine, to see with the eye of the human spirit.

It's one thing to compare our mind to a computer storage system; it is entirely different to ascribe the ability to imagine as purely a biological function. Human beings have an ability to imagine, design, and create in ways so far beyond anything else found in nature that it makes us "god-like". We are the only creatures found in nature that can massively alter our environment and create entirely new environments—such as a space capsule that enables us to explore space or the depths of oceans—that would not be possible without these human-engineered micro environments.

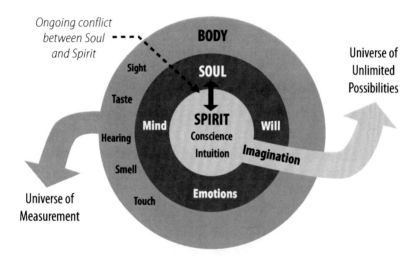

Figure 8.1 - Tripartite Nature of Humans

So how do we activate our imagination to see the future? Remember an *Imaginal* leader is like an imaginal cell in the pupa that has the ability to see and create the butterfly.

Previously, I introduced the concept of the brain as a pattern producing and pattern recognition instrument with a phenomenal degree of complexity. These patterns enable us to interpret what is happening in the world and in so doing limit our ability to have foresight. Since these patterns are formed through life experiences, and through the knowledge we have accumulated in school and elsewhere, our foresight is constrained by them. So how do we break free from these constraints?

Let's go back to Figure 10.1, The Tripartite Nature of Humans Model, which shows the nature of human beings. Our body perceives the natural world, the Universe of Measurement through the five senses. With the exception of sensory illusions, such as optical, by and large data we receive from these senses are being mapped into our brains and interpreted to provide some kind of meaning. There is some universality as to how all this works, otherwise we could never go to see a movie. The visual colors, shapes, and sounds are more or less interpreted by our brains in the same way, hence our movie experience can be viewed as a shared experience. Now, your emotional response to scenes can vary greatly depending on your personal experience. If a movie has a scene involving an abuse similar to one that you may have experienced it will trigger a strong emotion that may be unique to you, and so in that context every movie experience is unique.

It is the soul aspect of human beings—our minds, emotions, and will—that need to be examined if we are to learn how to activate our imagination. Each part of our soul has its own unique voice that can either free us to see with our imagination or limit our sight. And in particular there are three voices that will hinder our ability to engage with the Universe of Unlimited Possibilities: the voice of limitation, the voice of cynicism, and the voice of fear. All three voices can be unified under the voice of judgment, as used by Michael Ray, but each unique voice targets and seeks to immobilize a certain aspect of our soul.[14] To get to the place of seeing with our imagination we must overcome these voices of judgment within our soul.

Overcoming our Limiters

Overcoming Limitation with Faith

Our mindsets by definition are limited, because they are represented by neurological patterns in our brain, as we saw in Chapter 6. Every new experience is judged or filtered by these limited patterns which we perceive as thoughts. When a new idea is shared with you, immediately your mind will create a judgment that tells you if this new idea is possible and or desirable. For most adults, the default mode of thinking is always constrained by what we perceive as being possible. As adults we live in the real world, and, for many, success and happiness come from our ability to navigate through this world with the least amount of pain as possible.

There is an interesting story in the Bible about Jesus feeding the five thousand. I know that some may question if this really happened, but this is not the point I am trying to make. Let's assume for one moment that it really *did* happen. In the story, Jesus approached some of his disciples with a problem he wanted them to solve: he had been teaching to a large crowd of people all day, and they were getting hungry. Jesus asked his close disciples if they could find a way to feed all these people. So the disciples held a meeting to discuss this matter further. They analyzed the situation from their vantage point and concluded that it was not possible: first they were not close to any town that had provision for such a large crowd, and second even if they were they simply did not have enough money to buy the large quantity of food required to feed the crowd. They reported back to Jesus that it could not be done. Then along came a little boy with five loaves and two fishes and he gave them to Jesus who blessed them; and, according to the Bible, a miracle occurred, for from these five loaves and two fishes the entire crowd was fed.

The question is this: What did the little boy see that the adults were unable to? Children have active imaginations, there is virtually no limits to what a child can imagine or even believe is possible. As we grow older we become immersed in the world of measurement—the world of limitation, the real world, which then governs every aspect of our life. The breakthrough will come when we learn to activate our imagination and become like a child again; for it is only when we can see the invisible that we can do the impossible. This book is about activating your imagination so that you can experience the joy of innovation and creativity resulting in the most adventuresome life.

The first step to seeing the invisible with an active imagination is to have an open mind, and be open to unlimited possibilities. Ben and

Rosa Zander in their book *The Art of Possibility* introduce the concept that "it's all invented"—our limited mindsets are mere inventions, so why not invent a new framework that alters our view of what is possible?[15] We all have a picture frame or a mental model of who we are, what we are good at, and what the future might look like personally. But that picture frame is only an invention, so why not invent a new frame that will hold another picture of who I am, or what is possible.

Every problem, every dilemma, every dead end we find ourselves facing in life, only appears unsolvable inside a particular frame or point of view. Enlarge that box, or create another frame around the data, and problems vanish, while new opportunities appear.[16]

Universe of Unlimited Possibilities

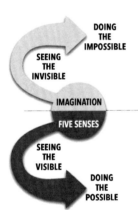

One enters the **Universe of Unlimited Possibilities** with your imagination- this is seeing the invisible. **Faith** is activated within the human spirit, it utilizes imagination to see into the future and uses **hope** to bring the future into the now. A unique transformation occurs when we engage the universe of unlimited possibilities with faith, the seemingly impossible becomes possible.

One engages with the **Universe of Measurement** by observation through the five senses. What we see is framed by our **past experiences**, which have created the lens through which we interpret the world. Creation is driven by the intent of one's ego, to build the biggest, the tallest, the best etc. Invariably, design defaults to status quo, what we know and feel secure about.

Universe of Measurement

Figure 8.2 - Seeing the Invisible

As we begin to imagine new possibilities, we can add hope to what we see, and bring that future into the now—this we call faith, which makes what we imagine real and tangible. A scientist who believes that we are all here on this earth as a result of a near infinite series of accidents requires faith to believe in evolutionary theory. Once that near impossible theory is accepted by faith the impossible turns into the possible and becomes the basis for much of the scientist's life work. Similarly, a person who adheres to the notion of intelligent design, a mysterious yet purposeful creator, must exercise great faith that makes that impossibility possible. Faith is not a religious concept, but rather a fundamental requirement for us as humans if we are to make any sense of our lives and ultimate purpose. We must learn to walk by faith and not just by sight.

To overcome the voice of limitation we must exercise faith, which will elevate us to a place of seeing and believing, contrary to the limiters embedded in the patterns of our minds that are shouting that it is impossible. History is full of men and women who have held on to beliefs that certain discoveries or accomplishments were possible even in the face of overwhelming odds and a sea of skeptics.

Dr. Blalock (1899-1964) was the first surgeon to successfully perform heart surgery on a living person. Dr. Blalock and his team at Johns Hopkins University were able to surgically fix a congenital heart defect for what was known as the blue baby syndrome. No one in modern medicine thought that it was possible to operate on a human heart, and some religious people fundamentally believed that it was wrong to tinker with *Something the Lord has Made* (which became the title of the 2004 HBO's docudrama on Dr. Blalock's and his assistant Vivien Thomas's lives). Dr. Blalock had this unquenchable faith that he was going to find a way to solve the problem of the blue baby syndrome, which, along with a deep sense of cause, created the perfect storm of drive that kept him on his path until he was able to solve the mystery. We need faith to do the seemingly impossible, for it is faith that sees what others consider impossible already made possible. In one scene in the movie, Dr. Blalock is playing pool with the head of Johns Hopkins Medical School. The senior hospital administrator asks Dr. Blalock to give up his quest of solving the blue baby syndrome—that it is impossible to operate on a human heart. Dr. Blalock dryly but passionately responds, "Where you see impossibility, I see opportunity."

Overcoming Cynicism with Trust and Hope

The voice of skepticism or doubt can arise from our mind when we experience cognitive dissonance, and when our mental models cannot reconcile the situation we are facing. A good response is to engage in an inquiry, to seek to understand and learn more. Perhaps there is a gap in your understanding, or you may be operating from an obsolete paradigm. Years ago, I was presented with an opportunity to invest in a company that appeared to have an amazing breakthrough technology. They claimed that by using a specific high frequency wave they were able to break the molecular bonding of hydrogen and oxygen in water, and that the release of hydrogen could in turn be captured and used as energy. I knew from my high school science days that through electrolysis this concept was possible. Imagine pouring water into your car tank and having it run with no pollution. I was shown videos of a device that supposedly was doing this very thing. But I was skeptical—it just didn't seem to add up. So I decided to take this video and documentation to an engineer friend to get his opinion on this world-changing invention. Immediately, he said this was economically impossible; that it was defying the laws of science. His analysis proved to be correct, and my skepticism saved me from making an investment into a scam.

Cynicism, however, is entirely different from skepticism. Cynicism is an emotional judgment on yourself or others. In many ways it is a cancer of the soul. Cynicism is paralyzing, since at its core is some past experience or number of experiences that have so jaded your life that you default to negativity. We all have been around people whose first response to any new idea or opportunity is an objection or reason why it won't succeed. We label these people as pessimists. A lot has been written over the years about the power of positive thinking, and there is a lot of good in taking that perspective; but I really do not want to advocate a dishonest view of life or a life that is more like a masquerade party where we put on the mask of positive thinking.

The voice of cynicism that arises from our emotions is a self protective measure. Going back to our Centers Model in Chapter 3, whatever is at your center will be your source of security, power, comfort and wisdom. A self-centered person who may be carrying a lot of past hurts may naturally become cynical, and lose trust in others or in one's self. Suppose you were an employee at Enron. You trusted your senior management, and placed your entire retirement into the ongoing success of your company. Then you find out that they were lying to you, and that the company is bankrupt. As you move on with your life, you have a whole new set of lenses by which you will view your new company's leadership. You are a lot less likely to trust what they are saying to you even though they have done nothing to warrant your distrust.

Years ago I was working with a highly experienced financial expert, and every time I suggested a different approach to what she was recommending, she responded by saying, "We have tried that before and it doesn't work." There was only one correct approach and that was what she had learned over the years worked for her. Not only was she cynical of any new approach, she had elevated her thinking to the place of near infallibility.

As humans we must be on guard against the pride of opinion. We all have opinions about virtually everything in life, whether they be about politics, education, the environment, war or religion. No one will espouse a view that he or she knows is wrong—only a fool would advocate falsehoods as truth, unless playing a con. So every opinion I hold, I believe to be true. Trouble arises when I elevate my opinion on a subject above everyone else's—this I call the pride of opinion. Opinions expressed are to be understood as a partial glimpse or explanation of the world we live in, but they cannot contain all that there is to know.

In education, with so many initiatives that have been tried over the past number of decades, there is such strong cynicism built into the system. "Oh we have tried that before!" or, "That sure isn't going to work!" or, "Here we go again!" There are so many assumptions one makes when voicing one's cynicism, such as:

- The proposed approach is the same as the one tried previously.

- The conditions that led to the failure previously are the same today.

- We are no smarter today than we were decades ago.

- No new learning or understanding can be applied to this initiative that could lead to its success.

- I know more than the people proposing this new approach.

Not only does the voice of cynicism paralyze you from acting, it will become a self fulfilling prophecy in your life. Whether consciously or un-consciously you will undermine any initiative to prove your own cynicism. You will demonstrate either grudging compliance or outright defiance, but in a most subtle way so as to protect your self.

Back in the late 1960s and early 1970s, schools were being designed and built based on the "open concept philosophy". The idea of the open classroom was that a large group of students of varying skill levels would be in a single, large classroom with several teachers overseeing them. After years of experimentation, these schools began to build walls and returned to a more traditional approach of command and control and teacher-centered learning. In the 1980s no one dared to talk about open concept schools, it was clearly put into a category of being a fad that failed. But why did it fail? Was it a flawed model or was something else at play? Without going into deep analysis, the open learning model was sound pedagogically, which was the reason why it was so widely accepted, but it was implemented without truly understanding how the system would push back. There were too many assumptions made as to the ability of teachers to implement the new model. The open concept model required a significant shift in the understanding of teacher and student roles as well as the overall cultural shift that needed to take place in the classroom. Today you will find schools all over Australia successfully implementing the open classroom concept with a high level of buy-in by all the stakeholders. The Profound Learning Model, referred to in Appendix A, is optimized by having open classrooms. At Master's Academy and College we are tearing down the old factory model of classrooms and building new, larger, and more free flowing spaces. In addition, we have designed and built web-based software that enables the management of personalized learning of large groups of students by teachers. We have designed system transformation strategies that anticipate and addresses most of the areas of system push back. When we introduce the Profound Learning model to schools, we anticipate that there will be some cynicism, such as, "This has been tried before—just another fad coming our way."

For you to see and design the future as an *Imaginal* leader you must be able to extinguish the voice of cynicism in your own soul. A cynic has been let down many times in life, whether having been hurt by broken promises, or a failed relationship. Self protectionism sets in and says, "I will not be hurt again. I cannot trust what others say they will do." But you can break free from the prison of your past and begin again to trust others. For trust says, "I am willing to engage in a relationship even though there is a chance of being hurt again." We all know that trust is something that is earned and established over time, particularly after trust has been broken, but ultimately trusting others is a choice we need to make.

The voice of cynicism will often be prevalent with people who have shame-based identities. People who have been told time after time that they are not good enough, or that something is wrong with them will have a difficult time entering the Universe of Unlimited Possibilities. They have accepted the lies about who they are and have become prisoners to those lies. It is time for a prison break.

The fact is, we are all flawed human beings. We will all fall short of living 100% to the ideals that someone may have of us. In my own life I have had to look beyond that to find my natural place of rest. I have found that as I place my trust in a Higher Power, I need not be so demanding on others around me. I can live in the world of imperfection, including my own. As I place my trust in a Higher Power a supernatural transaction occurs, and I am able to find peace and hope for the future. As you engage in your future with hope, cynicism will soon fade away.

Overcoming Fear with Love

The third part of the human soul is our will, which is the volitional part of our being that can choose how we act. The voice of fear attempts to neutralize or limit your ability to act. "What if I were to fail, what would others say?" This voice, although coming from within our soul, may in fact be the voice that has been spoken over us by parents and others. Even well-intentioned people who do not want to see us fail, may cast fear into our soul.

Let's start by defining failure. There is more that one definition of failure, since we have different values and beliefs about life. Failure is simply falling short of expectations. Failure to one person may simply be a great learning experience to someone else. Perhaps one of the great examples of persistence is Abraham Lincoln. The following is what it took for Lincoln to eventually become the President of the United States:

- Lost job in 1832
- Defeated for state legislature in 1832
- Failed in business in 1833
- Elected to state legislature in 1834
- Sweetheart died in 1835
- Had nervous breakdown in 1836
- Defeated for Speaker in 1838
- Defeated for nomination for Congress in 1843
- Elected to Congress in 1846
- Lost renomination in 1848
- Rejected for land officer in 1849
- Defeated for U.S. Senate in 1854
- Defeated for nomination for Vice President in 1856
- Again defeated for U.S. Senate in 1858
- Elected President in 1860

We all know of these great inspirational stories of people overcoming adversity to accomplish great things in life, but how do I deal with my fear?

Let me take you back to the first key of finding your Big WHY and second key of activating drive. Throughout history we have seen people demonstrate a great amount of courage in the face of fearful circumstances. The reason for such tremendous courage is that these people had found their Big WHY of life that was ultimately attached to a cause that was bigger than they were. The Big WHY was calling for sacrifice and to take risks, and, even after failure, to be persistent and exhibit perseverance.

Even though fear can be a debilitating emotion, there is one emotion that can neutralize fear—it is LOVE. Parents out of love will put their own lives at risk if their child's life is in danger. Many soldiers put their lives at risk out of love for their country. Martyrs over the years have been willing to lay down their lives as an act of love for the cause they believe in. Love is the most powerful motivating force in the universe. It is what motives acts of creation by parents, artists, architects, and visionary *Imaginal* leaders—it is what drives people to do extra-ordinary feats.

Find your Big WHY and you will find the antidote to fear.

The Open Principle

The Open Principle is a model that shows how we can get to a place of seeing with our imagination and translate that seeing into something tangible and remarkable.

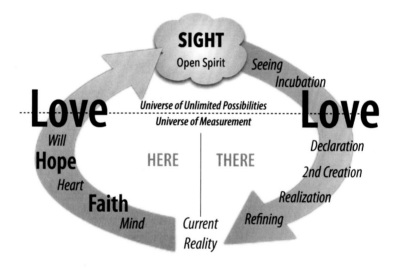

Figure 8.3 - The Open Principle

In Chapter 2, I introduced you to the Vision Formation Model, where vision begins as a burning desire and a generalized concept; and through incubation the burning desire becomes a dream—still a pie in the sky concept, but perhaps with a little more certainty as to its viability. Eventually a vision is formed into a mature picture of the future with some real tangible steps. All through this process you are engaging in the Universe of Unlimited Possibilities with your imagination.

Albert Einstein spent years conducting thought experiments with his imagination, which eventually led to some of the most amazing discoveries in scientific history. For him, "Logic plays within boundaries, imagination plays *with* boundaries."

The Open Principle is designed to help you sustain long periods of imagining your future. For imagination to be most effective, you must enter the space of imagining by quieting the three voices of judgment. Take the time to quiet your soul by meditating on your Big WHY and your calling in life. Open up your mind by welcoming faith to come; faith that nothing is impossible to those that believe. Open up your heart, and allow hope for a better future to permeate your inner being, and, finally, open up your will and allow love to conquer every thought of fear.

Allow the love of your Big WHY to fuel your imagination and creativity. You are now entering the zone of innovation and creativity. Enter into your vision, that specific aspect of the cause you have been called to advance. What does it look like? How does it feel? See it working through the eyes of faith. Seeing with your imagination is the first act of creation. Remember: if you cannot see the invisible, you cannot do the impossible!

All creations start in one's imagination in the Universe of Unlimited Possibilities. Through a period of incubation, your vision will become more and more tangible. The day will come when you step back into the Universe of Measurement and with some trepidation begin sharing your vision. You are now beginning to make visible the invisible which is the fourth key, Create.

This is the act of creating. For seeing the future is fundamental to becoming *Imaginal*, but to bring THERE to HERE will demand that you understand and can struggle through the creation process.

Part III: Creating

9.

Creation

"The creation of something new is not accomplished by the intellect but by the play instinct acting from inner necessity. The creative mind plays with the objects it loves."

- Carl Jung

The *Imaginal* leader creates a vision in the midst of a world of overwhelming change and complexity; and yet, unlike most, he or she has a way of overcoming the tendency to become trapped in the hopeless state of mere reaction. In the face of adversity, the *Imaginal* leader finds the courage to create, thus avoiding the negativity of complacency and compliance. How does the *Imaginal* leader do this?

As argued throughout this book, such an orientation to create is not simply a genetic one, but also a way of being, a habit, that the *Imaginal* leader has learned and honed over the years: it is called *the Creation Orientation.*

The Creative Age

One benefit of the 21st Century to the *Imaginal* leader is that we are living in the creative age as described by Richard Florida and others, which has emerged rapidly and radically over the past 100 years since the industrial age. This creative age is a response to the world of massive change. We take for granted the speed of innovation that has created the world around us; however, over the next ten to fifteen years we will see an acceleration of innovation, change and disruptions on a scale no civilization has ever experienced. The struggle of daily business will be won by the people and the organizations that adapt most successfully to the new world that is unfolding.

Having the ability to adapt quickly will enable you to *survive* the world of massive change, but those that can innovate and create the future will *thrive*. Your future can be by design or by default, but one thing is for certain, you cannot stop it from coming.

The first generation of the information age was launched by the pervasive use of the personal computers in the workplace in the 1980s. The mid 1990s ushered in the second generation of the information age, the communication age, with wide scale adoption of mobile technologies and the internet. We are now living in the third generation of the information age, called the creative age.

The creative age puts the power to create in the hands of virtually every designer and innovator. In the past there were a few dominant newspapers and TV stations, today anyone can create a news organization by launching a blog or video channel on YouTube. Three dimensional (3D) printing is now affordable enabling designers to rapidly prototype objects that previously required expensive machining. New upstart authors can self publish and print books at low volumes and low costs, which previously was unthinkable. Musicians can create and record their own music and establish their own distribution channel on various online music vendors.

International CEO surveys over the past decade, by IBM and others, have shown that the majority of the CEOs anticipate major disruptive changes to occur in their industry in a period of a few short years. CEOs routinely state that they are planning for radical changes in their business models over the coming years fearing that changes from a competitor could likely result in a radical change to the entire landscape of their industry.

Yet when asked in one study if they had a handle on the transformation process fueled by innovation and creativity, only 6% felt like they really knew what they were doing. (Financial Post, Tuesday, October 3, 2000)

James Canton wrote the following in his book *Extreme Future*:

The creative economy represents the largest future threat or opportunity for your career or business—depending on whether or not you prepare for it. "Are you ready? [17]

Why is there such a deficiency when it comes to innovation and creativity? Otto Sharmer, a professor at MIT, and author of the book *Theory U*, states that:

We pour considerable amounts of money into our educational systems, but we haven't been able to create schools and institutions of higher education that develop people's innate capacity to sense and shape their future, which I view as the single most important core capability for this century's knowledge and co-creation economy.[18]

How prepared are you for the creative age? How well are schools preparing students for the creative age? The world has changed—opportunities exist today that were not even imagined 10 or 15 years ago. We need to ensure that students graduating from our schools are truly FUTURE READY!

Reactive / Responsive

In his book *The Path of Least Resistance*, Robert Fritz introduces two orientations to the world: the reactive-responsive orientation and the creative orientation.[19] Most people live their lives reacting against or responding to life circumstances. Parents teach their children that there are things to avoid, such as playing on the street or playing with a sharp knife; and there are rules to be obeyed, such as no shouting and how to be polite. As a child you learn how to modify your behavior to fit the circumstances you are in. To succeed in school, the child learns further how to conform and comply to the circumstances that the teacher has created. The most successful students within this system of conformity often get recognized as valedictorians—they are considered the best of the best. But how well do valedictorians actually do in life?

Karen Arnold, Associate Professor from Boston College, conducted a research study of 81 Illinois valedictorians. After 14 years and over 11,000 pages of interview transcripts, she concluded that these valedictorians worked best within the system and were not likely to change it. They became good accountants, lawyers, and doctors, but they never devoted themselves to a single area in which they could invest their passion. There was also a significant number of valedictorians who struggle with depression since they were never able to succeed in the world of work as they did in the world of school. Doing well in a linguistic test-oriented academic environment does not necessarily prepare students for the world of tomorrow.

To excel in the traditional education system a student learns to conform and comply to the external conditions that are created by the school system itself. To succeed in school you learn how to perform and respond to the demands of the system.

Instead of responding positively to the circumstances, you may become rebellious, and react against the circumstances of life. This orientation often will lead to a deep rooted cynicism, an anti-establishment mentality with a conspiratorial view of the world. Reactive people are viewed as being difficult and often get ostracized. Many reactive people have learned how to be subtle and contain their reactions so as to better fit in, hence they become conformists and responsive.

Reactive / Responsive Orientation

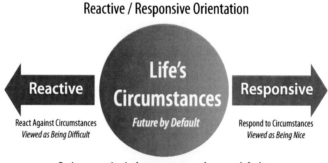

Figure 9.1- Reactive / Responsive Orientation

The reactive/responsive orientation maintains that you are powerless, and that the power lies outside of you in your circumstances. You become the victim to your circumstances, hence adopt an attitude that shifts the blame for your life situation on others. Your future is by default, and your life's goal is to make the best of what comes your way. Failed attempts to break free from this sense of powerlessness has further reinforced the truth of this belief, and has led to hopelessness and despair. No amount of positive thinking will change this basic orientation toward life because deep inside of you is the belief that you are powerless. The reactive-responsive orientation tends to oscillate between being responsive and being reactive. People have learned how to manipulate situations with their responses to get what they want. However, at the end of the day there is still a sense of powerlessness they feel, since the circumstance they are still in holds all the power. They are not actually changing anything, but merely using the circumstance to their benefit.

In July 2012, I spoke at the West African Education Transformation Conference in Lagos, Nigeria. During a panel discussion, the very first question I was asked was, "How can we implement Profound Learning in our schools if the government doesn't recognize the need to change the model of education?" The assumption of powerlessness was evident, as she continued by asking, "What can we do as individuals or as schools as part of a larger system that is broken?" My response was first to challenge the assumption she was making, namely that her behavior is determined by others and that she was powerless to make any significant changes. I began to explain how one can go about transforming one's school within a system that is broken. History is full of examples of how individuals or groups who decided to "buck" the system and change the world that they had control over. All revolutions started with a small group of people who believed that they can change their world. Martin Luther King Jr. led the civil rights movement with a belief that the broken system he lived in could be changed. And he was right, even though many people thought it would never happen, at least not as quickly as it did.

The Creation Orientation

Robert Fritz introduces a second orientation, the creation orientation, that lifts you out of the reactive-responsive orientation. The creator has the ability to see a different future and is able to establish a new dominant structure, the creation process, which lifts the creator above the circumstances of everyday life. The creator is motivated by the desire to have something come into existence. The creator loves the creation enough to see it exist. The creator learns how to create the future separate from personal circumstances, feelings, or even identity. The love creators possess for their creations allows them to transcend their circumstances and create. The creator is not in denial, as you will discover. Rather the creator simply begins to act in ways that will cause the creation to come into fulfillment.

An *Imaginal* leader is not only able to see the future but also able to create it. The heart of *Imaginal* leadership is the ability to be a creator, to break free from the reactive-responsive world that most people live in. *Imaginal* leaders posses an unwavering commitment and passion for their visions, which is reflective of the deep love they carry for their creations. The love parents have for their children enables them to endure many challenges and hardships; and so it is with *Imaginal* leaders, but in their case their "child" is their vision. An *Imaginal* leader does not have to live in denial of circumstances; as a matter of fact being truthful about one's circumstance will further foster along the creation process. The *Imaginal* leader simply will not allow circumstances to derail what is in the process of being created.

Table 9.1- Imaginal Leader Comparison

Reactive/Response Person	Imaginal Leader
Reacting and responding to circumstances as the primary orientation	Circumstances do not limit or control what can be created
Limited possibilities, trapped by circumstances	Creator of the future, sees unlimited possibilities
Happiness is the avoidance of negative circumstances	Happiness is in creating the future regardless of the circumstances
Living in the Universe of Measurement	Living in the Universe of Unlimited Possibilities and Measurement
Despair for the future, because of powerlessness	Hope for the future, because it can be created
Emotions become a strong driver	I can create despite my emotions
Motivated by trying to think positively	Motivated by one's calling and strong desire for the vision to exist

Reactive/Response Person	Imaginal Leader
Motivated by obligation of doing the right thing	Motivated by love not obligation
Uses emotions as a gauge whether one is in the "right" circumstance	Engages in the creation process regardless of emotions, feeling good is not a prerequisite for action
Victim of circumstances	Lives above circumstances
Identity is defined by external circumstances	Separates one's identity from the creation

Creation versus Creativity

Creativity is a popular topic in today's highly competitive world. Often creativity and innovation are used together indicating a tight relationship between the two concepts. One can be creative but not necessarily innovative; but it is hard to be innovative without being creative.

To be creative means that one is unusually inventive, and able to create a large number of options which can be distilled into viable concepts. Being creative does not mean one can innovate. Innovation is the development of new systems or solutions that are beneficial and desired by others. Designing something that is highly creative may not be useful, and hence would not qualify as being an innovation. Innovation creates value and advances a field, an organization, or goods and services. One can be very creative in designing a portable electronic device that dangles from your earlobe, like an earring; however if there is no one interested in buying or using such a creative product, then there is no innovation—you have just been creative.

Years ago, Apple created a first generation tablet or personal organizer called the Newton in response to a whole field of electronic devices spurred on by the success of the Palm Pilot, but it really went nowhere. It simply did not have what consumers were looking for. Years later Apple launched the iPod, the iPhone and the iPad that became game changers for mobile telecommunications and computing. The Newton was simply a concept that was ahead of its time. The iPhone and the iPad are excellent examples of a creative idea that became a revolutionary innovation.

There are a lot of books and seminars on increasing your creativity. The fact that we are living in the creative age is further calling for books and programs on creativity. Richard Florida and others have written books about living in the creative age, some stating that the wealth generators come from the creative class. Everyone understands the negative impact that traditional education has on children's creativity, hence the need for all these programs. In many ways creativity has been elevated to the same level as positive thinking in the human potential movement. Creativity is viewed as something we add on to our lives that will make them richer and more fulfilling.

This is not a book on creativity, rather it is about you becoming a designer and creator of your future as an *Imaginal* leader who understands the creation process, and is able to create the result you want and need. What makes certain people *Imaginal* is that they are creating something that is transformational; they are able to see and create a "butterfly" from a "caterpillar".

The skill of creating will enable you to create solutions, disruptive technologies, new businesses, better relationships, and breakthrough systems such as a 21st century model of education. The creative age is fueled by knowledge—there is no shortage of fuel, it is widely available and more is being created everyday. But, how does knowledge fuel the creative age? At the heart of the creative age is innovation, the ability to combine ideas and knowledge in new and novel ways that results in solutions that bring value and benefit.

Tim Brown wrote in "Change by Design",

The myth of innovation is that brilliant ideas leap fully formed from the minds of geniuses. In reality, most innovations are born from rigor and discipline. Breakthrough ideas—whether for a new bicycle, an advertising campaign, a treatment plan for diabetes, or a program aimed at tracking the national obesity epidemic—emerge not by chance, but by studying and embracing the immediate challenges we encounter every day in our offices and homes, laboratories and hospitals, classrooms and conference rooms, and in all the spaces between. We don't simply realize solutions; we design them.[20]

The Creation Orientation is the difference that makes a difference for the *Imaginal* leader. It removes the creator from the creation itself, which helps ward off those feelings of vulnerability and hopelessness that the creative act at times invokes. In the Creation Orientation, one does not become reactionary to the challenges one sees, but rather is motivated by a desire to see and create something new.

There is something else that drives the creation orientation to one's world that must be ventured into and gleaned that further explains and pinpoints this difference. It is a driver that you may not think relates to the creation process and the act of creation, but indeed lies at the very core of becoming *Imaginal* itself: It is LOVE.

10.

Built on Love

"The whole difference between construction and creation is exactly this: that a thing constructed can only be loved after it is constructed; but a thing created is loved before it exists."

- Charles Dickens

Imaginal leaders create from a different center than those who create things that are simply pretty or cool but ultimately without substance. What is the difference that makes a difference between *Imaginal* leaders and the rest?

LOVE is the Reason We Create

Robert Fritz, in his book *Creating*, eloquently lays out the importance of love while creating.[21] Some may find it strange to talk about love as the reason we create, after all isn't love a feeling that comes and goes? For many people love is a feeling or response we get when we meet someone special and we "fall" in love, or we just finished attending an amazing concert that we "loved." For most people, love is a response to something we like; we experience something good and feel happy.

The *love to create* flips this around where love becomes the motivation for our behavior, and the experience comes after we have created. Previously, in Chapter 4, I presented the Back to Egypt Syndrome, where people's commitment to a vision journey is made explicit when they face "Red Sea" moments. During these moments one makes a decision to either press on despite obvious threats, or retreat back to Egypt, which represents the status quo. Those who decide to go back to Egypt would rather experience the certainty of slavery in Egypt, rather than the uncertainty of moving forward and facing even worse conditions. The syndrome proposes that one's dissatisfaction with living in "Egypt" will not be the driver that keeps one moving towards the "Promise Land," which is the vision itself.

Dissatisfaction is not what drives *Imaginal* leaders to create. Dissatisfaction may initiate the envisioning process, imagining a future that is different than your current reality, but it rarely is powerful enough to drive people to do extraordinary feats. Dissatisfaction will not fuel creation, but *love* will. People who pursue their vision, their Big WHY, are willing to endure incredible hardships, uncertainty of success, and a sense of inadequacy in light of the vision they carry. *Imaginal* leaders understand that how they feel about themselves really doesn't matter. The calling to a vision, to advance a cause, is fueled by the deep love they have for what they are about to create.

In Chapter 4, we explored courage and where it comes from. The courage to create is activated by the love the creator has for the creation. The focus of love is not on the creator, but on the creation itself. It is this sacrificial nature of the creator that explains why people like Mother Teresa and many others like her gave up all comforts of life to help the poor and needy in India. Not all creation requires that kind of sacrifice; however the common thread is that vision-led people have their focus on what they are creating and not on themselves.

I have written many articles over my lifetime, but this will be my first book. The process of writing this book has stretched over many years, having started and stopped several times. It was only until recently that the love of this creation kicked in, which compelled me to finish my creation. This book is part of a bigger vision of transforming education around the world. Recently, while sharing in Nigeria to a group of education leaders, I heard myself saying that we must equip educators to become *Imaginal* leaders so they can transfer this ability to their students. I said specifically, " You can't give what you don't have." Immediately I was convicted to finish my book and create an online training program for people who want to become *Imaginal* leaders. Why? Because of my love for the vision I carry. But it takes courage to do something for the first time: What if I fail? What if nobody likes what I create? All of these thoughts have entered my mind. But it is the love for my vision that is driving me to create, not some positive thinking mantra, such as "I can do this" or, "I am a winner" or, "I am a history-maker."

The *Imaginal* leader who sees the future, who wants to begin pulling that future into the now, will always be in tension with others who may not share the same passion and love for what needs to be created. The hallmark of *Imaginal* leaders is the courage they exhibit even in the midst of apathy within their own organization. For the *Imaginal* leader there is no compromise. The vision needs to be created, there really is no option to quit.

Creator vs Creation

Before we introduce the creation process through which you make visible the invisible, it is important to establish the dividing line between the creator and the creation.

In today's world we are often led to believe through powerful advertising and marketing campaigns that we are what we possess. We all know that we are not our cars, but too often we equate our identity with things we possess or even create. We even equate our future happiness by obtaining more things.

A few years ago I was shopping for a new car and happened to drop in on a particular foreign automobile manufacturer that had a less that stellar reputation for quality cars. I found it difficult to visit the showroom of this car manufacturer because of strong mental scripting. It did help, however, that the particular car I was investigating was voted the car of the year by automobile journalists; nevertheless it was quite difficult for me to conjure up the "courage" to visit the showroom. I spent hours reading reviews on this particular car, trying to find reasons not to pursue this option. Finally, I mustered up enough courage to visit the showroom and take the vehicle for a test ride. *Wow*, what an amazing car! It exceeded all of my expectations, so I leased it; however, my emotional roller coaster was not over. I made sure that all references to the manufacturer were removed. The car had its own branding, so I had it placed on the wheels as well as on the rear of the car. I ordered from eBay a metal badge that perfectly hid the car manufacturer logo on my steering wheel. It was the perfect coverup. One time while in a supermarket parking lot a person walked by my car and said, "I like your Bentley." Now what do I do? My deception worked perfectly! I felt really good about who I was—at least for a fleeting moment—but then it hit me: Why am I feeling this way? What have I done? About four or five seconds had passed by, so I had to intentionally walk over to the person that was a few cars down from me and explain that my car was not a Bentley.

Whether we are aware or not, so much of our identity is derived by things we own or the recognition we receive for our accomplishments. I found it difficult to consider leasing this car because of how it might impact what others would think of me. Certainly, if I drove a well recognized luxury brand then that would clearly mean that I am significant, that I am successful—why else would people spend enormous amounts of money to buy luxury brands, whether it be cars, purses, clothing and so on? I am not against luxury brands, I am just reflecting on the motive behind why we buy them. I was so impressed with the vehicle I had leased that when the time came for me to find a new car, without hesitation I went back to the same dealership and leased the same one, brand new of course—only this time I did not order the badge from eBay.

It is equally important to understand that just as our true identity is not derived from what we possess, it is also not derived from what we create. As an *Imaginal* leader you will be designing and creating your future, but it is important for you to separate yourself from what you are about to design and create. A painting is not the painter, and a building is not the architect. They may tell us something about how the artist or architect thinks, but the creation is not the creator. Our creation is motivated by our love for the creation, but our identity is not what we create. Parents should love their children, but they are not their children, nor should they try to control their lives as if they were.

Why is this important? What is the danger of wrapping your identity around what you create? If what you create is flawed, which invariably it will be, you will feel bad. This is why it takes courage to create, as mentioned previously in Chapter 4. For many people, feelings become synonymous with who they are. If what you create is rejected, then you will feel rejected. Fear of rejection will prevent you from designing a different future particularly if it involves the risk of failure.

If you are what you feel then you will stop the creation process to resolve how you are feeling. Separating your identity from your creation will:

- Free you up to make mistakes, and learn from them.

- Enable you to carry on with the design process. Creators have learned that what fuels their actions are not temporal feelings, whether good or bad, but rather a powerful desire to create an end result that they love. This separation will free you from the compulsion of feeling good before you start to take action.

At the center of our feel-good society is self. As a creator of the future, you will shift the focus on to your creation and away from self. You will also not be adversely affected if people reject your creation. You will no longer be dominated by the fear of what others think or the fear of failure.

This book is not about pumping you up to believe that you can do anything you set your mind to. It is about finding your Big WHY and through intentional design begin to take action toward your vision. It is seeing the invisible and doing the impossible.

Probletunity

I first heard the term "Probletunity" from David P. Langford back in 1993. As you can imagine, this word is the result of combining the words *problem* and *opportunity* into one word. This word suggests that a situation can be both a problem and an opportunity. The reason why we are creating a new word is because of the mental models people carry when the word "problem" is mentioned. Some people have very strong scripting in avoiding problems while others may revert to problem solving approaches that may not be helpful in designing what they want. Therefore this new word allows us to apply an intentional response of design in seeking resolution to what is being viewed as a probletunity.

When a vision emerges it invariable creates a gap between your current reality and the picture of your preferred future. Your current reality is made up of conditions that describe where you are today. *The conditions are not your probletunity, they are mere statements of reality.* A probletunity emerges when you have a vision for something different than your current reality. This creates a gap that generates the creative tension and energy to resolve the probletunity.

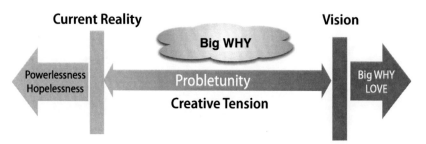

CONDITIONS describe the current reality before you begin the creative process. Conditions are descriptive statements of reality and are not the problem. Conditions are in constant flux and will change as the creative process advances.

VISION is a picture of your preferred future – this is what you wish to create and become.

A **"PROBLETUNITY"** is created when you discover a gap between reality and your vision for a new reality. The "probletunity" is neither current conditions nor the vision, rather, it is the discrepancy between them.

CREATIVE TENSION is generated, when you decide to resolve the probletunity, which is the interplay between your vision and current reality.

Figure 10.1 - Probletunity- Creative Tension

Here's how this works. In my current reality, I do not possess a rocket, but this is not a probletunity, it is merely an accurate statement of my current condition. Nobody is going to come up to me and say, "Hey Tom you don't have a rocket, what's wrong with you!" If, however, I had a vision to travel into space, then all of a sudden not having a rocket becomes an issue. The gap between my vision and my current reality creates the probletunity. I must find a way to create a new condition in which space travel becomes possible.

The probletunity creates the structural tension that elicits the actions needed that will enable me to create new conditions that bring me closer to my vision.

Vision and our Big WHY have a natural tendency to pull us forward. These are the driving forces that answer the question, "Why do this?" There are, however, restraining forces that want to pull us back or keep us in the status quo. In system dynamics these restraining forces act as balancing loops, constantly bringing you back to where you were. These restraining forces are either real limiting factors or just imagined; nevertheless they are constantly pulling us back to the status quo of comfort. As humans we seek comfort and have many conscious and unconscious strategies designed to maintain it. If we can identify these comfort-maintaining strategies, and come up with ways of minimizing their power over our lives, then the driving forces will do their job in pulling us closer to our vision.

It is important to emphasize that you do not have to eliminate all of the restraining forces in your life first before you can move forward towards your Big WHY. On the contrary, you can begin creating your future now because of the LOVE you have for your vision and Big WHY.

The Creation Process

The creation process is dynamic and iterative, and cannot be distilled into a linear process or formula. That being said, creation is a discipline that is not limited to the arts. It is a process that can be learned, developed, and matured. Professional writers, artists, architects, filmmakers, to name a few, are able to create consistently time after time. They have mastered the creation process in a way that is unique to them. One masters the creation process through the power of use. The more books I write, the better I will become at creating them.

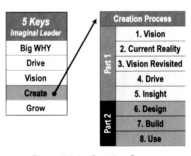

Figure 10.2 - Creation Process

Even though the creation process is shown in eight steps, it is to be understood as a form or pattern and not a fixed process. The first time you engage in the creation process, I recommend that you follow the steps as shown, but over time you will develop your own approach that invariably works for you. Steps 1-5 will form the first part of the creation process, which is Seeing the Invisible. The second part of the creation process, steps 6-8, is the Actualization of your Vision, which is when you become the designer and creator of the future.

1. Vision (There)

In this phase—preferably starting with a blank canvas—you seek what you want to create. Often this is an image of the end-state you want to achieve, with hardly a clue as to how to get there. The process may begin with recognizing a lack that's based on your experience of something being missing or incomplete. Recognizing a need could cause you to imagine a different future; however, dissatisfaction will not drive the creation process, *but love will.* Your sense of satisfaction or dissatisfaction with your current condition is merely your response to the current condition itself; but it will not have the *energy* to drive the creation process. Love, however, is generative; it has the power to create your vision.

Table 10.1 - Vision Activation Steps

Step	Action
Imagination Activation	• What cause am I most passionate about? • What is it that I want to create that would bring me a real sense of joy that advances the cause? • What aspects of this cause need to change? • Imagine an ideal scenario. • Imagine yourself in that scenario. • Imagine yourself creating that change. What has changed? • Imagine yourself presenting your breakthrough at a conference. • Imagine yourself being interviewed on television. What did you say?
Incubation of Outrageous Ideas	• Allow breakthrough thoughts to incubate. • Continue imagining your vision working and build up your faith. • Try not to rush to solutions. It is too early to have limiting mindsets constrain your vision. • Go beyond what your mind is saying is possible. • What needs to be created to make it possible?

Step	Action
Tell Somebody	• Selectively tell somebody your breakthrough idea. • Be passionate when you share. • Do not discount your idea for fear of being judged. • Let people know that you are not in the design phase, you are not able to answer *how* questions, but you welcome any insight that might advance your vision. • Add other people's faith to yours. • Reject cynicism, and avoid cynics if possible. • When you share, you are hearing yourself speak, and, in doing so, elevating your faith. • Invite people to join your Dream Team. • Take rejection with humility. People are not rejecting you, only your idea.
Write down your vision and make it plain	• Writing down your vision is the first step in pulling the future into the now. • What know-how will I need? • What questions do I need to answer?

As vision forms, it shifts from being a "cool" idea ("Won't it be a nice dream?") to an actual entity with its own identity. (See Fig. 5.2- Vision Formation Model.) For the *Imaginal* leader the vision of the "butterfly" is as real as any tangible object, for the *Imaginal* leader can live with one foot in the Universe of Unlimited Possibilities and one foot in the Universe of Measurement without any conflict. The *Imaginal* leader can see what isn't there yet, and beyond to what has never been seen before. It is truly an incredible gift to create what hasn't been done before. Anne Sullivan was able to see something in Helen Keller that even her parents were unable to see.

Vision pulls you out of the mundane and into the extraordinary. It begins to focus your values and your actions on clearly seeing what your current reality requires. Vision can be somewhat magical as well. You can see the results of your vision without actually seeing the process behind the "illusion". Vision doesn't demand that you have your "how" figured out—that will come during the design phase. In fact, prematurely entertaining the "how" of your vision has the potential to limit it's extraordinary nature.

2. Current Reality (Here)

One day a lion approached a monkey and asked, "Who is the king of the jungle?" The monkey answered with a timid voice, "Why of course you are." Then the lion met a zebra, and asked the same question. The zebra answered with a quivering voice, "You are your highness." Later the lion met an elephant, and asked with no hesitation, "Who's the king of the jungle?" At first there was no response, but all of a sudden the elephant picked up the lion with his trunk and threw him against a tree. The lion brushed off the dust and walked away, muttering to himself, "I guess he didn't know the answer." That lion definitely needed to adjust his thinking about his current reality.

In the current reality stage, you study the world around you and observe data, facts, and feelings. Your task is to identify your conditions and your relationship to them. Unfortunately, the ability to define truthfully your currently reality is not as simple as it sounds. Our tendency is not to describe currently reality, but rather explain why it is the way it is. Often we get defensive when describing our current reality, or we describe what we would like it to be. The ability to accurately describe your current reality will only help you in the creation process. You don't need to ascribe blame, you just need to know the truth.

As we previously described, our mind is a pattern producing mechanism that uses these neurological networks to interpret reality. It requires intentional discipline to make current reality statements that are truthful, rather than mere inferences your mind wants to make. Most often when you interpret your current reality as to why it is the way it is, you are really speculating which may very likely be incorrect. If this is the case, then the plan of implementing your vision could be thwarted by surprises from those areas of your current reality that lay outside of your interpretation of it.

The skill of sight, and more specifically *insight*, is critical for this step to be executed well. Using the strategies and tools from Chapter 7 (reflective thinking, systems thinking, seeing at various levels of recursion, modeling, and knowing the "real" problem) will be helpful for you to accurately define your current reality.

While understanding in more detail the underlying causes for system behaviors will come in step 5, it is important to know your current reality as best you can. Indeed, in the first iteration of your current reality it is best to avoid simply explaining it away. *This is a trap you must avoid.* You have to properly *look at* where you are for the creative tension to arise.

3. Vision Revisited (There)

Following a thorough vetting of your current condition, without getting into the blame game, you will want to revisit and further refine your vision. Vision is always morphing as you gain greater clarity around your current conditions and the needs of the future. Throughout the design process you continue revisiting your vision, which keeps on gaining clarity and refinement.

When you revisit your vision there may be a tendency to lower it in order to reduce the structural tension that is generated by the creation process. Such lowering happens often with organizations, while individuals often quit the endeavor completely. You will come up with all the reasons why your vision will not work—if your reactive-responsive orientation has been, to this point, a powerful limiter in your life. Steve Jobs was constantly challenging his development team at Apple with what they thought was possible. As an *Imaginal* leader you have the ability to rise above your circumstances. You can make the choice to pursue your vision because of the love you have for your creation. Let your Big WHY guide you and it will.

4. Drive

Here you size up the situation and decide to *do something* about it. This phase involves clarifying what you have gained from the preceding explorations. Primarily this is the phase of personal ownership and commitment in which you make it your personal quest to resolve the creative tension between your current condition and your vision. The deeper the vision connects with one's meaning network and one's Big WHY, the more likely drive will be activated. The deeper the love is for the creation, the more likely that circumstances can be transcended.

Parable of the Deck

This is the parable of the deck. The names have not been changed, so as not to protect the guilty person.

There once was a man named Tom(me). Tom was a man of vision and action. He would lead people to take on seemingly impossible journeys, such as the transformation of education. He would teach people

Parable of the Deck

to cast off all of the constraints that are holding them back, and pursue their unique visions relentlessly.

Tom is married to his lovely wife Silvia. Long ago, when Silvia and Tom got married, they both vowed that they would never live a life of mediocrity—after all, Silvia married Tom, a man of great vision and action.

Tom and Silvia had a deck. It was a good deck. The deck never complained, even when it was under a foot of snow. The deck loved it when family and friends would come together; and there were many moments of joy as we shared our deck with our friends.

Just like all of us, the deck was getting older. And then it happened: Tom was barbecuing one day when suddenly one leg fell through the deck. It was excruciatingly painful, not only to Tom, but also to Tom's deck. So Tom began envisioning a new deck, after all he was a man of great vision and action. But after much deliberation he decided to do what most men would do in this situation—it was time for a cover up. Tom went and purchased an outdoor carpet and covered up the hole and a good part of the deck. Tom reckoned that even if the deck is rotting away there is no way anyone will fall through with the rug in place. And so Tom's vision of a new deck quickly was replaced with a cover up rug.

After a couple of years, Tom's lovely wife, in a most gentle and kind way, began to nudge him towards his vision: "Tom our second son's wedding is coming up in a few months. Don't you think it is time to repair the deck?"

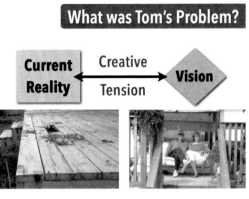

Suddenly, intent came—the reason Tom needed to move out of his comfort zone and toward his vision had come. Now Tom was on a mission, since once he started he knew there would be no turning back. So Tom drew up his plans and the man of vision became the man of action.

Tom was hoping that the building of the new deck merely required a new decking, that the main joists and beams would be fine. Unfortunately this was not the case, and he was greatly disappointed. Building a completely new deck required Tom to remove all of the old structure and start over again. This was twice that amount of work than building a new deck from scratch. Often with any vision you get unexpected surprises, and so it was with Tom.

Finally everything was ripped out, and there was nothing left but an empty hole.

And now began the building of the new. Tom was able to find a little bit of help along the way—he wasn't totally on his own.

As with any vision, one soon finds out that it takes teamwork to make a dream work. A vision

as compelling as a deck required the backing of the family.

Tom even had time to enjoy the journey. Even though the deck was not completed he and his sons were able to have a game of poker on the partially completed deck, just to have a sense of accomplishment of what had been done up to that point. Tom had learned that one should "smell the roses" once in a while—it can't be *all* hard work!

Well the big day came. It was now Tom's son's wedding and the deck was completed.

Silvia was a happy wife, and so Tom and Silvia lived happily ever after.

What is the moral of the parable?

And they lived happily ever after

Having a vision for something as well as a clear understanding of the current condition is not enough to cause the action to close the gap between these two.

One has to activate drive, and take action to move toward the vision. What's it going to take for you to activate your drive toward achieving your Big WHY and the vision that is generated by it? Moving out of your comfort zone is not as easy as it sounds. If so, then everyone would be doing it. The hardest part of the journey is to simply begin.

5. Sight

This is the "Aha!" stage in which a synthesis occurs between all that has gone before. The confusion starts to make sense. Having created the "probletunity" through clarifying your current condition and your preferred future, the solution usually becomes obvious. If no obvious solution has emerged, you need to continue to envision many possible solutions and systematically explore their potential. By using the third key of VISION (SIGHT), you are able to see hidden assumptions and mental models that have created your current condition and the thinking that is being applied to your vision.

Vision Deployment Matrix

The Vision Deployment Matrix (VDM), is an extension of the System Levels Model found in Chapter 7. We have found this tool to be one of the most useful tools for gaining insight into the current reality, as well as gaining understanding of what needs to change in the system as we move towards the vision.

Table 10.2- Vision Deployment Matrix

Level of Perspective	Current Reality	Vision
Vision	What is the current vision in use?	What is the espoused vision of the future?
Mental Models	What are the prevailing assumptions, beliefs, and values that sustain the systemic structures?	What is the espoused vision of the future?
System Structures	Which system structures are producing the most dominant pattern of behavior in the current system?	What kinds of systemic structures (either invented or redesigned) are required to operationalize the new mental models and achieve the vision?
Patterns	What is the behavior over time of key indicators in the current system? Select key variables and research the patterns over time	What are some key indicators whose pattern of behavior shows that the desired vision is a reality?
Events	What are some specific events that characterize the current reality? Are they individual events or stories of a larger pattern that has been unfolding over time? Resist any temptation to sanitize it for political reasons or bias it towards a particular solution.	What are some specific events that illustrate how the vision is operating on a day-to-day basis?

The power of the VDM is to compare your vision with your current reality at the various system recursion levels. One starts at the events level within the current reality and works up the levels of perspective to vision. Once the current reality has been thoroughly vetted, one moves to the vision side of the matrix and works down towards the events. You are now envisioning what kind of mental models and structures are needed to support your preferred future, your vision.

Table 10.3- Closing Gap between Vision and Current Reality

Levels of Perspective	Current Reality	Gap or Barrier	Strategy	Vision
Vision		Step 3	Step 4	Step 2
Mental Models				
Structures				
Patterns				
Events	Start			

Now that you have gained this valuable insight, the next step is to analyze that gap between each of the levels of perspective. To do this, you identify the barriers that are what prevent you from implementing your vision. For every barrier a specific strategy can be created that will enable you to begin the journey of implementing your vision.

As we have seen, the *Imaginal* leader creates out of Love for the vision, and not out of ego or self-love. This orientation mitigates the fear of failure and opens up the courage to create. The creation process is not the exclusive right of the creative or artistic elite; in fact, they have simply honed the skills of the creation process that is granted to all. Again, the creation process is all about determining the probletunity, namely the tension between the There and the Here.

To put this into practice is the beginning of the act of designing the future of education. But this kind of designing is different from cars and fashion—in the words of Bruce Mau, it is not about the world of design, but about *the design of the world*. To become *Imaginal*, entails becoming a DESIGNER.

11.

Your Future...by Design

*"A cathedral of this magnificence cannot be built without people be-
lieving in it so deeply and so truly that their belief becomes contagious.
It had to have taken more than salesmanship and communications
skills to convince citizens across five centuries to bring the vision of this
cathedral to fruition. There had to have been an authenticity that reso-
nated in the hearts of others."*

- Bill Shore, The Cathedral Within.

The dawning of the creative age was ushered in by the advent of the personal computer. When Steve Jobs first introduced the Apple Macintosh
to the world, whether knowingly or unknowingly, he unleashed the
power to create within millions of people. I remember back in the late
1980s learning desktop publishing and feeling so proud of the brochures
I had created. Virtually overnight desktop publishing companies
sprouted throughout the world. The ability to design a poster or a bro-
chure using WYSIWYG (what you see is what you get) software became
an overnight phenomenon. Combining this new desktop publishing
capability with laser printers, one was able not only to create nice looking brochures but also print them. Advancements in technology were
clearly putting the creative tools in the hands of anyone who desired to
use them. Musicians were now able to write music simply by connecting
their electronic keyboard via midi to a computer using some very powerful music creation software.

By the 1990s, a new revolution began to explode onto the scene. It
was a similar revolution that was ignited by the invention of the Guten-
berg's printing press in the 1400s, but on a much larger scale: the World

Wide Web. Finally, the internet was accessible by everyone and not just the academic elite.

User-created content and social networking characterized the emergence of Web 2.0 during the first decade of the 21st century, which has created a cultural shift by empowering millions of content creators. Now anyone can write a blog, capture a video and publish it on YouTube. This emergence has disrupted the media elite who are now being threatened by this new sense of empowerment of the masses to create all forms of media and news. In addition, the rise of terms like *design thinking* that attempts to combine both convergent and divergent thinking into one discipline has now become common place, thus merging change agency with creativity. So what now is design?

The Design of the World

When you hear the word "design" a myriad of images probably pops into your head, mostly about *stuff*: iPhones, Lamborghinis, fashion runways peddling the latest in urban garb from design masters like Prada or Versace, perhaps architectural masterpieces like Frank Lloyd Wright's Falling Water. Perhaps you think of the latest piece of furniture you picked up at IKEA, such as a lamp or bookshelf. This is nothing new. We live in a world of design; of objects that perpetually help us do things, seduce us with their opulence, or lie unnoticed below our noses hidden by their own banal ubiquity. In fact, more and more of our world is being designed, or, as the title of the design documentary by Gary Hustwit reveals, *Objectified.*

But there is another understanding of design than merely that of widgets and websites that is just as critical, if not more so: a process of thinking and working that leads to changes in our world—that is, *the design of the world itself.* This more authentic way of understanding and applying design addresses the perpetually complex sense in which the world, as a landscape of our own design actions, is in fact designing us. We live most of our days indoors under artificial lighting; we drive in our cars through streets already designed and engineered for us, and breathe in the refuse that our cars exhale; we eat food that is becoming more *product* than produce; we have conversations with others through devices and 3rd party interfaces that have designed the experience for us. All of these factors of our lives are intricately woven into an emerging system that we are intimately a part of; and that system in turn is designing us. The more we design the world, the more we are designed by it. Our lives are thus immediately and perennially directed by what we design.

As designer and academic, Tony Fry, maintains, this makes designers of all of us, for it is fundamental to what it means to be human.

Anthropologically, designing is able to be recognized as omnipresent and integral to every intentional act we take. It is therefore elemental to our being and, as such, is one of the defining characteristics of what we [as human beings] are. In this respect we are all designers. We live in and by design—our choices, be they of homes, lifestyle, dress, actions, perceptions, employment practices or environments are directed by the employment and consequences of design.[22]

Design is thus a fundamental orientation to the future of our world. Its importance lies beyond the capricious trending of it by well-known business schools to that which *provides tools and a way of being for creating a better future.* As Canadian designer Bruce Mau explains,

Design is a method by which we change things. So if you're going to think about changing things you're going to use a design method or it's going to be accidental. Accidental may or may not be helpful, but design certainly will be. Design is about making things exactly as you want them."[23]

Further to Mau's point, design is a way of creating what is deeply *intentional.* Much of decision-making, whether in boardrooms or conference rooms, lacks good design process, which is a problem given the complexity of our world. As complexity surges, a greater premium is placed on decision-making processes that can factor the complexity into it, thus amplifying the intentionality of the decisions themselves. As Mau and others advise, you need design to both understand your world and make the most intentional decisions to change it.

Design is thus an *Imaginal* activity, rather than a mere cosmetic one. *"Good design,"* Tony Fry states, *"is an opening into the future"*—it intentionally imagines an ideal place or scenario, and seeks through the process of conceptualizing, prototyping, and iterating to bring it into reality.

And as such design is "redirective," moving us away from accidental unsustainable responses to intentional design decisions:

We all confront an unavoidable choice: we either support the status quo (a choice so often made unknowingly) or we choose a path of change (which few do). Change only occurs in two ways: by accident or by prefigured intent (which is...design). To choose change means knowing how to identify, create and become an agent of change who is able to mobilize design to this end. For designers and non-designers, the potential...capability of design as an instrument of change must be grasped. [Design] needs to become a redirective practice. [24]

Hence, the *Imaginal* ability of seeing and creating the future is indeed deeply fused together with design. To orientate yourself to the world in such a way is, in essence, to be a designer—even if you've never thought of yourself as one.

"Design is really a way of looking at the world with an eye toward changing it. To do that, a designer must be able to see not just what is, but what might be." [25]

In fact, to become *Imaginal* is to become a designer of the future, which is a greater way to live than by compliance or conformity. Bruce Mau further elucidates this point in the following narrative:

In the process [of creating Massive Change] we met a couple of hundred of the world's greatest innovators, people like Dean Kamen who created a robotic arm so sensitive it can pick up a grape without breaking the skin, because he saw people coming back from Iraq without limbs.... 'It's a way of thinking,' Dean said, 'If this isn't going to change the world, let's move on.' That's how to live. Let's live like that. [22]

That design is an *Imaginal* activity fundamental to who we are as human beings is the reason why I argue its critical applicability to seeing and creating the future of education. Far beyond the fading trends of business schools looking for the latest thing with which to teach strategy, scale, and profitability, design is a way of seeing and creating the future.

It is no longer acceptable for our children to be learning within an obsolete system designed for an age long since past and profoundly different from our own. As we look into the future we see the complexity of challenges intensifying, which demands our children to be able to think and create in ways that will solve them. By designing the future of education, we have an opportunity to create the conditions for the next generation to become *Imaginal*, thus redirecting how they relate to and work in and around their world. The current design that prevails in education—all the way from the physical design of our schools to the way students experience their learning—is all a product of intentional design for an era that no longer exists. Not only do we need to design a new system of education, but also our students need to become designers of their world and their future.

Here design is understood and taught as a fundamental way of being—a set of tools to design the world. Tim Brown, CEO of the high-profile design firm IDEO, makes a similar case here in the following:

[Principles] of design thinking [are] applicable to a wide range of organizations, not just to companies in search of new product offerings. A competent designer can always improve upon last year's new widget, but an interdisciplinary team of skilled design thinkers is in a position to tackle more complex problems. From pediatric obesity to crime prevention to climate change, design thinking is being applied to a range of challenges that bear little resemblance to the covetable objects that fill the pages of today's coffee table publications [26]

However, while the potential of design lies inside us perhaps untapped, like our own creativity, it must be actualized and honed as a skillful and intentional way of being in the world. If you've never thought of yourself as a designer before, then think again. In what follows, you will engage in a process through which the tools and skills that designers use will be available for you to learn and apply to the complex challenges you and your organization, or team, are facing.

6. Design: Making Visible the Invisible

This chapter introduces you to the second part of the creation process, steps 6-8, which is the actualization of your vision. Through DESIGN you will make visible the invisible, by BUILDING you will actualize your vision, and through USE you will refine your creation. In this phase, you will be making visible the invisible, as you put ideas into practice.

We are now ready to apply design processes to the probletunity that will resolve the structural tension generated by steps 1-5 of the creation process. The focus of design is on the vision—what it is that you want to create, as well as your current reality, namely where are you at today. Both ends of the structural tension will inform the design of the solution being contemplated. Solutions being designed need to be implemented within the context of your current reality.

Table 11.1- The Creative and Design Processes

The design process differs from the more structured problem-solving approach of the scientific method, which starts with defining a problem and a hypothesis that is tested through a series of experiments. You will draw your conclusion at the end of your experimentation phase. The design process starts with what you want to create, your end state; and in order to start, you need to define enough of the parameters to optimize the path to the goal. What you what to create is actually the starting point.

The creation process starts with the "end in mind," which is one of the Steven Covey's seven habits of highly effective people. You will be designing a solution or a series of solutions to the design "problem" generated by the creative tension between your vision and current reality.

Table 11.2- Scientific Method vs the Design Process

Structured Problem Solving Scientific Method	Solution Based Design Process
State your question	Start with what you want to create
Do background research	Research gathered from steps 1-5 of the creation process
Formulate your hypothesis, identify variables	Specify requirements
Design experiment, establish procedure	Create options and choose the best one and develop it
Test your hypothesis by doing an experiment	Rapid prototyping
Analyze your results and draw conclusions	Test and redesign as necessary

Design process

One puts on the engineering hat as one begins the design phase of the creation process. There is enough clarity to what needs to be created that the time has come to design your creation. I will introduce the design process as a series of steps, but it would be too simplistic to suggest that, within the larger creation process, design is simply linear—not at all. It is quite cyclical, meaning that you will constantly be moving back and forth through various steps.

Step 1: Clearly stating what you want to create

Although much of the research and development of your vision has already taken place in steps 1-5 of the creation process, it is time to write down specifically what you want to create. You can write each statement to include the following:

1. What is it you want to create?
2. What is the intended outcome of your creation?
3. How will you know if you have accomplished your outcome?

Your creation may have a varying degree of complexity and thus require you to stage it. With more complex solutions you may need to create a system diagram of your creation showing how various parts of your solution are interrelated. Given the limits of your resources, you may need to make a decision about which part of the solution you need to design and build first. There may be a need to outsource part of your creation to a third party, which introduces a whole new set of design constraints. Outsourcing has both pros and cons, but one thing for certain, it will require you to create a very detailed and rigid set of specifications, which will create further tension within the creation process. I would recommend, if at all possible, anything that is foundational to your creation should not be outsourced.

Step 2: Determine specifications for your creation

Now that you have your game plan, you need to begin the specification process. In software development there are a number of best practices, such as developing *use cases*, that aide in the specification process. This book is not an engineering book, hence I will distill the specification process to six basic questions.

Table 11.3- Six Questions when Starting to Design

Type	Question
Who & What	• Who are the players? What do they do? • What makes their roles different? Where does responsibility lie? • What is it that I want to create? • What are the technical specifications?
How Much	• How much will it cost? • What is the budget? • How well will our solution scale?
When	• What comes first? What's next? • Is the order important? • When is the best timing?
Where	• Where do they fit? • Where does it work best? • Are we moving in the right direction?

Type	Question
How	• What happens if we did this...? • How are various parts connected? • How do parts effect other parts? • How do our actions affect the outcome?
Why	• Why are we doing this? • Is it the right thing to do? • How does it fit my Big WHY? • Are there better options?

Step 3: Creating Design Options

Creativity is the elimination of options. Without options you have most likely not designed an innovative solution. There is a danger that you fall into the trap of "paralysis by analysis" by spending too much time considering too many options, or even worse over-analyzing *too few* options. However, there is a sweet spot where you begin to act in the "action zone."

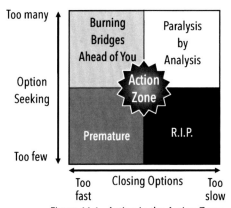

Figure 11.1 - Acting in the Action Zone

Step 4: Rapid Prototyping

The ability to rapidly prototype your solution will greatly save you both time and money. Depending on what you want to create, and the amount of innovation you have incorporated into your design, getting early feedback is essential in determining whether or not you have made the right design decisions. All design decisions are based on a number of untested assumptions. It is in the prototype stage that we get to test those assumptions.

For Tim Brown, the CEO and President of IDEO, the goal of designers is to match the desires of humans with the available technical resources within the constraints of business. Rapid prototyping allows you to test whatever assumptions you are making in all three of these domains.

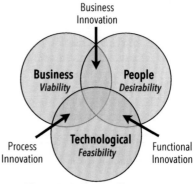

Figure 11.2- Zones of Innovation

Step 5: Feedback and Refinement

Rapid prototyping allows you to gather valuable feedback fairly early in the design/build phase of your creation. Should you need to pivot and make a major change to your design, now is the time to do so. Years ago in software development, it would take months and even years before you were able to get a beta product into the marketplace for testing. We have seen many failed launches of new software products over the past decade. With newer software development tools, companies are now able to rapidly prototype concepts in a matter of weeks and in some cases even in a matter of a few days, and the cost of pivoting on a particular design direction is not very high.

7. Build

The seventh step of the creation process is to build your creation. You have moved out of the design, rapid prototyping phase into the actualization of your vision.

This is the phase of production, marketing, entrepreneurship, and personal growth. When the building phase is done well, the solution resolves the creative tension that drove the creation process from the beginning—it is now time to celebrate.

The envisioning and design phase, or the creation process, are the most arduous and time consuming steps. In software development often the first six steps take up to as much as 80% of the time to the completion of the project, meaning that the actual programming is really only a small fraction of the overall development schedule.

Again, the creation process is not linear, so even in the build phase there are still some tweaking and design decisions that have to be made or altered.

In the development of Profound Learning, we spent over 10 years investigating and testing various elements that today are a part of our model. The emergence and building of the Profound Learning model have taken another three years which has included the design and development of a series of major software systems. Sometimes the build phase can take years and usually more than double the time of what you may have initially thought.

Table 11.4 - The Creation

Creation Process	
Part 1	1. Vision
	2. Current Reality
	3. Vision Revisited
	4. Drive
	5. Insight
Part 2	6. Design
	7. Build
	8. Use

Become a cathedral builder. Build something great that will last—that will "rock" your world. A builder of a vision needs to have the patience of a cathedral builder. In today's rapid-paced world of instant gratification, we have lost the sense of investing into something that will take time to build. But what in life is worth having that doesn't require an investment of time?

There once was a traveler who journeyed all over the globe in search of wisdom and enlightenment. In the midst of one village, he came upon a great deal of noise, dust, and commotion.

He approached the nearest laborer and asked, "Excuse me, I'm not from this village. May I ask what's going on here?" The laborer replied curtly, "Can't you see? I'm busting rocks."

The traveler approached a second laborer doing the same thing and asked the same question. The second laborer replied, "Can't you see? I'm earning a living to support my family."

The traveler then approached a third laborer who was also breaking up rocks and posed the question a third time. With a broad smile and a gleam in his eye, the third laborer replied with great pride, "Can't you see? We're building a cathedral."

As mentioned earlier, it takes courage to create since the creation seldom measures up to the expectations of the creator. This is when you need to remember that you are not your creation—be certain to separate your identity from your creation.

You and others will see all of the deficiencies, but take the time to celebrate your creation even though it may not yet be where you would like it to be. I have often used the nursery rhyme "Pussy Cat Pussy Cat" to remind people that there is a time to focus on the Queen, your creation, and there is a time to focus on the mouse, the defects.

Pussy cat, pussy cat, where have you been?

I've been to London to look at the Queen.

Pussy cat, pussy cat, what did you do there?

I frightened a little mouse, under the chair.

Hold a party and celebrate your creation. Enjoy the moment. On occasion I have seen creators almost apologetically present their creation to others. They will talk about why the creation isn't what it should be. This comes from a fear of judgment from others, since they still have not been able to separate their identity from their creation. Celebrate—you have accomplished something very special. All the naysayers have not created anything. Who cares what others think—you are a creator. Let the love you have for your creation be your reward.

At Master's we have often met as a leadership team to reflect on the journey, remember milestones and accomplishments, and express our gratitude for the journey. There were many moments in our early years in which seemingly impossible things happened, and everytime we reflected on our past it gave us the courage and faith to press on to the future.

8. Use (Feedback and Re-Design)

This is often the forgotten part of the creation process. It is when the creation is put into use that you can truly evaluate the success of what you created. Inevitably, this process brings new insight that will lead to redesign and further improvements through which a new "probletunity" will begin to emerge.

You create prototypes during the design phase to gather valuable feedback before you commit to the building of your creation. But no prototype can fully replicate the real life conditions that you will experience when you put your creation through the rigor of normal use.

To conclude, design is inside all of us, and fundamental to seeing and creating the future of education. As we've seen, it is not merely about making things look cool or expensive, but rather about the application of creativity and collaboration to bring change to the world and your future. In fact, becoming *Imaginal* means becoming a designer of the future.

Now that you've learned about design as a powerful iterative way to create the future, you're ready to look at what it takes to grow your vision.

Part IV: Growing

12.

GROW

It always seems impossible until it's done!
– Nelson Mandela

Imaginal leaders are not only able to see and create but also GROW their vision. All living things grow and replicate, which is the order of life. Once a vision has been actualized—the baby has been born—it will require nurturing and care. As an *Imaginal* leader you are now responsible for your creation. You need to ensure that your new "baby" is properly nurtured to the point that it will sustain itself.

Nurturing Phase

Just as a new born baby, your creation will require special attention. Over the years I have learned that the rollout of vision happens in stages. There will always be the early adopters that are able to take the early creation and run with it. These early adopters are not deterred by the incompleteness of the first generation creation, but actually revel in these conditions. As the creation continues to mature, more and more people are able to join the deployment of your vision.

During the nurturing phase you want to set realistic expectations. Overselling and under delivering in the early rollout could be devastating to your vision. Be very cautious what you promise early on. Invite people to be a part of your early rollout strategy, and make it a privilege to be included in such a venture. Microsoft, as well as many other software companies, have thousands of beta testers of their new products. It is a privilege to be a beta tester, knowing that the product is not quite ready for prime time, and expecting to find some bugs. This is all part of the nurturing phase.

Growth Phase

In most living organisms, there are various stages of growth from birth to adulthood and eventually death. During the growth phase your vision requires a lot of attention. This chapter will explore growth from the following two perspectives:

- Growing in size or scale

- Maturing your initial creation

Revisiting and refining vision happens naturally the more you become focused on what you want to create. As new insight is gained through the creation process, your vision continues to mature. At some point, the vision begins to grow in scope and scale, and you cast your gaze beyond the instance of your first creation.

Growing in Size

At Master's, our vision is to produce Profound Learning: a 21st century model of education that truly prepares students to be Future Ready. Master's Academy and College was established to be a research and development "laboratory" for Profound Learning. But what happens once Profound Learning has been developed? Do we declare mission accomplished and settle into a maintenance mode?

Back in November 1999, I shared at a Master's board retreat that one day we will be taking Profound Learning around the world. We were only two years into our journey, barely crawling, yet I felt compelled to share the vision of transforming education around the world. Our vision was not only revisited, but elevated to a whole new level. In hindsight I could imagine what some might have been thinking; nevertheless, *Imaginal* leadership is all about seeing the invisible and doing the impossible. Having this global vision allowed us to find our Big WHY that not only would continually stretch our thinking and abilities, but also put our vision into the realm that required us to walk in faith and not just by sight. This second level of recursion of our vision, to take Profound Learning to the world, takes us beyond making a difference with 750 students in Calgary, Alberta to tens of millions of students around the world. This aspect of the vision is quite a bit more challenging than the creation of Profound Learning in the first place. There are plenty of model schools around the world that have successfully implemented their vision for education in a local school setting; but seldom have these schools made a difference in a broader context. I would even argue that having a model school may even make matters worse, for it further reinforces the powerlessness and hopelessness of those visiting these schools. There is a human tendency to discount or rationalize away a successful model to justify one's sense of powerlessness. I have seen this happen many times.

Fours Levels of Sustainable Transformation

Given the complexity of education, we needed to see and create solutions to support the transformation of education at multiple levels of recursion (as shown in Figure 12.1). Advanced software systems that enable customization and tracking of learning needed to be developed that would enable schools to shift from the assembly line approach to education (the caterpillar) to that which is optimized and customized for the individual learner (the butterfly). To further support this transformation, powerful processes have been created that help shift the thinking and behaviors of people to seeing how a new system through incremental transformation can implemented.

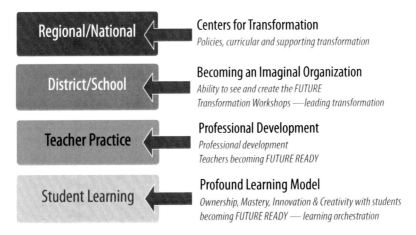

Figure 12.1 - Four System Levels for Sustainable Transformation

Level 1 Transformation: Student Learning

For almost twenty years, we have been developing and field testing Profound Learning, not only at Master's Academy and College but also around the world with schools that have been implementing Langford's Quality Learning philosophy and tools. We have developed a powerful Profound Learning Orchestration System (PLOS) that enables schools to shift student learning from the assembly line, factory approach to a more personalized 21st century approach. This system supports the creation of individualized learning roadmaps and itineraries that can be tracked concurrently by the teacher. As mentioned previously, system transformation requires new system structures that will generate the new kinds of behavior we envision. If we have a vision for a butterfly, then we need to create the requisite structures, for example wings, that did not exist before.

The use of technology coordinates with the engagement of students in learning adventures, while at the same time assisting them with the development of their Future Ready skills. The technology solution allows students to take ownership of their learning, while giving the teacher both the capability to mentor and guide them through their learning process, and monitor each student's progress in real time.

Profound Learning is about releasing JOY for both students and teachers. Joy is released when students engage in learning experiences that are meaningful and personalized to their learning style. Joy for teachers is released when students are enabled to be autonomous in their learning experiences and their planning time is reduced due to a streamlined system. Our PLOS guides teachers through the design of learning experiences by providing various tools that incorporate key elements of J.W. Wilson's Learning Code and the Essential Future Ready skills. These strategically designed experiences will result in greater student JOY, relevance, and a higher retention level of learning. (You will find more information about PLOS in Appendix C.)

Level 2 Transformation: Teacher Practice

A key aspect of how we can grow our vision is the development of the Profound Learning Odyssey for Teacher Transformation (PLOTT), a comprehensive professional development program, with professional practices and the supportive philosophy based on brain research, tools for designing rich learning experiences, and examples of how other teachers have implemented these student learning practices. Who the teachers are becoming is as significant as who the students are becoming. At the core of the transformation strategy is professional development.

Our professional development program (PLOTT) will include the following:

- Necessary training to be a practitioner of Profound Learning.

- Establishment of culture and climate.

- Linking of professional practice with neuroscience.

- Designing engaging Learning Adventures.

- Customized teacher professional growth plan.

- Developing teachers in "Who they are Becoming" by using the 5 Keys to develop teachers into *Imaginal* leaders, who will be able to instill that visionary spirit into their students.

- Recognition for teachers as they advance in the various levels of their own professional development.

- Tracking of teacher professional growth as an accountability factor for school administrators.

- Bringing district alignment into practice eliminating wasted time and grid-lock.

Learning Adventure Exchange

What if teachers created rich Learning Adventures that can be packaged and shared, or sold, through a Learning Adventure Exchange similar to an Apple App Store? Teachers would be able to deposit and acquire Learning Adventures, modify them, and disseminate them to their students.

The sharing of Learning Adventures between teachers will elevate the learning of all students particularly in those countries that have challenges with a sizable number of teachers lacking professional competencies.

Level 3 Transformation: Becoming an Imaginal Organization

Developing the capacities of organization to become *Imaginal* is the objective of Level 3. But where do we find these *Imaginal* schools and leaders that are willing to take the leap into the future with Profound Learning? To this end we have developed a powerful three day *Imaginal* Transformation Workshop, in which we begin developing the *Imaginal* leadership abilities of the participants. During this workshop, leaders create a bold vision for a *new* system of education, and in turn, become designers of the future for their school, district and nation. The *Imaginal* Transformation Workshop is a three day process of discovering, defining and designing the *future*. As *Imaginal* leaders, they learn how to incrementally pull the future into the now, and how to lead transformation with their key stakeholders. The key to our vision is our ability to activate and develop *Imaginal* leaders. The *Imaginal* Transformation Workshop can be used by any organization that wants to Discover, Define, and Design its vision to become a butterfly.

Imaginal Transformation Workshop is recommended to all school districts that are implementing Profound Learning. Transformation is fueled by the leadership's commitment to its vision of the future. Without a vision of the future, the system will continue doing what it has always done: trying to improve something that is obsolete.

Level 4 Transformation: Regional/National

Our model for scaling our vision requires us to establish, in partnership with local visionaries, Centers for Transformation. In the spring of 2013, we formed a strategic partnership with Incubator Africa Limited in Nigeria to establish our first Center for Transformation. The Center for Transformation will have the ability to conduct *Imaginal* Transformation Workshops, Profound Learning Teacher conferences, provide consultative support to the *Imaginal* schools that have joined the Profound Learning network, and influence policy and curricular changes with the government. The goal is to have dozens of Centers for Transformation strategically positioned in countries around the world. With this growth model, we will be able to support millions of teachers and tens of millions of students implementing Profound Learning.

Maturity Models

The second principle of growing your vision is rooted in a core principle of life, which I call the Maturity Principle. The Maturity Principle takes the pressure off the Creator or Innovator to get it right the first time, which seldom happens when creating. This is why it takes courage to create as I shared in Chapter 4, since the creation seldom meets the expectation of what the creator sees. The creator has to understand that the creation needs to mature over time.

The Maturity Principle helps those who create to accept the first creation as an iteration of what has been envisioned, hence the need for further work and refinement. The pressure of creating something that is just right or perfect is alleviated when one accepts that, as an innovator and inventor, it is just not possible to get it right the first time. The other element that comes into play is that the user feedback typically has some surprises that were not anticipated.

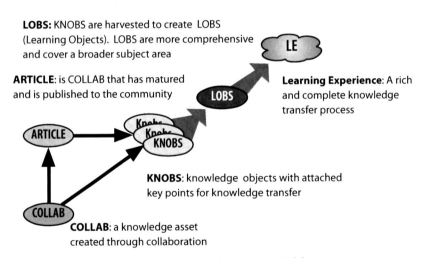

Figure 12.2 - Knowledge Maturity Model

Over the years we have used this fifth key of GROW to develop various maturity models that allow people to engage with processes with the view that they will grow their skill and competencies over time. For example, years ago we developed the Knowledge Maturity Model that looked at the development and maturing of learning experiences over time. This Knowledge Maturity Model clearly conveys the notion that the ability to design and create powerful learning experiences is a maturing process.

Similarly we developed an Organizational Brilliance model that looks at how we can grow the brilliance or overall "intelligence" of an organization. The intent of this book is not to go into detail about the processes we developed, but rather to convey the idea that most every aspect of your creation needs to mature over time. Every system and subsystem we have developed, or are currently developing for education, is incomplete and needs to mature, which can only happen when these systems are put into use. As an *Imaginal* leader, developing maturity models around your creation will greatly alleviate the emotional tension you feel when your first generation creation is being realized.

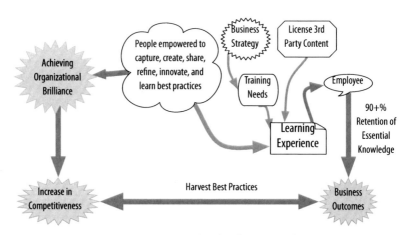

Figure 12.3 - Organizational Brilliance Model

The essence of education is to grow students in their knowledge of the world and the development of skills essential for their future. We have taken a deeper look at who the students are becoming by creating a system of personal development that goes beyond the curriculum. You can learn more about our student development model in Appendix A: Profound Learning

Just as technical systems have maturity models, so does the human development component of our learning model. For centuries people have started as apprentices working under a master craftsman with the vision of becoming a master craftsman. We have created a system in which the student as an Apprentice Learner becomes a Master Learner or teacher by the age of ten, eleven or twelve (see Appendix A, Figure A.3). Similarly, we have developed a growth model around who the teacher is becoming. If one can create such a maturity model for who the student or teacher is becoming, then one needs to be able to make that growth explicit. Through our self reflection tools, students and teachers can track their progress of who they are becoming.

Becoming an Adaptive Imaginal Organization

Let's assume that you got lucky and what you created was exactly what you envisioned, or over time your system matured to exactly what you envisioned. Things are working perfectly; however the dynamics of living in a world of massive change, with new technologies, new jobs requiring different skills, and new economic realities, will continually put pressure on your creation to adapt. Adaptation is the key to sustainability of life on this planet earth. If life forms were unable to adapt to changing conditions then we would all have gone the way of the dinosaurs.

It is commonly understood that education as a system has been highly resilient to change thus making adaptation very difficult. The next couple of chapters outline what it means to become an *Imaginal* adaptive organization that embraces the tension of predictability and control with ambiguity and innovation.

13.

Becoming an Imaginal Organization

"Innovation is definitely not self-starting or self-perpetuating. People make it happen through their imagination, willpower, and perseverance. And whether you are a team member, a group leader, or an executive, your only real path to innovation is through people. You can't really do it alone."

- Tom Kelly

Most organizations maintain their existence by serving their primary purpose. In the business world, often that purpose is defined by profitability and creating shareholder value—after all why else would a business be in business? Employees of these businesses view their time at work as a means of exchanging time for money, which is necessary to sustain the standard of living they expect. This transactional approach to work and life does not provide a deep sense of fulfillment; it does not inspire people to greatness. David Shapiro, in his book *Repacking Your Bags,* elucidates this point in the following:

> *We've discovered that many people are laboring through their lives, weighed down by attachments that no longer serve them. Patterns of behavior that have helped them get where they are, aren't helping them get where they want to be. As a result, many people feel desperate. They are grieving over the loss of life—their own.[27]*

Shapiro continues,

> *Many people are worn down with trying so hard, while the oasis of life that was promised is still tantalizing inches beyond the reach of their dry, thirsty souls.[28]*

For educators, job satisfaction seems to be diminishing, and higher levels of tension and stress in the system are not leading to greater joy.

The focus on raising test scores tied to teacher performance has fundamentally placed the system into a negative tailspin. If, as Deming taught, the system causes 90% of the system variation, then how is a teacher able to respond effectively when the majority of the performance issues are system derived? What is needed is the creation of a new system made up of *Imaginal* leaders and *Imaginal* organizations beginning the process of system transformation. And we need teacher professional development programs to be focused on training teachers to function effectively in the new emerging model of education. I will share more on this in the Epilogue.

The same Five Keys to Becoming *Imaginal* apply to organizations. *Imaginal* Organizations have the following characteristics:

- Have found their Big WHY

- Know how to activate DRIVE

- Operate with a compelling VISION that energizes their stakeholders

- See and CREATE their future.

- Know how to GROW

Primary Purpose vs Big WHY

Every organization has a primary purpose or reason for existence. In a competitive business landscape, that primary purpose is often viewed in terms of staying ahead of the competition and maximizing profits. In education, where the competitive forces are not as severe, incrementalism has become the accepted norm. The incremental improvement method presupposes that the structure of the system is fine, but by exerting enough pressure through reward and punishment, the system will be forced to improve. The generalized presupposition is that the main culprit for performance variation are people and not the system itself. This is a failed theory, yet it continues to be the main strategy for education reform.

What is the primary purpose of schools and of education? Most people would answer that schools are preparing students for the next level of education, which ultimately results in a career. Schools are preparing students for a life time of work. But obviously we know that there are other areas in which students must be prepared, such as citizenship, and various social skills necessary to succeed in today's world. To accomplish this primary purpose, countries have prepared curriculums that supposedly contain the knowledge and some of the skills that a student would need to succeed in the world of tomorrow. The role of the educator is to deliver the curriculum that meets the expectation of the district. Unfortunately, the identity of many educators has diminished to that of an assembly line worker: they do their part on a vast assembly line of educators trying to *install* curriculum outcomes into the students. By stating this I am in no way trying to diminish the nobility of the teaching profession, for the system is full of educators who have found ways to work within it while instilling the love of learning into their students.

Is it possible for a school, district, or state to have a Big WHY that fundamentally changes the orientation and behavior of those in the system? It is not just possible—*it is absolutely necessary*. When there is an organizational Big WHY, a shift takes place from a sense of powerlessness and hopelessness to one of hope and faith. You and your organization will no longer feel like victims of a failing system, but rather empowered to create the future you collectively envision and need to became designers and creators of the future.

What if we added to the primary purpose of a school jurisdiction researching and developing the future model of education? What if system transformation was part of the primary purpose of the jurisdiction? I can hear the naysayers, "Come on Tom, teachers are not trained in system redesign, and certainly this would not fall into their collective bargaining agreement. Teachers are already overloaded—*now* you expect them to be visionary designers and creators of the future?" My response is YES, but it will take some time to realign the system's primary purpose and create appropriate structures to support this new thinking. I will share more in the Epilogue about what I envision for this.

Creating Your Own Transformation Roadmap

We have discovered that before an organization can engage with a serious transformation initiative it needs to have its core leadership aligned with the future vision it sees, needs and wants to create. Transformation is fueled by leadership who are committed to its vision of the future. Without a vision of the future, the system will continue doing what it has always done, namely trying to improve something that is obsolete.

True transformation comes from *Imaginal* leaders who have the passion, courage, and vision to engage in the process of seeing the invisible and doing the impossible. (See Appendix D: *Imaginal* Transformation Workshop.)

Drive 4.0

The second key to Becoming an *Imaginal* Organization is DRIVE. Daniel Pink's book, *Drive: The Surprising Truth About What Motivates Us*, lays out the premise that extrinsic motivation using the carrot and stick approach does not drive people to do extra-ordinary things. Other authors, such as Alfie Kohn, have advocated for years a departure from the industrial age reward and punishment model of education toward a model that empowers students to intrinsically own and direct their learning.

In *Drive*, Pink examines the three elements of true motivation — autonomy, mastery, and purpose. Organizations that incorporate these three elements into their corporate operating system, as shown in Figure 13.1, have highly motivated employees. In addition to Pink's 3 elements, there is a *fourth* that takes an organization's motivation to a whole new level: a *calling* to a vision. A vision is that specific future we have been called to create that advances a particular cause. Vision and purpose are not the same. An organization can be very purposeful and not command a compelling vision, but a visionary organization cannot exist without a clearly understood purpose.

Vision calls forth *Imaginal* leadership from everyone in the organization—they are asked see the invisible and do the impossible. *Imaginal* Organizations know what it means to hold onto an extra-ordinary vision that is beyond most of its reach, and collectively, as a vision community, begin to pull the future into the now.

Calling

People are not hired into an *Imaginal* Organization, they are *called!* Being called to an *Imaginal* Organization is more than a job, you have a sense of destiny, and the joy of being a part of something that is bigger than anyone in the organization—you are serving a cause that is worthy of your time and sacrifice.

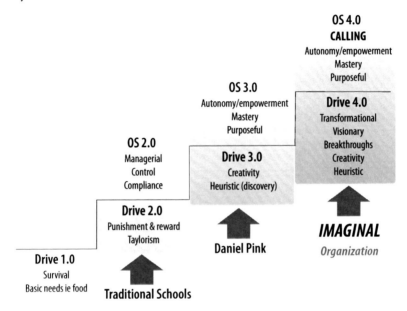

Figure 13.1- Imaginal Organization and Calling

The calling is a *spiritual commodity*. It is the culmination of your identity, who you are, your passions and gifts, your purpose for life, the cause you feel connected with, and the dream you have for advancing it. The combination of these five elements results in your life's Big WHY.

Back in 1997 when we launched Master's Academy and College, we introduced the "Call" process. Every year, faculty members were asked to reflect on their calling to be a part of the Master's vision community and our vision of developing Profound Learning. No two years of the "Call" were the same. We framed different questions and processes that forced faculty members to reflect deeply on their calling. One cannot assume that once someone feels called to a vision that decision remains the same forever.

We have found that some of our faculty have been called for a season, while others have become lifers. Everyone is treated with the highest respect, but everyone is expected to view their employment at Master's as more than a job.

The importance of understanding your calling is underscored when the tough times hit you. It is your calling to the vision that helps give you the determination to endure the hardship you face from time to time. One of the great defining attributes of history-makers is an unshakeable commitment to their vision and calling. It is also your calling that enables you to intentionally enter into the "pupa" stage of system transformation.

Why Organizations Die?

Organizations, like people, go through various stages of development. The early years of many organizations, particularly those with a vision to make a difference, are earmarked by innovation. Startup companies will almost always out-innovate larger more established companies, not because of their size, but because they have not yet tasted success. But eventually an organization achieves a degree of success, begins to mature, and eventually dies.

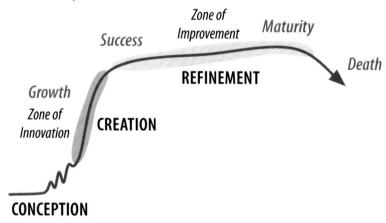

Figure 13.2 - Organization Lifecycle Model

But why do successful organizations die? It is because they stopped innovating. In the early years, innovation was a primary driver for success, but once success was attained, the fear of losing what the organization worked so hard to achieve caused it to shift from an innovative to an improvement orientation. This would be fine if we lived in the 1950s, but in today's rapidly changing world obsolescence can come quickly even to the most successful enterprise. When the relevance gap becomes too large, obsolescence and ultimately death will occur. The tipping point for obsolescence comes when the relevance gap becomes too large to close by using conventional improvement strategies. The system has become obsolete and needs major transformation if it is to endure. The education system has long reached the point of obsolescence; and the reason it has survived so long is that there has been no real alternative, at least for the majority of people.

Transforming education from a voracious caterpillar into a beautiful elegant butterfly is immensely challenging—if it were not so, our educational reality would be substantially different than what it is today. The very nature of the complexity of the system of education is what makes transformation such a formidable challenge, but not impossible.

Figure 13.3- Obsolescence Tipping Point

Incremental Transformation

Transformation begins with a vision of the future, the butterfly. A core team of leaders needs to be fully invested in seeing that butterfly it loves comes into reality. There is a misconception that for a vision to be shared it must be created by a group or by a committee. *Imaginal* leadership is not leadership by committee. A compelling vision is birthed from the spirit of an *Imaginal* leader, it is not reached through consensus, which typically reduces the vision to the lowest common denominator. *Imaginal* leaders are able to see the future and inspire others to follow their vision.

In education, it is very hard to reach consensus on any reform initiative. Invariable it gets watered down to improving the system incrementally and treating symptoms as problems. The *Imaginal* Organization recognizes that the role of leadership is to clearly define not only the vision for the future, which provides direction, but also the boundaries of behavior within which empowerment is created for people.

At the foundation of Profound Learning is student empowerment, which is clearly defined by intentional processes and system structures. If you want to create an empowerment model of learning for students, then you need to have an empowerment culture for teachers. Teachers need to feel empowered to implement Profound Learning in their classrooms, which can only happen with clear boundaries that define their empowerment.

Imaginal teachers are not asked to be visionaries for the entire system of education—although some may gravitate toward that thinking—they need to be *Imaginal* leaders of their own classroom. They need to see the butterfly and be willing to go through the pupa stage of seeing it begin to take shape.

Inspiration versus Motivation

Imaginal leaders lead by inspiration, which is rooted in their deep love for the vision they desire to create. When we try to motivate people to a vision, we often default to the use of manipulation which is rooted in fear not love. Great *Imaginal* leaders like Martin Luther King Jr. boldly declared their dream of the future with unreserved passion, and people followed. There was no manipulation, no threats, no fear—just a powerful invitation to join something that at its heart was just and right. John Kennedy inspired a nation with the challenge of going to the moon before the end of the decade, which mobilized the imagination and creative spirit of the whole nation. Too many politicians try with one hand to create a positive picture of the future with inspiring rhetoric, and with the other hand present a doom and gloom scenario if the current policies were to continue. Doom and gloom and hope and vision simply do not work together, which is why very few political leaders have the capacity to be real nation builders. The same applies to education, in which *Imaginal* leaders hold a compelling vision of the future birthed not out of ego, but out of love for the vision and the people it will serve. The greatest leaders all saw a beacon beckoning them from the future. They had a clear vision of the world they sought to create, and a burning passion to bring that world into existence.

The Pupa Stage

Once *Imaginal* leadership has established a compelling vision of the future, and has successfully communicated this vision to its key stakeholders, it is time to begin the transformation process.

In education, the transformation process will take several years—involving a series of three to five years transformation initiatives. There is no quick fix if one is serious about addressing the real problem of education, which is system transformation.

There is no set formula for how this process works, since it needs to be customized to fit the local needs and conditions. A transformation

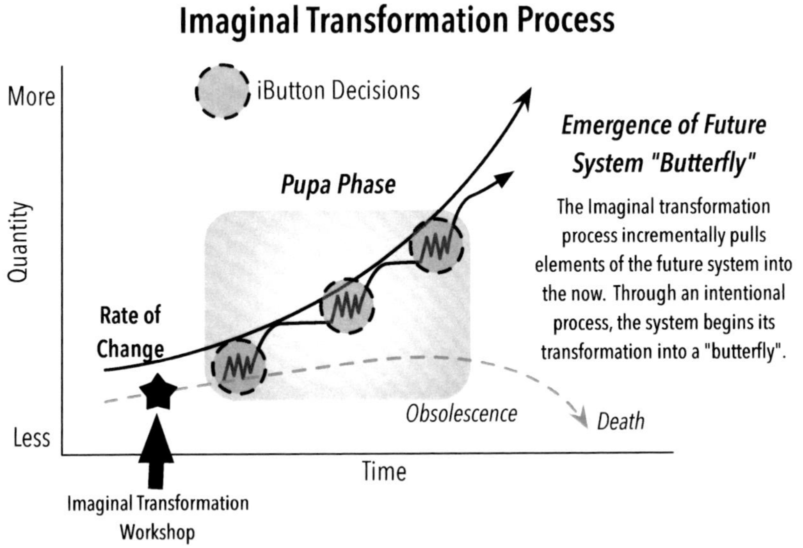

Imaginal Transformation Process

Figure 13.4- Incremental Transformation

plan for a school in Canada will look different than a transformation plan in Nigeria. This is why we are strongly advocating the *Imaginal* Transformation Workshop as a needful first step in launching the transformation process. The next table gives an idea of the various stages of the transformation process.

Table 13.1 Stages of the Transformation Process

Stages	Description
1. Envisioning the Butterfly	Transformation Workshop • create a compelling vision of the future • define the process for transformation • strategize for communicating to stakeholders • strategize for system pushback
2. Entering the Pupa Stage	Share compelling vision of the future Select parts of the butterfly that will be focused on first • the whole system cannot be transformed at once • decisions will be made as to what parts of the future will be developed now that fit the overall transformation plan Initial staff professional development on Profound Learning • Why we are going to succeed • Staff are invited to be a part of the journey • Establishing a culture of empowerment and begin using some basic tools and strategies with all faculty • Early adopters will be asked to take on more responsibility during this early stage launch
3. Formation of parts in the Pupa	This is the messy stage of transformation • parts of the butterfly are being formed but still in an immature stage • parts do not yet resemble the butterfly • handling system push backs • continue to add more faculty to the rollout until 100% are involved.
4. Exiting the Pupa	There will be some pain as the butterfly exits the pupa • some new system structures will be foreign to the stakeholders, for it is not the caterpillar they were accustomed to seeing • Will the butterfly survive, will it fly? • Need to ensure all the support mechanisms are in place to enable survival • Celebrate for the amazing accomplishment that has taken place, no turning back

Stages	Description
5. Stabilize and Standardize	It will take some time for the new system to stabilize. The goal is to bring vision alignment of all the stakeholders. Strategies will have been developed as to how to bring professional practice of all teachers into alignment with the new system
6. Start a new Transformation Initiative	Start envisioning the next butterfly. A whole new world of opportunities will emerge as the initial success has led to further envisioning of what could be.

System transformation requires shifting the thinking of your practitioners, the teachers, along with the development of new structures that will generate and support the new behaviors desired. New teachers will be mentored by veteran teachers, thus reducing their anxiety as well as increasing their success. The process also applies to students.

A powerful aspect of the Profound Learning model is the grouping of multiple classes of students within a particular grade, thus allowing for a greater level of teaming of teachers and differentiation of learning experiences for the students.

For education as a system to transform, we need *Imaginal* leaders to facilitate organizations in becoming *Imaginal,* or indeed create *Imaginal* organizations themselves. This will bring about a system of education that is *Imaginal,* and therefore able to see and adapt to the world of massive change. Accordingly, students who graduate from such institutions will have become *Imaginal* themselves through the power of transference, and thus Future Ready.

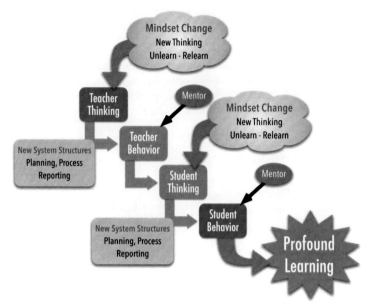

Figure 13.5 -New System Structures Generate New Behaviors

Master's Academy and College has spent the last 17 years becoming an *Imaginal* Organization. It has been years of victories and defeats, and trials and errors, but one thing we have not done is deviated from the vision with which we opened the doors of the school on its very first day.

The following story of our journey is entered in what follows to encourage you and show a possible way forward. It is the reason why Master's, as a prototype school for Profound Learning, was founded in the first place.

14.

The Imaginal Prototype

One enters the Universe of Unlimited possibilities with one's imagination; this is seeing the invisible. Faith is activated within the human spirit. It utilizes imagination to see into the future and uses hope to bring it into the now. A unique transformation occurs when we engage the universe of unlimited possibilities with faith: the seemingly impossible becomes possible.

- Tom Rudmik, 2006

Over the years, Master's Academy and College has gained success and recognition as a leading academic institution in the province of Alberta by the Fraser Institute. Many of the Profound Learning initiatives have resulted in professional practices, and an overall learning model, that consistently lead Master's students to the achievement of top scores on Provincial Achievement Tests. With a solid focus on core competencies and the early closing of gaps, Master's students have consistently scored above provincial norms for excellence. However, we needed to go beyond being one of the the best within an obsolete system—the butterfly had yet to emerge.

On April 30th, 2011, the Master's leadership invited all its stakeholders to an evening event in which its 3-year journey of Rebirth (Master's 2014) was publicly declared. This rebirth called for, as stated, an alignment of vision to practice, and taking Profound Learning to a whole new level to see the emergence of the butterfly and not mere elements of it. Master's publicly pushed the innovation button to engage in the incremental transformation process to become the "butterfly." Why do this? After all, there was no driving external force that was compelling this kind of initiative. The school was highly successful and could easily coast for a number of years without any real major issues to deal with. The reason was simple: the LOVE for the vision to become a butterfly would not allow us to stop with anything less than seeing it come into being.

To really understand the launching of the 2014 initiative we have to go back and review the history of Master's.

1997-99- Launch with Great Enthusiasm

Master's was launched in 1997 with a vision to create Profound Learning; however the vision was only at the DREAM stage of the Vision Formation Model. We established the school on Quality Learning principles, and experienced great success in those early days.

1999-2005 - Discovery and Defining of Innovation and Creativity

Having had my epiphany moment with the revelation of the iCubed model in June 1999, it was obvious that Quality Learning would only form a subset of a bigger picture of Profound Learning. We forged important strategic relationships with thought leaders in the area of design and innovation, and built our first Innovation Center. During this time we had become an iCubed organization, having established a culture around innovation and creativity, which we made the signature of our school. We began developing various models around innovation, which resulted in a unique assessment framework called EQS (Exceeding Quality Standards) which we implemented along with innovation and creativity.

2006-10 - Defining & Maturing the Vision for Profound Learning

Early in 2006, we introduced the Five Keys to Becoming *Imaginal,* first to our faculty and then to our students. Becoming an *Imaginal* leader was now an intentional part of our professional development program. Using these keys we began developing advisory programs for our students that would build their capacity to become designers and creators of their future. We also developed the following graduate profile for our Grade 12 students.

Grade 12 Graduate Profile Statement

Master's College, graduates will be Master Learners who have developed skills in all four Future Ready Capacities. Graduates will be able to pursue their personal vision without limitation by becoming:

LEADERS / HISTORY MAKERS / IMAGINERS who:
- ★ serve others
- ★ leave a legacy

RISK-TAKERS who:
- ★ demonstrate personal drive
- ★ are courageous

EXPLORERS who:
- ★ explore unlimited possibilities
- ★ suspend fear, cynicism and judgment

INNOVATORS / INVENTORS who:
- ★ activate imagination
- ★ release creativity
- ★ engage in the world of design and design of the world

BUILDERS who:
- ★ act on a vision for what seems 'impossible

Our vision for Profound Learning really began to mature when we decided to invest more focused resources into our research and development team. In earnest, we began to bring clarity to all aspects of Profound Learning, not only alignment to vision but also alignment to practice. After all, if we are to create the butterfly we can't have some teachers still practicing as if they were a caterpillar. All this led us to April 30th, 2011 when we launched our becoming a butterfly with our parents. Needless to say, we had already been working behind the scenes for many months with our faculty, getting everyone ready for the transformation process.

During this three year window, we were implementing various new system structures, such as capacity maps, more engaging learning adventures integrating the latest neuroscience designed to ignite the learning of our students, some changes to our physical environment, and an intensive development of the Profound Learning Orchestration System.

Master's 2014 Journey

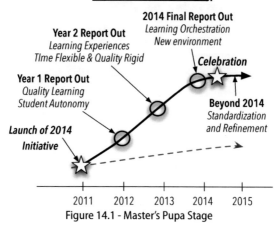

Figure 14.1 - Master's Pupa Stage

After this three year journey of elevating the model of learning, we will take a period of time to normalize—or to standardize and refine—our practice. At the end of all this, we expect to see greater JOY with students and teachers and an overall reduction of stress in the system. We know that when we go through systemic change the system will push back, but once these new structures mature the system will normalize.

How does one take an antiquated highly resistant to change system, such as education, and begin to transform it from a caterpillar into a butterfly? Previously, I wrote that system transformation must go beyond system improvement, and enter into incremental transformation. Incremental transformation sees an entirely new system, the THERE, and begins pulling new structures of the future model into the present, the HERE. Over a period of time a new system will emerge representing a significant leap into the FUTURE. You will learn, as an *Imaginal* leader, how to lead the transformation process even when the system begins to push back, which it will. You will learn how to set conditions for powerful transformation to occur in a way that is embraced by your key stakeholders. In essence you will be implementing disruptive change in your organization in a way that causes the least amount of disruption.

Those Early Years

In the Preface, I shared my epiphany experience when the iCubed model was conceived. Upon returning to Canada from Africa in June 1999, I shared with our faculty that quality principles alone were not sufficient to get us to our future. The Deming philosophy, I explained would continue to play a foundational role, but we needed to explore the broader playing field of innovation and creativity. Innovation and creativity were nowhere near as popular of a topic in education back then as it is today, so we were launching into brand new territory as an R&D school.

We began to explore and formulate the iCubed organizational model for Master's Academy and College. During the early years we referred to our school as becoming an iCubed Organization, which we now refer to as becoming an *Imaginal* organization. (I will use these terms interchangeably throughout this chapter.) Schools were not known as places of innovation and invention; as a matter of fact there were very few organizations anywhere that really understood how to intentional develop a culture that embraced continuous innovation. Educators are asked to work within a system, but very seldom are they asked to work on the system itself, particularly if it means the systematic dismantling of an obsolete system and the recreation of a new one. For this we would need *Imaginal* leadership and *Imaginal* organizations.

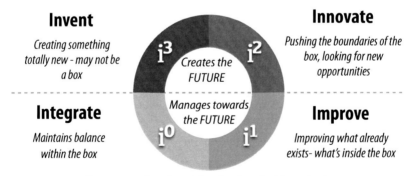

Invent
Creating something totally new - may not be a box

i³ Creates the FUTURE i²

Innovate
Pushing the boundaries of the box, looking for new opportunities

Manages towards the FUTURE

Integrate
Maintains balance within the box

i⁰ i¹

Improve
Improving what already exists- what's inside the box

Figure 14.2 - Four Capacities of an Imaginal Organization

It took several months to distill the essential elements to become an iCubed Organization, an organization that has the capacity to function in all four iCubed capacities to integrate, improve, innovate, and invent.

There were some examples of companies that had a reputation for innovation, such as 3M, Apple, IBM, GE, Sony, and Samsung (to name a few), but most of these companies were in the business of producing products, for which having an R&D department or division that looked after innovation and invention was necessary. But what about education? Where was the R&D, the innovation and invention occurring in that sector, particularly in K-12? Yes, there was some research taking place at the university level, but most of it was focused on various aspects of the learning process; but those that were trying to innovate and invent a new system of education were few and far between.

Who is responsible for the research and development of the future system of education? Since the vast majority of schools fall under the domain of public education, which fall under district and state or provincial jurisdiction, there was no real mandate towards the R&D of the future of education. Many states and provinces provided grants for schools to engage in some innovation, but most of these were small incremental improvements designed to raise academic performance and not to transform the system itself.

Is it even possible that a school can be both an academic institution and an R&D entity without having large amounts of resources and money thrown into R&D itself ? Well we were about to find out. This chapter is a summary of what we have learned over the years about what it means for a school to become an *Imaginal* organization, and to intentionally design and architect a culture of innovation and invention that is able to see and create the butterfly, the future of education.

Master's Story

Master's vision is to produce Profound Learning, an empowerment model of education elevating the learning of all students to heights not achievable in a traditional command and control system with an intentional focus on preparing students with Future Ready skills. With the fundamental belief that there is ample room for advancement in student performance in learning, we undertook the challenge of removing barriers to learning, discovering breakthroughs, and implementing real systemic change. We needed to engage in the I^2 and I^3 capacities of innovation and invention along with the creation process.

The dynamics of working in an *Imaginal* organization will invariably create anxiety and discomfort. Implicit in this assumption is that vision is about change. The willingness to engage actively in our vision with commitment and not compliance was based on a basic dissatisfaction with the status quo of education, as well as the belief that the pain and discomfort associated with change is less than the eventual cost of not changing or remaining status quo. As vision is being implemented, negative emotions often will come into play that will cause us to want to pull back from it. In Chapter 4 you learned that dissatisfaction alone is not strong enough to drive system transformation, rather people need to become *Imaginal*, they need to see and create the future they love.

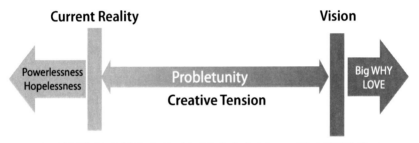

CREATIVE TENSION is generated when you decide to resolve the probletunity, which is the interplay between your vision and current reality.

Figure 14.3 - Tension within iCubed Organization

Zone of Innovation

So much of what we do everyday, whether at work or at home, is repetitive. We are not looking to innovate or invent, we simply are in maintenance mode, or being good managers. The integrator/manager role is extremely important since systems need to maintain a sense of balance and cohesiveness. The role of the manager is to maintain the system's overall purpose. There remains, however, a need for the other three capacities, namely the ability to improve, innovate, and invent. Very few people will resist the notion of improvement since these tend to be incremental with minimal disruption. Innovation and invention are quite different; for they create a whole new system dynamic that typically is not found in most organizations. How do we create an organizational dynamic that embraces all four iCubed capacities particularly if the organization is a school or district?

The next illustration was named by teachers as the "Bow Tie" Model. This model expands our understanding of the organizational dynamics that are involved when one embraces the need to become an *Imaginal* iCubed Organization. An iCubed organization will want to operate in the Zone of Innovation, knowing that a healthy level of anxiety resulting from ambiguity is needful to drive creativity and innovation.

The natural tendency of most systems and organizations is to gravitate to the left side of the "Bow Tie" model, particularly in education. Our human body is a perfect example of a system that wants to maintain homeostasis with its many elaborate systems designed to maintain that balance. The job of an educator is to produce predictable results which they have control over, at least to some degree. Traditional education is all about controlling outcomes, through command and control.

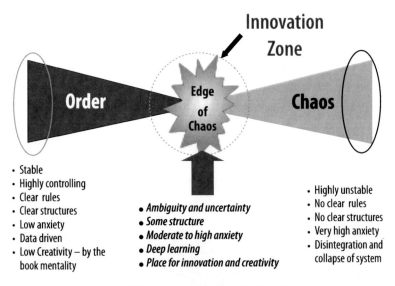

Figure 14.4 - iCubed "Bow Tie" Model

Moving a school to the edge of chaos, which I prefer to call the *Zone of Innovation,* is not something schools and educators will do easily. This is complicated by the fact that parents really don't want you to be tinkering with a system that possibly may put the learning of their children at risk. Parents do not want their child to be a "guinea pig" in some kind of grand educational experiment. However, parents do not really know how great the risk currently is in having their children in the old system of education that is not adequately preparing them for the world of massive change. Parents' views of education are primarily formed by their own past experience: if the old system was adequate enough for them, then why would it be any different for their children?

We needed to create a culture within our school community that would embrace innovation, creativity, and the necessary ambiguity that they would elicit. How do you find the balance between clarity and ambiguity, structured and unstructured, control and no control, order and chaos? This was the challenge we faced on an ongoing basis.

Vision is a powerful motivating force in an organization as well as in individuals. Victor Frankl discovered that we change by envisioning very intensely what we want to happen in the future. Once that picture or vision is clear in our minds, a creative tension is generated that calls for us to engage in the creation process to make the vision reality, which becomes the path of least resistance. Organizations that succeed in changing are those that have mastered the art of seeing the future and pulling that future into the *now*. They are able to convert the friction of resistance into positive propulsion—they have become iCubed Organizations.

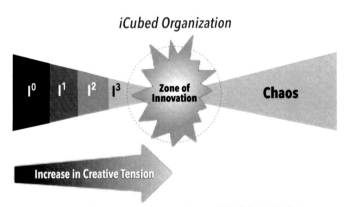

Figure 14.5- Tension Generated in an iCubed Organization

The iCubed Organization utilizes systems theory and the theory of complexity to transform from a traditional command-and-control organization into an adaptive learning enterprise. We used many of the concepts from Stephan Haechkel's book *The Adaptive Enterprise*, to design what it means to become an iCubed organization.[29]

The iCubed Organization has the capability to anticipate and identify emerging trends, to sense the weak signals that appear on the horizon of a rapidly changing global business landscape, and enable organizations and schools to be more responsive and adaptive. Within the iCubed Organization model, we needed to create a culture and supporting systems that encouraged the release of those particular creative, innovative talents to sense and respond more quickly to a rapidly changing world that are latent within every organization.

In 2010 the Alberta government released its 25 year vision document, *Inspiring Education: A Dialogue with Albertans*, calling for system transformation. As in most education systems around the world it is the curriculum that drives much of the system behavior. Not only is Alberta Education redesigning the content of the curriculum but also the very framework of the curriculum is being redesigned to enable a more rapid nimble adoption. A new curriculum in the old framework takes about 10 years to implement across the entire province, hence by the time it is fully adopted it will already be obsolete. School systems need to develop strategies to become more nimble, they need to become iCubed Organizations.

Imaginal Organizations as Early Adopters

Before any new idea or concept can become accepted by the majority of the population, a unique group of people, whom Everett Rogers called "the innovators," must first adopt this new way of thinking. [30] The innovators are pioneers. They are the first ones over the mountain. They are the first to tell the rest of society that a brave new world exists on the other side. Often these individuals do not see themselves as leaders or trendsetters; they feel quite ordinary. Yet it is their unique ability to see the value of a new idea that ultimately transforms our world.

Over the years we have found in a similar way that only a small subset of teachers are able to pioneer new practices. Typically these teachers are chosen to lead certain pilots as we explore new territory of learning. We have found approximately 20% of the faculty are able to function in the I^2 and I^3 capacities which are required in the early stage of system transformation. These are the *Imaginal* teachers that begin creating the first evidence of the future butterfly within the "pupa" stage of system transformation. The vast majority of teachers are able to be involved in I^0 and I^1 implementation of new teaching practices. The classification of teachers into these four categories is not necessarily a judgment of a teacher's efficacy in the classroom. This classification serves one real purpose and that is to convey the notion that only a small subset of teachers fit the pioneer category thus willing to go where no one has gone before. It would be totally counter productive to assume that all teachers are willing to take on higher levels of ambiguity and uncertainty when they are not. Let the pioneers be the pioneers and let the settlers arrive when it is time for settlement.

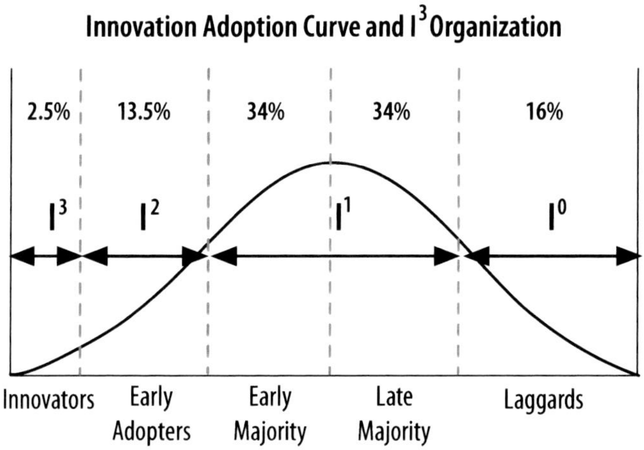

Innovation Adoption Curve and I^3 Organization

Figure 14.6- Everett Rogers Innovation Adoption Curve Mapping into the Four iCubed Capacities

Table 14.1- iCubed Organization Demographics

Type	%	Description
I^0	15%	Able to implement proven practices but not likely to pioneer new ones
I^1	65%	Able to be involved in system improvement initiatives even when data may point to a deficiency with the teacher's practice
I^2	15%	Able to innovate and explore new practices, extending existing practices into new areas
I^3	5%	Able to pioneer completely new practices within a new emerging system

10 Characteristics of an Imaginal iCubed Organization

We have developed and refined 10 characteristics to becoming an iCubed Organization. With the intentional cultivation and development of these 10 characteristics we were ready to take the leap into the abyss, in becoming a school that embraces innovation and creativity as a core competency. At the time we really did not fully understand what we were moving into, for it was certainly not the norm for schools to be doing what we had undertaken. Nevertheless, we had a dream and this was the path that we needed to go down. The key was that we would integrate all four iCubed capacities into these ten characteristics of an iCubed Organization.

Table 14.2- Ten Characteristics of an iCubed Organization

Characteristic	Description
Complex Adaptive System	• A world of interdependence and interrelationships • An adaptive learning enterprise
Clarity	• Provide focus and reduce ambiguity of the context
Context	• Reason-for-Being • That which surrounds and gives meaning to a situation and event • Governing Principles that are drawn from values that form non-negotiable boundaries

Characteristic	Description
Continuous Innovation	• To innovate and see opportunities; to envision solutions that are outside our mental models • Outside of the box thinking
Commitment	• A process that embraces breakthrough thinking and stretched goals
Coherence	• An alignment of context, viewpoint, purpose and action that enables further purposive action • It's getting everyone moving in the same direction
Coordination	• An effective system of commitment management • Communication of progress
Competence	• Individual and organizational capabilities to achieve its goals
Continuous Improvement	• Meeting and exceeding customer satisfaction • Process improvement and systemic change
Courage	• Willingness to risk, endure hardship and exercise faith

For a more detailed description see Appendix E: 10 Characteristics of an iCubed Organization.

Dealing with Anxiety

An iCubed Organization understands that there will be a level of anxiety that is generated by pursuing breakthroughs within a culture that embraces innovation and creativity. Strategies need to be developed that will help contain the inherent anxiety that will arise and that is necessary to drive the creation process.

One of the key strategies for anxiety containment is the role of leadership in the early stage development and adoption of new learning practices. Leadership needs to be in front of the early adopters, taking the "hits" that invariably will come from parents and others who may not fully understand or agree with what is happening in the classroom.

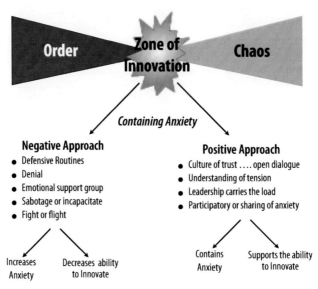

Figure 14.7 - Strategies to Contain Anxiety

People naturally want to contain anxiety that makes them feel uncomfortable or insecure. We as humans have developed many strategies for containment of anxiety, which are illustrated in Figure 14.6 below. The leadership of an iCubed Organization understands these dynamics and proactively, and in a positive way, helps people contain anxiety.

Back in 2001, we wanted to better understand the dynamics of stress and anxiety within the context of Master's as we were becoming an iCubed Organization. We created an extensive survey for our faculty who responded anonymously. (see Appendix F.)

As with any survey of this kind, other factors come into play that create anxiety and stress that lay outside of the parameters of the workplace. But given some obvious challenges we were able to gain valuable insights into the emotional aspects of working in an iCubed Organization. It is our vision to create an ongoing anxiety or well being monitoring system that will help promote a healthy environment in which the pursuit of breakthroughs in innovation and creativity is not only embraced but also flourishes.

The mission of Master's Academy & College has always been to create a breakthrough model of education and share it with the world—that is, to become *Imaginal.* The purpose of Master's, as with this book, is to create Hope in the lives of others who are fed up with an obsolete system and who see a better way forward but may not know how to bring it to fruition. This has been our vision, our BIG WHY. May you find yours, and those with whom you can join in this critical moment of transforming the system of education so that HOPE and JOY can be brought to *Imaginal* leaders, teachers, and, especially, children—the future *Imaginal* leaders of our world.

Epilogue: I Have a DREAM

"This is our hope. This is the faith that I go back to the South with. With this faith we will be able to hew out of the mountain of despair a stone of hope. With this faith we will be able to transform the jangling discords of our nation into a beautiful symphony of brotherhood. With this faith we will be able to work together, to pray together, to struggle together, to go to jail together, to stand up for freedom together, knowing that we will be free one day."

- Martin Luther King, Jr.

What will the future look like? How does anyone know? We don't have a crystal ball that magically shows us the future. The future is coming and there is nothing we can do to stop it. The question is, can we create the future we want or do we inherit someone else's? Either way it will come, but will it be by design or default?

I am purposefully calling the Epilogue "I have a DREAM" rather than "I have a VISION." A dream needs to be grandiose, it needs to inspire people, it is not a clearly defined future that can be designed and built using the creation process. Some aspects of the dream are clearer than others, and may be approaching the executable vision stage. Nevertheless, I will call this my dream for the future.

Martin Luther King Jr. gave one of the most electrifying speeches in modern history back in 1963, in which he laid forth his dream for a country where all people were treated equally regardless of race. In a similar spirit, I have a dream for education. It is a dream not just for one nation, but for all the nations of this world, and especially for the children of this world.

To my fellow educators, I have a dream for you.

Let us not wallow in the valley of despair, I say to you my friends. [31]

And so even though we face the challenges of today and tomorrow, I still have a dream, a dream deeply rooted in the fundamental belief that all children are created equal and deserve the best possible education we can create.

I have a dream that educators around the world will rise up, not as a force of discontent, but rather as a voice of hope that the system of education can and *WILL BE* transformed much like a caterpillar is transformed into a butterfly.

I have a dream of an army of *Imaginal* educators willing to pay the price for freedom, freedom from the demands of a system that no longer serves the most precious of our society.

I have a dream of students around the world being set free from the bondages of a system that favors the few and banishes the many to lives of also rans.

I have a dream that in those places where educators have been downtrodden, they will be lifted up to a place of honor and esteem.

I have a dream that the vast majority of students succeed, that learning becomes the JOY it always was intended to be.

I have a dream that all teachers will experience a release of JOY not yet seen by the many who labor in this noble profession.

I have a dream that one day Profound Learning will be experienced from Canada to Argentina, from Nigeria to Ethiopia, from Singapore to the outback in Australia, and throughout all of this earth. I have a dream!

With the eyes of faith, I see a glorious future in which every child is given what he or she needs to succeed in their world. I have hope for the future and with faith I pull the future into the now.

With faith we will be able to transform education; we will create a better future for those we LOVE, the children of this world.

I have a dream that one day every valley shall be exalted, and every hill and mountain shall be made low, the rough places will be made plain, and the crooked places will be made straight; "and the glory of the Lord shall be revealed and all flesh shall see it together." [32]

What We SEE and WANT to CREATE

The dream we have for the future of education is for schools and children around the world. You can only build that which you see working through the eyes of faith. As I previously wrote in Chapter 8, you see your future with your imagination and hope brings that future back to your now. These two working together generate the faith to act towards your vision, to begin the creation process. Here are some aspects of the future that we see and will actively moving towards by faith.

We See ... Academic Excellence for Vast majority

We see a system in which learning excellence is achieved by the vast majority and not the few, as is the case in most systems of education. We have demonstrated at Master's Academy and College, by focusing on real systemic change and not focusing on test scores, that academic excellence by many is possible, where *four out of five* students attain "excellence" standing on provincial achievement tests versus the provincial average of one out of five.

We believe in the giftedness of all students around the world, and that the system is the primary cause of performance variation. Therefore, we must transform the systems of education into that which will enable the release of brilliance and joy of all students. We have proven that by changing the system we can change its output. But who will take up the challenge of the dream of transforming education? We need thousands of *Imaginal* leaders in every country to join us in making this dream a reality.

We SEE ... a Global Network of schools for Profound Learning

Our dream includes creating a global network of schools, districts, states and countries that share a common goal of transforming education as described in this book. In Chapter 12, we outlined a number of strategies for how we can grow this movement, which include,

- Transforming the factory model of education with breakthrough technologies that enable the personalization of student learning thus releasing JOY and BRILLIANCE.

- Transforming teacher practices with a comprehensive professional development plan focusing on the future and not the past.

- Processes for school district transformation.

- Establishing Centers for Transformation to spur regional and national transformation.

The personalization of education should not be interpreted as a sterile delivery of educational content using technology. What we envision is an environment full of human interaction of teachers, students, outside collaborators, and technology supporting the orchestration and management of personalized learning.

We see ... a Global Learning Adventure Exchange

In Chapter 13 we introduced the concept of a Learning Adventure Exchange. A Learning Adventure can be thought of as a highly engaging unit of study comprised of numerous smaller experiences and steps. Teachers create these Learning Adventures using the Profound Learning Orchestration System (PLOS) and can share them with other teachers within a district, state, or country, provided they share the same or similar Journey Maps .

Our vision is to create a Global Learning Adventure Exchange allowing teachers to share Learning Adventures with other teachers around the world. To allow this kind of ubiquitous exchange we will need to map each nation's or state's curriculum to a common reference Global Learning Map. Over the next few years as Profound Learning spreads throughout the world we will see the development of Journey Maps specific to each country. With our research team we will be able to map all of the national curriculums to a Global Learning Map that will enable Learning Adventures to be shared by teachers around the world. This kind of project is somewhat analogous to the ENCODE (ENCyclopedia Of DNA Elements) project, through which scientists are defining the 20,000 genes that make up the human genome. Analogously, we will be creating the Encyclopedia of Curricular Elements resulting in a Global Learning Map.

This Global Learning Map will help developing countries to shift their curriculum to a more modern one. Transforming education will require us to create a more agile curricular framework that can more readily adapt to the rapidly change world we live in. Our Global Learning Map will provide an international standard that will help elevate all national curriculums. This is a mammoth project for which we will be looking to partner with organizations that would share this dream with us.

The sharing of Learning Adventures between teachers will elevate the learning of all students particularly in those countries that have challenges with a sizable number of teachers below the poverty line. Just imagine when learning is being orchestrated by great Learning Adventures developed by great teachers. These teachers can now learn the curriculum along side of their students, and school jurisdictions can assign these Learning Adventures to their teachers as part of their overall professional development requirements.

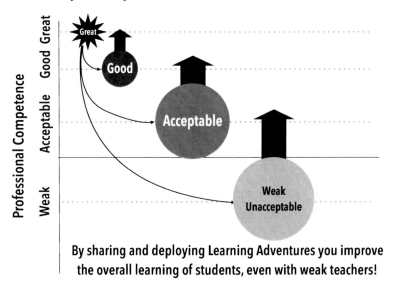

By sharing and deploying Learning Adventures you improve the overall learning of students, even with weak teachers!

Figure E.1: Transforming Student Learning with Learning Adventures

We envision a grass roots movement of entrepreneurship with educators who can create high quality Learning Adventures and sell them in the Learning Adventure Exchange. This is analogous to the marketplace Apple created with its App Store. Great teachers can supplement their income as well as being a part of transforming education around the world.

We See .. a Technology Explosion

It goes without saying that we are living in a time of massive technological advancements and a connected world unimagined just a few years ago. The growth of mobile devices and connectivity to the internet is experiencing explosive growth as shown below. [33]

- 2011: 5.8 billion mobile subscriptions - 85% of earth's population.
- 2017: internet connectivity will increase 3000 times.
- 92% of the world will have mobile coverage.
- 2011: 85% of all the phones sold have internet access.
- Internet will be available to 93% of the world's population.
- 2020: 50 billion connected devices.

We are preparing for a world in the near future in which every student will have access to affordable web-enabled tablet technologies that will give them access to systems like the Profound Learning Orchestration System.

We See ... Transformation of Teacher Practice

As with any movement it is imperative that the practitioners are well trained in the core precepts and practices that will elevate the movement to the global stage. In Chapter 13, we introduce the Profound Learning Odyssey for Teacher Transformation (PLOTT). It is our vision to train and certify one million teachers around the world as Master Teachers of Profound Learning. Whether this takes five years or 10 years is dependent on how rapidly we can scale our training programs.

We will be using both online training and live seminars to equip teachers in the practices of Profound Learning. But to scale to one or more million teachers we will need to transfer the live training to our Centers for Transformation located throughout the world.

We See ... a Network of Centers for Transformation

We envision at least three levels of Profound Learning Centers for Transformation.

1. The Global Center for Transformation will be found in Calgary, Canada where the Profound Learning Research Team resides. The Global Center will continue to refine the practices of Profound Learning and the training required by teachers around the world

2. Several International Centers for Transformation (ICT) will be strategically positioned throughout the world. The role of the ICT is to become the hub from which satellite centers are spun off. An ICT could have as many as 7-12 regional Centers of Transformation in its network.

3. Regional Center for Transformation (CT) will be responsible for training and equipping teachers, and providing support to local districts and schools.

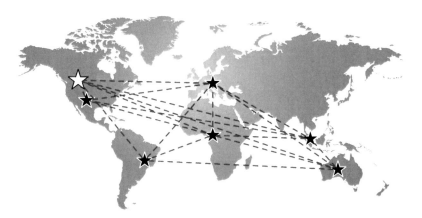

Figure E.2: Network of Centers for Transformation

If we were to establish seven ICTs, each having twelve satellite CTs making a total of thirteen for each region, then we would have a total of ninety-two CTs, including our Global Center. If each center were to train 2,000 teachers every year, then it would only take a few short years to train a million teachers. There are over 65 million teachers in the world today, so with a million teachers we are only scratching the surface of what needs to be done. I am confident, as the church leaders began building by faith the Santa Maria del Fiore Cathedral in Florence in 1296, knowing that at the time it was impossible to complete the dome, that when the time is right the pathway to reach millions of teachers will be made known to us.

I understand that mathematical modeling and reality are two different things. But what this kind of vision modeling does is create hope, and with hope and imagination comes faith to begin the creation process. The actual rollout may not look anything like the model presented here, but it doesn't matter. What matters is that there is a viable pathway to the fulfillment of the dream. The creation process will yield enough current reality feedback to inform the best path to take at any given time in the future.

We See … New Systems and Tools

Schools and other organizations needing to transform from a caterpillar to a butterfly need new tools and a system to support this transformation process. Many businesses die as a result of their inability to transform themselves fast enough in their highly competitive landscape. Education, however, continues to propagate its obsolescence, which is concealed under the guise of new reform initiatives that seldom, if at all, address the real problem.

I see the development of tools and systems that will help support districts and schools to become *Imaginal* Organizations and navigate the transformation process effectively. Years ago we piloted a process of gaining feedback on teacher anxiety levels (See Appendix F) as we were transforming our learning model. We will develop software systems that will enable us to gather this kind of information on an ongoing basis to help *Imaginal* administrators lead their school successfully through the "pupa" stage of incremental transformation.

We need to develop new management software tools and systems that support the pursuit of *breakthrough* goals rather than the mere management of those that maintain the status quo. An early version of such as system has already been prototyped at Master's. (See Appendix E.)

Our DREAM and Creative Tension

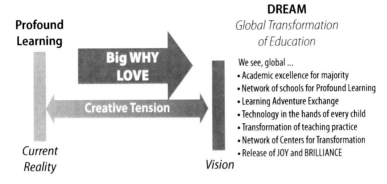

Figure E.3- Our DREAM and Creative Tension

The energy to engage in the creation process is generated from the structural tension between your current reality and the vision you hold for the future. This tension is resolved by creating the future you deeply desire. It is the love you have for your creation that elevates you above your circumstances, and enables you to proceed despite the challenges you face. You will find a more detailed description of our current learning model in Appendix A: Profound Learning.

System Transformation Laws and Principles

The following system principles support our global dream of transforming education.

Metcalfe's Law

Metcalfe's Law states that the value of a network increases with the square of the number of nodes in the network. If there are 5 computers in a network, then the value is 25. If there are 1000 computers in a network, then the value skyrockets to 1,000,000. It is this effect that has created the tremendous value of social networks.

In 2011, what was popularized as the Arab Spring uprising, activists were able to use social media to mobilize millions of people in a very short period of time in protest against their government. Eventually, several long standing governments were toppled by the power of a network that grew exponentially.

By applying Metcalfe's Law to our global vision for Centers of Transformation, even though our network may grow from 5 centers to 100 by a factor of 20, the value or the power of the network increases by a factor of 400.

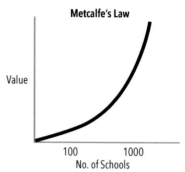

The power of the network grows exponentially with every new school that joins!

Figure E.4 - Metcalfe's Law

Table E.1- Metcalfe's Law and Global Transformation

No. of Centers for Transformation	Increase	Metcalfe Value (n^2)	Power of Network
5	0	25	0
25	5X	625	25
50	10X	2,500	100
100	20X	10,000	400

Shadow System

Previously in Chapter 9, I mentioned the question I was asked at the West African Education Transformation Conference in Lagos, Nigeria. The very first question I was asked was, "How can we implement Profound Learning in our schools if the government doesn't recognize the need to change the model of education?"

Beyond challenging the basic assumption of powerlessness I laid out the proposition of creating an education Shadow System. Before explaining this further, the table that follows contains some key terms:

Table E.2- System Terminology

Term	Definition
Schema	• Set of rules that reflect regularities in experience • Enables system to determine the nature of further experience and make sense of it • Rules are coded in a form of symbols, mental images, numbers, chemical interactions
Dominant Schema	• Set of rules, beliefs, assumptions, mental models • Models agent's perception of current primary task • Drives performance of currently perceived primary task • Expressed as routines, habits, procedures, theory in use, customs, rituals
Recessive Schema	• Part of the overall system schema that is not utilized in the Dominant Schema • Often takes the form of dreams, vision, imagination, ideas for improvement or innovation, metaphors, analogies, fantasies, myths, espoused theories • Can be employed in play • Challenges some portion of the Dominant Schema
Legitimate System	Defined By: • Policies • Hierarchical structure • Formal schema (informal) Goal: • Produce primary task • Surprise free • Controlled environment • Predictability and comfort
Shadow System	• Informal network of people possessing the same Recessive Schema • The goal is to transform or change the Legitimate System • Could be by destructive or constructive means

With these key terms in mind, here's what I mean when I stated that we could become a Shadow System. The Legitimate System in most countries is defined by schools that are accredited by the government, namely public and private schools. These schools usually operate government sanctioned curriculum and more or less have the same Dominant Schema or pedagogical framework that drives the factory model of education. There are those *Imaginal* schools that envision a different kind of system, for which they have adopted a Recessive Schema, and have become a Shadow System.

For years, Master's Academy and College was a Shadow System within the Legitimate System of Alberta Education. We were obligated to deliver the Alberta curriculum and thus were inspected regularly, but the *how* of curriculum delivery—namely, our Profound Learning model—was open for our Recessive Schema to interpret. The fact that we far exceeded the provincial norms with our student performance has now given us a platform to share our learning model with others. We chose the constructive route in the challenge of the Dominant Schema of the Legitimate System, which is the route that Martin Luther King and Mahatma Gandhi chose for their revolution. In today's world of viral marketing, a social revolution can spread much quicker than those a few decades ago. Further, the pervasiveness and low cost of technology enable this revolution in education to gain acceptance and adoption much quicker than in days gone by. We can now train millions of teachers online instead of having to conduct live in-person workshops and seminars.

Tipping Point

In any country, regardless of its standard of living, schools can form their own informal network around a vision of transforming education. Our strategy is to establish Centers for Transformation that will work with early adopter *Imaginal* schools of Profound Learning to facilitate the formation of their Shadow System Network.

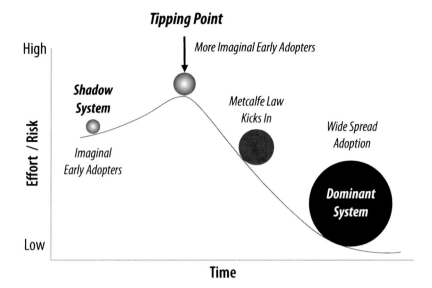

Figure E.5 - Tipping Point for Transforming Education

A tipping point will be reached when the level of effort to transform schools begins to diminish as the resistance from the Dominant System diminishes. Research has shown that the tipping point in social systems is around ten percent of the population.

Scientists at Rensselaer Polytechnic Institute, in New York, have found that when just 10 percent of the population holds an unshakable belief, their belief will always be adopted by the majority of the society. The scientists, who are members of the Social Cognitive Networks Academic Research Center (SCNARC) at Rensselaer, used computational and analytical methods to discover the tipping point where a minority belief becomes the majority opinion. The finding has implications for the study and influence of societal interactions ranging from the spread of innovations to the movement of political ideals.

"When the number of committed opinion holders is below 10 percent, there is no visible progress in the spread of ideas. It would literally take the amount of time comparable to the age of the universe for this size group to reach the majority," said SCNARC Director Boleslaw Szymanski, the Claire and Roland Schmitt Distinguished Professor at Rensselaer. "Once that number grows above 10 percent, the idea spreads like flame."[34]

This should bring hope that transforming education is doable. We need to reach a critical mass of 10% of the educators to create the tipping point, and once this happens Metcalfe's law will kick in and the shadow system will begin to gain rapid acceptance.

The Greatest of these is LOVE

This book has laid out the case that if we truly want to transform education then we will need *Imaginal* leadership at all levels of the system. We need *Imaginal* politicians, *Imaginal* administrators, *Imaginal* teachers, *Imaginal* students, *Imaginal* parents, and *Imaginal* business leaders. Incremental improvement at best can only lead to the reformation of a system; what is needed is a *new system* of education that can only be created through *IMAGINAL* TRANSFORMATION.

One of the purposes of this book is to create hope in the hearts and minds of the others that real transformation can happen; that we are not relegated to an endless cycle of failed initiatives attempting to reform what's obsolete. But hope itself is not sufficient—we need a compelling vision of the future which can only be seen with one's imagination. And the combination of hope and a vision of the future creates faith. With faith we can begin to take action to create the future we love. The Bible states, "These three remain, faith, hope and love and the greatest of these is love." The power to rise above one's circumstances, to engage in doing the impossible, comes from the love the creator has for the creation. Love is what empowers people to take on the giants in the land and to go where no one has gone before.

The courage, passion, initiative, perseverance, and persistence required for the journey of transforming education come when you can find your Big WHY, the first key to *Imaginal* leadership. When you understand that the calling of your life is connected to the vision you carry to advance the cause that is bigger than yourself, that is tied to a purpose that truly is meaningful and is synchronous to who you are, then there is nothing that will stop you from seeing that vision fulfilled. Steve Jobs best sums all this up in his 2005 commencement address at Stanford University, of which the following is an excerpt from his address,

I'm pretty sure none of this would have happened if I hadn't been fired from Apple. It was awful tasting medicine, but I guess the patient needed it. Sometimes life hits you in the head with a brick. Don't lose faith. I'm convinced that the only thing that kept me going was that I loved what I did. YOU'VE GOT TO FIND WHAT YOU LOVE. *And that is as true for your work as it is for your lovers. Your work is going to fill a large part of your life, and the only way to be truly satisfied is to do what you believe is great work. And the only way to do great work is to love what you do. If you haven't found it yet, keep looking. Don't settle. As with all matters of the heart, you'll know when you find it. And, like any great relationship, it just gets better and better as the years roll on. So keep looking until you find it. Don't settle…. Your time is limited, so don't waste it living someone else's life. Don't be trapped by dogma—which is living with the results of other people's thinking. Don't let the noise of others' opinions drown out your own inner voice. And most important, have the courage to follow your heart and intuition. They somehow already know what you truly want to become. Everything else is secondary."*

It is our love for what our vision will do for the children of the world that will drive us to CREATE and GROW the future we want. Go and transform your world by BECOMING IMAGINAL!

Dream big dreams. Nothing is impossible to them that believe.

Appendix A: Profound Learning

Profound Learning Today – Our Current Reality

The first generation of the Profound Learning model has emerged. It is no longer a future hope, but a current reality.

Profound learning can be viewed as a 'three layered cake' with student Ownership as the foundation layer, followed by Mastery, and, finally, Innovation and Creativity. The icing on the cake, and between all the layers, is Who I'm Becoming, which is the intentional development of students with Future Ready skills.

Figure A.A.1 - Profound Learning Model

The foundation layer of student Ownership is achieved by implementing Quality Learning tools and processes, as pioneered by David Langford. A powerful learning orchestration system with tracking tools enables students to track their own learning, thus creating a greater sense of ownership and awareness of what needs improving with their own learning.

The second layer is Mastery, by which the vast majority of students attain a high level of academic proficiency by engaging in meaningful learning experiences, self-assessment vis-a-vis benchmarks, differentiated instruction and formative assessment throughout the learning process. Learning adventures are designed taking into account the latest neuroscience.

The third layer is Innovation and Creativity. The design-based learning context seeks to identify a scenario in the future, the THERE, that is quite removed from the constraints of the current condition, the HERE. Students become designers of the future by envisioning the future first, which creates the tension between the THERE and the HERE that will drive the design process. Since students are designing relevant solutions, the process is driven by their own passion that helps to create a sense of purpose and vision.

The icing not only on the top of the cake but well spread between each of the layers is Who I'm Becoming, the intentional preparation of students with Future Ready skills.

We have developed the Profound Learning Orchestration System (see Appendix C) with advanced design tools, guidance, and integration of the Learning Code and latest neuroscience enabling teachers to design and deliver rich learning adventures. (See Appendix B for a detailed description of J.W. Wilson's Learning Code.)

Two Dimensions of Who I'm Becoming

Preparing students to be Future Ready involves the development of the whole person and not just a student's academic abilities. "Who a Student is Becoming" has both an inner dimension and an outer one.

Inner Dimension

The inner dimension of a student's life is all about his or her IDENTITY; who a student is on the inside. The deepest sense of a person's identity is all about character, values, beliefs, principles, talents, gifts, and personality.

We have focused attention on identity formation as informed by Erik Erikson's psychosocial development theory, John Bowlby's Attachment Theory and brain science. Summarily, Erikson's theory traces the development of one's identity through a series of tasks, that, when successfully completed, result in a healthy personality and meaningful engagement with others. The atmosphere of acceptance and empowerment is key to the development of healthy attachment bonds and a sense of security, which then impacts academic performance. More so, according to recent advances in neuroscience, the experience of empathic and attuned connection facilitates neural integration necessary for personality development, character formation, principled-centered living, and adoption of pro-social values.

As students progress into the higher grades, they are introduced to the the 5 Keys to Becoming *Imaginal*. We begin to build the capacity of students to be visionary, designers, and creators of their future within the context of a secure and enriched school environment.

Outer Dimension

The tending and nourishment of the inner ground of identity inevitably leads to the flourishing of the outer and more visible embodiment of Future Ready skills or capacities. Embedded in the teaching and learning of these Future Ready capacities are principles critically derived from Piaget's cognitive developmental theory, Vygotsky's social development theory, and Wilson's brain science of learning. Creating the conditions for students to grow cognitively that are developmentally appropriate, gaining knowledge through collaboration with teachers and peers, and attending to students' brain health is paramount. This integrated approach to teaching and learning expands students' capacity to integrate, improve, innovate, and invent that will prepare them to meet the challenges of the future with a posture of curiosity, creativity, and confidence.

The outer dimension of who students are uniquely becoming is all about what they are capable of doing, namely their Future Ready skills. In our elementary school the focus is on developing students as Master Learners to become principle centered:

- Leader
- Independent Worker
- Collaborative Worker
- Quality Producer
- Life Long Learner
- Critical and Creative Thinker

As students progress into the older grades they will more intentionally begin developing their four Future Ready Capacities: to integrate, improve, innovate, and invent.

Four Future Ready Capacities

Since the creation of the iCubed Model by Tom Rudmik in 1999, teachers at Master's Academy and College have been implementing strategies that develop the creative and innovative capabilities of students. The following are the four Future Ready Capacities:

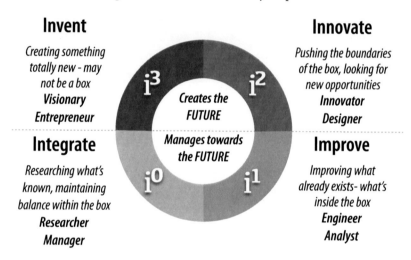

Invent
Creating something totally new - may not be a box
Visionary
Entrepreneur

Creates the FUTURE

Innovate
Pushing the boundaries of the box, looking for new opportunities
Innovator
Designer

Integrate
Researching what's known, maintaining balance within the box
Researcher
Manager

Manages towards the FUTURE

Improve
Improving what already exists- what's inside the box
Engineer
Analyst

Figure A.A.2 - Four Future Ready Capacities

Teachers intentionally design learning experiences that incorporate roles and skills from one or more of the four Future Ready capacities.

Becoming Future Ready

Developing students' inner identity and outer Future Ready skills is as important as academic preparation. The Seven Habits of the Master Learner are integrated into the elementary experience, which starts in Kindergarten. The four Future Ready Capacities to Integrate, Improve, Innovate, and Invent and their corresponding roles and skills, are integrated as the student reaches the higher grades in elementary, and junior and senior high.

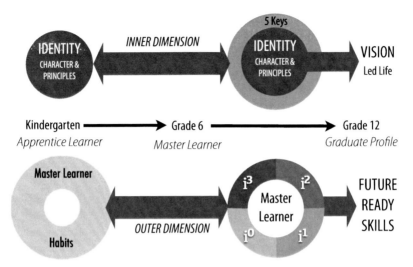

Figure A.A.3 - Who the Students are Becoming

5 Keys to Becoming an Imaginal Leader

In addition, we have developed specialized junior/senior high school programs. One of these programs is i.d.School (Innovation & Design School) which is designed to equip students to become leaders, history-makers, visionaries, and innovators and inventors. The program focuses on students becoming designers of the future and the five keys to un-locking the *Imaginal* leader within everyone—those who have the passion, courage and vision to engage in the process of seeing the invisible and doing the impossible.

Appendix B: The Learning Code

What is the Learning Code?

The Learning Code is simply: "The special code in your DNA that must be switched on before learning, memory formation, and behavioral change can take place."

- The key finding is that, in each one of us, there is a genetically implanted Learning Code.

- Before we can create learning systems that produce profound memory formation and lasting behavioral change in learners, we have to understand that we must first create biological change at the level of their genes and neural tissues.

- Failure to recognize that learning, memory formation, and behavioral change are biological processes is the primary cause of our existing learning problems.

Changing Your Paradigm

The information presented in what follows will forever reframe how you look at implementing learning and behavioral change within your organization.

Having a more scientific perspective allows us to grasp that our past learning/training failures have not been a result of our lack of effort. No, our past learning failures have arisen because we did not know that this Learning Code existed, and that we lacked the knowledge to turn it on.

Unfortunately, the reason we experience such high levels of learning failure in our scholastic and corporate institutions is that our existing educational methods fail to effectively turn on this Learning Code.

What is Learning?

When we have a firm understanding of what learning actually is, and how it is best facilitated, it is much easier to develop learning programs that work. From the scientific perspective, the ultimate goal of any learning/training program must be to create genetic and neurological change in the biology of the learner. Why?

Because without genetic and neurological change in the learner, there can be neither long-term memory formation nor lasting behavioral change. The reason most learning programs fail to live up to our expectations is that our learning process has not been based on science; we have focused on getting learners to pass tests rather than on creating biological change within them.

The Scientific Explanation:

Temporary vs. Long-Term

The main reason we experience such a high level of learning failure is that virtually all traditional 'stand and deliver' and e-learning programs only create low level electrochemical change within the neurons of learners. This low-level change is called temporary potentiation. Temporary potentiation fails to create genetic change within a neuron.

Long-term memory formation can only occur when higher-level neurological and genetic change occur in a neuron which leads it to change its shape and function. This high-level biological change in a neuron is called *long-term potentiation.*

Why do learners forget 85% of what a typical training/learning program presents? Because most learning/training programs are designed in a way that creates only *temporary* potentiation in a learner's neurons, not long-term potentiation.

In order to be successful, the goal of any learning/behavioral/training program must be to create long-term potentiation in the neurons of learners. Once you make the paradigm shift from designing learning programs that get learners to memorize facts and pass tests, to developing learning programs that create biological change, a whole new world of learning/behavioral change opportunities opens up.

The Learning Code Check List:

1. Meaning

Have you turned on the learner's Meaning Network? Meaning is the Holy Grail of learning. Why? Because before new information can be efficiently selected into long-term memory, it must first stimulate a group of neurological structures called the "Meaning Network." If you do not switch on the brain structures that code for personal meaning, you cannot create the neurochemical climate that allows neurological change and profound learning to occur.

2. Hebbian Learning Rule

In building learning programs, are you implementing the Hebbian Synaptual Learning Rule? This rule has become the basis for the 21st century neuroscientific view of how learning, memory, and behavioral change take place. The Hebb rule maintains that, 1) in order for learning to occur, large diverse numbers of neurons in the brain must be activated at the same time, and 2) this simultaneous activation produces the neurochemical/genetic changes in neurons, which leads to long term memory formation. If your learning programs are ignoring the Hebbian Synaptual Learning Rule, they will not be successful.

3. Habituation

Have you caused neurons in a learner's brain to enter habituation? (A Psychological process in humans and animals in which there is a decrease in behavioral response to a stimulus after repeated exposure to that stimulus over a duration of time.) Habituation is the down regulation of receptor sites that make a neuron much less sensitive to environmental input. Habituation occurs when there is too much sameness in a presentation. When a course is designed in a way that causes habituation in a learner's brain, long-term potentiation in a neuron is severely compromised.

4. Two-Phase Learning Programs

Have you implemented a two-phase learning program? One phase to purposefully create Temporary Potentiation in learner's neurons, and a second stage to create Long-Term Potentiation. Most learning programs treat learner's brains like vessels, trying to fill them up with as much information as possible, as fast as possible, with stand and deliver, video and e-learning programs. We then test them to make sure what we poured in remained. But from a scientific perspective, all we have done is activated and measured the Temporary Potentiation of their neurons. And we all know this strategy has not been as successful as we would have liked. To ensure that neurons make the jump from Temporary Potentiation to Long-Term Potentiation, (the basis of all long-term memory formation and lasting behavioral change) a very sophisticated and scientific follow-up learning phase must be designed and implemented.

5. Mirror Neurons

Have you stimulated the Mirror Neuron ("Mirrons") System? This system forces us to imitate certain languages, behaviors, and emotions of others (positive and negative), even if we don't want to. Activating the Mirror Neuron System is one of the fastest ways to create behavioral change in individuals and organizations. If your organization is engaged in change management, to be successful, you must positively activate the Mirror Neuron System. Like the activation of Alpha Dog genes (discussed below), the stimulation of these brain areas by apprenticeship/mentorship programs can dramatically accelerate learning and change management programs.

6. Concept Before Details

Have you implanted firm concept networks in learners' brains before details are introduced? Details do not float about in our brains like many loose butterflies; they must physically attach themselves to strong preexisting neurological structures before they can be remembered. Concept networks provide 3 main benefits for detail acquisition.

- They provide the stable landing pad upon which details can attach themselves.

- The neurons and connections that make up concept networks supply mass, which then acts like a magnet, attracting details that resonate with them.

- When concept networks are activated, they demand large amounts of glucose and oxygen, which, in turn, provide the fuel necessary to power the neurochemical processes that allow details to be incorporated into long-term memory.

Any learning program that does not follow the "Concept Before Details" rule will limit Long-Term Potentiation in the neurons.

7. The Four Stages of Learning

Have you activated all four stages of the learning process? New research demonstrates that learning and memory do not occur "bam" all at once in one fell swoop. Instead, in order to form lasting memories, your brain must go through four distinct stages of the learning process, marked by the alternating dominance of different neurotransmitter systems. Limiting learners' exposure to less than the four stages of learning hinders the stimulation of the correct neurotransmitters at the correct times, which, in turn, dramatically limits the efficiency of memory formation.

1. Information

2. action

3. feedback

4. integration

Most traditional stand-and-deliver, video and e-learning programs only activate the first stage (the Information stage) of the four-stage learning process. The root of much learning failure can be traced to the inability to activate the other three vitally important stages of the learning process.

8. Over-Packing Working Memory

Have you over-packed working memory with too much information? This is one of the greatest sins of traditional learning/educational programs. Working memory has very limited space. These areas are very small, about the size of tiny thimbles in your frontal lobes, and coordinate with the hippocampus in the limbic system. Most learning programs fail because they continue to pack information into working memory before evoking the process that allows this information to flow back into the learner's long-term memory banks, which are located in the rear associative areas of the brain.

9. Maintaining Monoamines

Have you depleted the learner's mono aiming system (Dopamine, serotonin, Neuro-epinephrine)? Most traditional learning systems over-stimulate the mono aiming system to such a point that these valuable neurons become depleted. Why is it important not to deplete this monoamine system? Because without the correct levels of dopamine, serotonin, and neuro-epinephrine, neither working memory nor long-term memory can be efficiently formed.

10. Quick Adaptors

"If we take a serious look around us, the entire fiction that the IQ ... fully measures intelligence rapidly disintegrates."
    —Daniel Goleman, author of *Emotional Intelligence*

Are you designing your learning programs to mold workers into Quick Adaptors? As management guru, Peter Drucker pointed out, we now live in a Knowledge Society. All the knowledge in the world is estimated to be doubling at the phenomenal rate of once every 18 months. In 7 years all the knowledge in the world will be doubling at the incredible rate of once every 35 days! This makes it clear; knowledge has become the most valuable asset any worker can possess. The new sciences are forcing trainers and educators to embrace more biological and evolutionary views of intelligence. The research is revealing intelligence is not best described by our scores on tests, instead it is now best defined as your ability to successfully adapt to the rapidly changing world around you. Learning programs based on the Learning Code apply principles that help learners become not just good test takers but also Quick Adaptors. It is critical to do this so that companies can be staffed with the kinds of individuals who can add to organizational productivity

11. Beta Too Long

Have you kept the learner's brain in focused forced-attentive wave states, called Beta, for too long a period? Research reveals that when we are in focused attentive states, the brain produces a very specific neurochemical signature, which in turn can be measured non-invasively by EEG (electroencephalogram) readings. Beta wave forms are fast frequency, unsynchronized brain waves that range from 13 to 30 cycles per second. When we keep learner's brain in these high frequency brain wave states for too long, Long-Term Potentiation is again severely compromised.

12. Intrinsic vs. Extrinsic Motivators

Have the correct balance of extrinsic and intrinsic motivators being implemented into the learning program? Most learning systems rely too aggressively on extrinsic motivators (passing tests and qualifications). This creates what is called a Neurological Downshift in learners' brains. What this means is that the blood flow, which contains vital glucose and oxygen, shifts from the upper and frontal neurocortical areas of the learner's brain down to the lower more ridged limbic and reptilian brain areas. This shift in blood flow not only compromises working memory but also negatively affects one's ability to manage and relate to others. This Downshift affects their capacities for empathy, compassion, big-picture thinking, and planning for the future. To keep learners' brains in the most effective learning state, the correct balance of intrinsic and extrinsic motivators must be maintained with the goal of keeping their upper and frontal cortical areas engaged.

13. Access Triggers

In your training presentation, have you implanted conscious and unconscious Access Triggers? These Access Triggers are tags, which, when implanted at an initial learning session, can be reactivated in secondary followup learning sessions and automatically stimulate neurons prompting them to make the jump from temporary potentiation to long-term potentiation. Often, trainers and educators do develop follow-up learning programs. But failure to design follow-up programs with well-defined Access Triggers implanted within them is a primary reason why 85% of the information presented in most training programs is forgotten within a few short weeks.

14. Novelty

Has novelty been strategically implemented into the learning/training session so that neurons are pulled out of habituation, thus increasing the attention and focus of the learner? It is important that when novelty is activated, it is not purely for entertainment value. Whenever possible, novelty must stimulate the learner's Meaning Network. We will show you how to implement the "Red Tree" strategy of novelty implementation, so that your learners will remain engaged throughout the memory formation and behavioral change process.

15. Orchestrated Alpha and Theta Time

Have you implanted Alpha and Theta wave form time into learning sessions? Like a fresh flower bud, newly learned information is very fragile. Precious information placed into working memory must be cultivated before it can become a hardy part of your long-term memory networks (sleep). To allow information in working memory to flow back into our long term memory banks, the brain must drop into spindles of the synchronized and slower frequency alpha (8 to 12 cycles per second [cps]) and theta (4 to 7 cps) brain wave states, otherwise Long-Term Potentiation will be impeded. In addition to facilitating long-term memory formation, these slower brain wave states have three other main advantages:

- They promote the protein synthesis that provides the construction of the physical structures of learning.

- They produce the brain wave rhythms that allow for heightened creativity.

- They replenish the aminergic system so that when we reenter the information, action, and feedback stages of learning we are more focused and attentive.

16. "Hot" Networks and Wrapping

Have you fired up "hot" networks in learners' brains in order to get them to remember information that previously held no value to them? As we all know too well, often what we want learners to remember has no value or meaning to them. Trying to get learners to remember what they consider valueless is a very, very difficult task. When preexisting networks that code for novelty, or what we find personally meaningful in life, are turned on and firing, they become what we at the Advanced Learning Institute call "hot." Once these networks are "hot", information that the learner has not previously valued can be wrapped into novel and meaningful stimuli so that it can more easily become a permanent part of the learners' long-term memory structures.

17. Blowing Magnesium Plugs Out

Have you created a learning environment where Magnesium plugs will be blown out of specific receptor sites prompting Long-Term Potentiation? A critical element of long-term memory formation is fulfilled when the brain's most abundant excitatory neurotransmitter, called glutamate, floods the brain and binds to a very special receptor on neurons, called the NMDA receptor. Normally, an NMDA receptor on an individual neuron is blocked by a magnesium plug. But if glutamate attaches to the NMDA receptor at the same time the neuron is being simultaneously stimulated by other neurons at other receptor sites, glutamate is able to blow the magnesium cork out of its NMDA socket. One way to look at this process is that the magnesium plugs act like boosters holding their power in reserve until an extraordinary response is required to remember special, important, and meaningful information.

- Kinesthetic
- Tactile
- Taste/smell
- Visual
- Audio
- Spatial

18. Immediate and Intense Feedback

Have you implanted immediate and intense feedback into your learning programs? The definition of feedback is any process where the result of your action serves to continually modify your future actions. Many memory researchers consider the following to be the most important discovery about learning and feedback: The more immediate and intense the feedback from an individual's actions, the more effective the learning; and, the converse, the lower the intensity and the longer the lag time between an action and feedback from the environment, the weaker the learning. Today, we know that the expression of the genetic code itself is dependent upon loops of feedback between an individual and his environment, and that without the right kind of feedback, learners will lack the production of enough dopamine, neuro-epinephrine, and serotonin to create efficient working and spatial memory formation.

19. The 11 Biological Intelligences

Have you designed the learning program to access the 11 Biological Intelligences of learners? To ensure the survival of the human species, evolution has selected genes that produce a limited number of general brain designs. These plans provide each of us with a primary modality in which we prefer to learn and adapt to our world. At The Advanced Learning Institute we call these learning modalities "Biological Intelligences." The evidence from brain imaging reveals that the brain areas that house our individual Biological Intelligence have more neurons and neural connections. Also, when we engage in specific tasks these Intelligence brain areas receive more of the brain's energy in the form of glucose and oxygen than other brain areas. Because of these factors, the most efficient way for us to learn new information is to have it delivered to your preferred biological intelligence. This is because accessing our primary intelligence helps commence the neurological cascade that is the basis of long-term memory formation. While there are conceded to be more than 11 Biological Intelligences, we emphasize the stimulation of the most common ones as follows:

- Linguistic

- Mathematical

- Emotional - internal

- Emotional - social

- Musical

20. Alpha Dog Genes

Have alpha dog ("follow the leader") genes in the learner been activated? Learning environments can be created that will activate specific genes in specific brain structures in such a manner that learners in training sessions will pay heightened attention to the presenter. When this learning environment is created, information that the learner believes will support his or her surviving and thriving will more quickly be logged into long-term memory. Like accessing the Mirror Neuron System, if your organization is engaged in change management, you must activate Alpha Dog genes in those whose behavior you are endeavoring to change. It is also important to note apprenticeship/mentorship programs accelerate change management implementations because they activate the Alpha Dog genes.

21. We Learn Through Selection Not Instruction

"Looking back into the history of biology, it appears that wherever a phenomenon resembles learning, an instructive theory was first proposed to account for the underlying mechanisms. In every case, this was later replaced by a selective theory."
　　—Niels Jerne, Nobel Laureate

Is your course being designed on the counterintuitive principle that all learning and neurological change occur through the process of selection and not instruction? Any learning system that fails to embrace this scientific principle will be inefficiently designed. From the fields of molecular biology, genetics, and neuroscience we are discovering that our previously held beliefs are off the mark. We learn though a selective process not an instructive one. At the Advanced Learning Institute, it is our sincere belief that this scientific concept will have a more profound impact on accelerating learning speed and increasing the joy of learning than any other previous learning advancement. Failure to understand this vital tenet of learning keeps us trapped in the world where painful and inefficient learning systems dominate.

22. Optimal Learning Stress

Has the course been designed so that Optimal Learning Stress is created? Low levels of learning stress actually help increase long-term memory formation. Yet extended or high levels of learning stress severely compromises long-term memory. How? Research shows that when stress levels are too high, or elevated for too long (just 20 minutes), the stress hormone cortisol impacts neural function by opening up a Pandora's Box of complications, such as the creation of neural tangles, the atrophy and withering of neural connections, and even the death of neurons, thus severely depressing long term memory formation. Excess stress also affects workers effectiveness by setting up a condition called a Neurological Downshift. (See Extrinsic vs. Intrinsic Motivators for explanation.) The stress levels in learning programs must therefore have the right amount of stress injected at the right times in order to accelerated learning to the maximum level.

23. Balance of Linearity and Complexity

Does your course design have the right balance of linearity and complexity? The new sciences are revealing that the brain's main job is to make order out of chaos. (Consider that your brain right now is processing literally billions of bits of data.) We now find that higher-ordered conceptual understanding can come about only after the brain experiences enough new input such that its existing neural order breaks down. (Similar to building new muscle mass) This breaking down of the existing physical order in the brain is often experienced by the learner as chaos or confusion. Yet, this untidy mental state is the rich soil from which higher-ordered conceptual thinking can arise (our "aha" moments). But, there is a danger in introducing too much complexity too quickly, for this can create a toxic learning environment. That is why there must be a delicate balance between linearity and complexity in any training/educational program in order to create profound learning and behavioral of change.

24. Real World Experience

Have you incorporated real world experience into your initial and secondary follow-up learning phases? Real experience is the fastest and most efficient way to access the Learning Code. Real world experience can increase the neurotransmitter activity necessary for the formation of long-term memory by as much as five hundred percent. From an evolutionarily biological view point, the idea that we can get organisms—whether they be amoebas, mice or men—to effectively learn in small rooms by just talking to them, having them watch a video or do e-learning programs far away from the natural world is a very new concept, indeed. Ever since lightning hit the primordial ooze 3.5 billion years ago, genes and nervous systems of all organisms have learned by moving through and getting rich feedback from real world environments. The genes and brains of learners are pre-set by evolution to learn most effectively in real world environments. Learning programs must take advantage of this genetic predisposition in order to maximize long-term memory formation. The reason that games and simulations are such efficient forms of learning is that they have the ability to mimic real world experience.

Consider the reasons experience is in fact the best teacher:

- At this point in human evolution, the brain centers that support linguistic processing are not mature enough to support learning solely through language.

- While experience automatically stimulates approximately 95 percent of all neurons that provide the massive neural firing that is the basis for all longterm memory in the brain, verbal presentation in general fires only 5 to 20 percent of neurons.

- Experience enhances working memory formation by stimulating the all important monoamine system by up to 500 percent.

- Experience naturally allows for the creation of personal meaning where no meaning previously existed.

- As we move through time and space, real world experience builds large spatial maps that provide substantial neurological structures upon which new information can easily attach itself.

Appendix C: Profound Learning Orchestration System

The Profound Learning model of education supports a blended approach to learning, which means that student learning has a variety of interactions with the teacher, other students, community members as well as technology. The Profound Learning model is not some kind of method in which a self-paced student sits in a cubicle behind a computer screen all day. The Profound Learning Orchestration System (PLOS) approaches learning from a vastly different perspective than traditional Learning Management Systems (LMS), which are primarily about delivery of content and assessment, and managing users using technology. Our philosophy is about creating rich and engaging learning adventures, which can be thought of as a larger unit of study containing many smaller learning experiences. The PLOS is used to orchestrate processes within the learning adventure where students accesses different kinds of learning content, either with or without technology. Our approach is to create learning adventures that can be personalized to the individual learner. The learning adventures designed within the PLOS can be implemented in the classroom without any available technology for the students—the teacher simply prints hard copies of the learning itineraries and corresponding capacity maps.

The following are some core structures that were created in PLOS that support the personalization of learning for students and teachers. The same system that orchestrates student learning can be used for teacher professional growth plans.

Journey Map

The student journey map lays the foundation on which all of the other PLOS components derive their meaning. The journey map is the entire learning journey of the student, usually found in the state or national curriculum. The curriculum is reduced to the essential learning elements that are entered into the journey map by grade, subject, unit, and strand. Knowing what is the essential learning in the curriculum is significant, since the majority of teachers simply teach from the textbook thus relying on the textbook writers to determine what is essential learning.

As students progress along their continuum of learning, the journey map is updated on a continuous basis upon successful completion of learning experiences. This process provides a high level of accountability that the student has both engaged and mastered the required curriculum.

Learning Adventure

Once the creation of the Journey Map has been completed, the teacher is ready to design the Learning Adventure. A Learning Adventure is like a unit of study, but on steroids. The role of the teacher is to design a sequence of engaging learning experiences that will cover the essential learning found in the journey map at a deep level of cognition. A Learning Adventure with its numerous experiences should be designed to be inter-disciplinary, pulling essential learning from numerous subject areas. Teachers will design the quality expectations or benchmarks that will enable students to self assess, whether or not they have met the learning outcome requirements. The system is designed to support formative assessment in which the teacher assigns various validation points throughout the Learning Adventure.

All Learning Adventures are easily configurable and customizable to meet the need of having differentiated experiences for various groups in a classroom.

When the teacher has completed the design of the Learning Adventure with its many experiences, he or she will have created a Learning Itinerary, a roadmap, that will help guide the students through the next weeks of their Learning Adventure. The system will also automatically generate a Capacity Map, which is described in what follows.

Capacity Map

The student Capacity Map is a multi-disciplinary subset of the Journey Map that is generated by the PLOS. The Capacity Map contains all of the essential learning that is being covered by the Learning Adventure. Students will self assess the depth of their learning using various metacognition scales, such as Bloom's Taxonomy of Thinking. Student self assessment provides the teacher with immediate feedback to gaps in learning and provides opportunity for immediate intervention in closing them.

Profound Learning Orchestration System

The Profound Learning Orchestration System (PLOS) enable:

- Teachers to easily translate the national or state curriculum into the Journey Map format.

- Teachers to use easy tools to create rich and engaging multi-disciplinary Learning Adventures.

- Teachers to create a "Who I'm Becoming" map which identifies both personal habits and FUTURE READY skills that are to be developed within a Learning Adventure.

- Learning Adventures to be customized to meet the needs of students and groups of students.

- Students to self-assesses their learning using higher-order meta-cognition scale, such as moving from understanding to application to mentoring others.

- Students to progress in their learning—both personally and in skill development—through our evidence-based tracking system.

- Teachers to track the progress of each student in his or her learning, who I'm becoming, and skill development allowing timely support when needed.

- Students to acquire long-term retention of essential knowledge, through our patented knowledge-transfer capability.

- Learning experiences to be integrated with the latest neuroscience, resulting in the biological change necessary for deep learning and behavioral change to take place.

Appendix D: Imaginal Transformation Workshops

We have designed processes and workshops in which leaders create a bold vision for a NEW system of education and thus become designers of the future for their schools, district and nation. For example, the *Imaginal* Transformation Workshop is a three day process of discovering, defining, and designing your FUTURE. *Imaginal* leaders learn how to incrementally pull the future into the now, and how to lead transformation with their key stakeholders. This process utilizes the Five Keys to Becoming *Imaginal* in a practical experience resulting in a customized transformation roadmap that the organization can take away.

A typical workshop is laid out as follows:

1. **Discover**: Your Compelling Vision of the Future - Designed to take teachers outside of their current comfort level, enabling them to see the future in a totally new way as follows:

   - Exploring the world of massive change.

   - Discovering some of the key trends that are shaping the world we live in.

   - Learning how to use the Open Principle to deal with Judgment, Cynicism and Fear.

   - Understanding the emergence of a compelling vision of the future.

   - Recreating your organization's primary purpose and discovering your Big WHY.

2. **Define**: What is the Real Problem? Participants in this stage will:

   - Use system tools to make explicit their current condition (Here).

   - Further refine their compelling vision of the future (There).

   - Discover a gap between the Here and the There that will drive the creation process for system transformation.

   - Be introduced to the vision deployment matrix.

3. **Design**: Transformation Plan – This final stage closes the gap between the There and Here. You will:

- Learn how to become an *Imaginal* leader and architect a culture that embraces the vision for transformation.

- Achieve alignment to vision and practice.

- Develop proactive strategies for when the system pushes back.

- Establish strategies for professional development.

- Be introduced to technologies that will enable you to customize student learning.

- Design an implementation plan.

Appendix E: 10 Characteristics of an iCubed Organization

1. Complex Adaptive System

A school as a Complex Adaptive System consists of a number of stakeholders interacting with each other according to schema; these are written or unwritten rules, beliefs and assumptions that everyone carries in their mind that define the organization's primary purpose.

Our brain is constantly sensing the environment for new information and responding to it as prescribed by some very strongly scripted rules, filters or mental models.

Two key aspects must be evaluated if we are to realize our vision for breakthroughs in learning. First, do our mental models enable us to see breakthrough opportunities? And, second, what should we be sensing that previously has been hidden in the background noise that may have a profound impact on our future? The Theory of Complexity presents the novel concept of the Butterfly Effect, which states that a very small influence in the environment, such as the flapping of butterfly wings, can begin a series of events that eventually may result in a hurricane. An iCubed Organization is constantly sensing information both inside the organization and outside that could lead to breakthroughs.

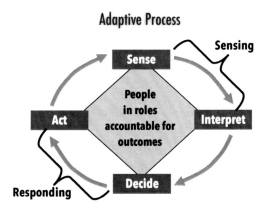

Figure A.E.1- Adaptive Process of Sensing

The underlying worldview from which the iCubed model has emerged is that organizations are more like living organisms than machines. The traditional mechanistic view of the world, from which modern command-and-control management theory has been derived, clearly no longer works. Only in those systems that are immune from the forces of change and the flood of new information is the future more or less predictable. Therefore, we must deal with the issue of emergence, that is new conditions that have emerged from the complexity of interactions that were neither predictable nor controllable. This is extremely difficult for those individuals who have a high need for stability and control to engage in, which often results in anxiety.

Members within an iCubed Organization are able to leverage this anxiety to drive the creation process resulting in innovation and invention. However, to maintain coherence, effective strategies need to be developed that will coordinate and focus thinking and activities.

2. Clarity

Clarity is bringing situations into focus. Clarity brings confidence to people's actions, lowers anxiety, eliminates mixed messages, saves time and energy, and eliminates fragmentation.

This does not mean an organization must become rule-based or defined by minute detail. Clarity must be with the "big rock" issues of purpose, boundaries, accountabilities and consequences for non-compliance. Empowerment can only function effectively when the boundaries, not the actions, have been clearly defined.

Herb Kelleher, chairman of Southwest Airlines said,

We don't have many rules because I think that rules, in a lot of cases, are substitutes for management. Somebody wants a manual to hide behind instead of evaluating something on its merits.... So we're not going to slavishly follow our remorseless rules.[35]

3. Context

Context is that which surrounds and gives meaning to a situation or event. Leadership addresses the guidance, creation, and shaping of context. It is about giving others an understanding about what they are doing regarding the entire organization—a coherent viewpoint. Leadership is about declaring a viable purpose and scope, defining capabilities, and ensuring coordination of capabilities. Leadership helps to architect a culture that nurtures innovation and creativity. Leadership answers questions similar to the following:

- Why are we here?
- How do we relate to one another?
- What limits our discretion to act?

As an example, I have included Master's organizational context:

1. Mission Statement

Master's mission is to prepare students to be FUTURE READY, which today includes:

A. The Seven Habits of the Master Learner

- Person of Character
- Life-Long Learner
- Independent Worker
- Quality Producer
- Creative and Critical Thinker
- Principle Centered Leader
- Collaborative Worker

B. The Four Future Ready Capacities:

- Integrate
- Improve
- Innovate
- Invent

C. The Five Keys to Becoming *Imaginal*:

- Finding Your Big WHY (Big WHY)
- Activating Your Drive (Drive)
- Seeing the Invisible (Vision)
- Making Visible the Invisible (Create)

- Doing the Impossible (Grow)

2. Vision Statement

Master's Vision is about transforming education from an industrial age assembly line approach to one that truly prepares students for a world of massive change.

Master's vision is to produce Profound Learning: an empowerment model of education that elevates student learning to heights not achievable through traditional command and control industrial age models of education. Our signature is innovation and creativity.

Profound Learning is:

- Exceeding all the current standards and expectations that have been set by provincial and state boards.

- Equipping students as knowledge workers with skill sets that will enable them to succeed in an ever changing world.

3. Signature

Master's signature is innovation and creativity. Master's recognizes that we no longer live in the Industrial age in which conformity, compliance and meeting standards were the desired virtues. We now live in the creative age that places a premium on the ability to think creatively, design solutions that are innovative, and see possibilities where others see impossibilities. This is the competitive advantage our students gain by attending Master's.

4. Reason for Being

Master's vision is to develop a breakthrough Future Ready Model of Education and to share it with schools and educators around the world. Even though Master's carries a vision of making a difference globally, it is predicated on creating value primarily for the students and parents of Master's. Master's is modeling to its students the importance of having a Big WHY—that making a difference is possible and even desirable.

5. Governing Principles

The following fourteen principles are non-negotiable benchmarks for Master's. These principles define the boundaries of empowerment and activities. These are *governing* principles as opposed to guiding principles. Guiding principles may or may not be implemented depending on the discretion of the employee. Governing principles, however, are not optional. Faculty at Master's must be committed to these principles so as to maximize their effectiveness in building the model of learning. The following are the 14 Governing Principles:

1. Our mission to prepare students to be FUTURE READY (which includes the Seven Habits of the Master Learner, Four Future Ready Capacities and Five Keys to Becoming *Imaginal*) will be intentionally integrated into daily instruction and activities.

2. Our values will be intentionally integrated into daily instruction and activities.

3. The role of leadership is to create clarity in context (the organization's Reason-for- Being, governing principles, and accountability structures), and to coordinate commitments (agreed outcomes) in fulfilling our Reason-for-Being.

4. We will always set a climate of mutual trust and respect wherein:
   i) Fear is driven out
   ii) There is no room for shame
   iii) Grace is extended
   iv) Discipline is administered with love

5. Empowerment will be given with a clear understanding of boundaries and expected outcomes within the context of who we are.

6. Pedagogy:
   i) We will always view *all* students as capable of meeting quality benchmarks, where time to learn is flexible and the quality of learning is rigid, thus driving out mediocrity.
   ii) Reward and punishment will never be the pathway to intrinsic motivation. Intrinsic motivation is achieved by bringing a learner to an experience of personal success.
   iii) The learning experience will always be rich and varied, meeting diverse needs within the classroom.

iv) Learning experiences will encourage creativity and innovation.

v) Technology will always be integrated as a learning tool in the classroom.

vi) Assessment will drive instruction.

vii) Assessment will always be a collaborative effort between teacher and student in the following ways:

  a. Assessment will always provide opportunities for reflection, rework, improvement, and analysis.

  b. The focus will be on the learning process and **not** the ranking process.

  c. Alberta Learning curricular expectations will not only be met but also exceeded.

  d. The collection of data using tracking tools will always be part of our problem solving and evaluation process.

7. Conduct will be aligned with the Seven Habits of the Master Learner.

8. We will use the continuous improvement philosophy utilizing quality tools and methods for process improvement.

9. There will be a strong commitment to ongoing training and development of staff/student competency.

10. An environment will be created to encourage innovation and risk taking in the pursuit of breakthroughs in learning.

11. We will always communicate on a "real time" basis key information to various stakeholders.

12. Since the whole is greater than the sum of the parts, sharing and collaboration are essential activities of all staff. Transformation of education is everybody's job; we need each other.

13. We will implement strategies to sense earlier and to respond faster to changes and needs of key stakeholders.

14. We will promote creativity within an environment that intentionally encourages a healthy balance between "clarity and ambiguity," and "structured and unstructured."

4. Continuous Innovation

Creativity is the cornerstone for innovation and invention. An iCubed Organization continuously encourages its adherents to think outside of the box. Designing a culture that embraces continuous innovation and change is an intentional act of the leadership.

Stakeholders are taught how to expose limiting mindsets and how to release creativity from the playing field of the mind. Specific tools and skills to enhance creative thinking are taught explicitly.

Individual as well as group expression of innovation becomes a cultural norm. Exceeding quality standards, as supported by the assessment and learning model, gives recognition to student's creativity. No longer will meeting benchmarks be good enough.

Conflicting Cultures and Schemas

Conflicting cultures will eventually collide

Figure A.E.2 - Clashing Cultures

Breakthrough Thinking

Breakthrough thinking can occur accidentally or at unexpected moments. However, if this were the case most innovations and breakthroughs would not occur. Most breakthroughs happen because of an intentional journey that may have taken years.

Three main components are usually involved in breakthrough thinking. First, there must be a healthy dissatisfaction with the status quo. Something within your world is causing you pain, discomfort, or anxiety, and you want to get rid it. Dissatisfaction is often the catalyst to begin envisioning a different future.

Second, the person must have a strong pull toward something better, such as a dream or compelling picture of the future that is linked to a cause he or she is passionate about.

Thirdly, the person or organization must possess know-how, or at least have the capacity to learn new skills and tools that will enable breakthroughs to occur.

1. Identify Need for a Breakthrough

The first step is to identify an area for which a breakthrough would have significant meaning to you and to others.

- What would happen if this were possible?
- If resources were not an issue could it be done?
- What would it be worth if it could be done?
- What realistically could be spent?
- Do others see the goal as impossible, difficult, inconvenient or discomforting?
- Does this change inspire you and others?
- What level of dissatisfaction would you feel with the way things are if there were no change?

2. Activate your imagination

- Imagine an ideal scenario or a worse case scenario
- Imagine yourself in that scenario
- What would have to change with your present situation?
- Imagine yourself creating that change
- Imagine yourself presenting your breakthrough at a conference

3. Incubation of outrageous dream or goals

- Allow these breakthrough thoughts to incubate
- Build up your faith by continuing to imagine with hope
- Do not try to create the solutions too early in your mind - limiting mindsets may cause you to abandon your dream

- What else do you see in your dream that is related to your break-through outcome?
- Spin off breakthroughs into a schematic or plan.

Typically, success is defined by achieving goals, what you said you would do. There is a tendency to aim low and over-deliver—nobody wants to fail in meeting a goal. This kind of thinking supports incrementalism and the status quo. Instead, be outrageous, reach for the stars. Set outrageous goals and measure success by the result itself and not with how it compares with the initial goal.

4. Tell somebody

There is tremendous power in verbalizing your dream. The following are tips for how to share your dream:

- Be selective about whom you tell—they need to be positive minded people.

- Be passionate when you share, after all this is a breakthrough dream, and, as we learned previously, it is passion that drives your early behaviors not knowledge—that comes later.

- Don't seek for immediate feedback. Instead, ask them to think about it.

- What limiting mindsets will people immediately go to when they hear your dream?

- In presenting your breakthrough mention these limiting mindsets as barriers, albeit which can be overcome. In doing so you defuse the power of those limiting mindsets.

- Each time your share your dream, you hear yourself speaking – this increases your faith.

- Build your dream team with those people who will support your efforts no matter how difficult it may be.

- Take rejection with humility.

- Listen for feedback that will enhance your dream.

5. Write it down and make it plain

Everything is created twice, first in the mind of the creator, then in reality. There comes a time with any dream or goal that it needs to be clearly stated in writing. As in the spoken word, there is tremendous power in placing your dream or outrageous goal on paper. You begin to flush out areas of weakness or gaps. Creating more than one scenario in which your goal can work is very helpful. It is very important that you do not commit too early in the thinking process to one particular solution. This will hinder creativity. Here are some tips when writing out your dream:

- Create your dream.
- Create multiple scenarios.
- Be specific.
- What know-how do I need?
- Increase your capacity: skills, knowledge, emotional intelligence.
- What outside expertise do I need to engage?
- Imagine yourself being Leonardo da Vinci or Thomas Edison.
- Be visual—using images and pictures to communicate your creative thoughts.

6. Act in the Action Zone

All of the previous steps lay the foundation for action. Without action one remains a dreamer. Many people are paralyzed by the fear of failure, and are more concerned with what others think than pursuing a dream or goal that could lead to a breakthrough.

In developing an action plan, one must consider multiple options. This takes time. The chart below shows the results of acting too slowly or too fast, with too few or too many options. The key is to find a balance between reasonable and unreasonable time and risk. Too many people are paralyzed by analysis. (See Figure 11.1 Acting in the Action Zone.)

Flexibility is essential if you are engaged in breakthrough thinking. New information, which is emerging from your action, will cause you to rethink and adjust your course of action. Double-loop learning (deep mental model level changes) must take place or else you will never accomplish your breakthrough. A breakthrough is something that no one else has been able to accomplish; and your ability to do so has every thing to do with eliminating limiting mindsets. You are now ready to engage in the creation process as outlined in Chapters 10 and 11. Your dream as matured into an executable vision.

5. Commitment

A commitment is defined as an agreement between two parties to produce a defined outcome, and to accept that outcome if it meets the agreed conditions. Since an iCubed Organization recognizes the issues surrounding complexity and non-linearity of cause and effect, managing outcomes becomes a vastly different scenario than the traditional Management By Objective (MBO).

Most people view their job merely as set of tasks. For instance, a teacher may say,

My job is teaching grade 7 math. Students come to class and learn on their own using the computer-based math program. My role is to monitor the student's progress and intervene where necessary to ensure everyone is moving at a reasonable pace. I will, on occasion, administer unit tests to assess their learning.

It is easy to define a job by the activities that are involved with it. If, however, we were to view this same job from the standpoint of outcomes and consequences of actions, it becomes much more difficult to define. It may go something like this,

My job commitment is to the following outcomes: All my students will complete the course in the prescribed time period achieving a minimum of 80% on unit tests. All my students must understand all core concepts at a 100% level. Those students that fail to meet this standard will be required to relearn the parts of the unit that are not understood, and will be tested again until the standard has been met. As a class, we will be engaged in at least two continuous improvement PDSA projects that will address various issues, such as whether the amount of time for home learning correlates with student success on test scores. These PDSA projects will be led by students. Each PDSA project will involve at least five different quality tools and five different complex thinking skills. Students will also use a Master Learner matrix that highlights the specific aspects of the Seven habits that are applicable to my class. All students will have met the grade level norm for development of Master Learner characteristics.

Looking at a job in terms of outcomes places it in a whole new perspective. For instance, the person is not in control over all the factors leading to success, which creates a higher level of anxiety and stress. How do I deal with an outcome that is falling short of the stated benchmark?

The natural tendency is to blame the student or someone else, but if we were to assume that vast majority of students, or nearly all, can learn at a high quality level, then we must look at system causes for the outcomes that fall short of the stated benchmarks. We now have a probletunity that calls for a creative solution.

6. Coherence

Organizational coherence happens when a shared vision is ignited with passion and faith. We may have an overall shared vision, yet have a vastly different view of how it is to be implemented or how it may ultimately look. The governing principles will help to define the boundaries for our behavior and actions. Governing principles can be reviewed and modified with only leadership approval. The role of leadership is to ensure that these principles are being upheld on an ongoing basis. This is not to be viewed as a command and control philosophy that is implemented using fear, it is rather a process to create system alignment and constancy of purpose.

Our mental models, the filters we use to interpret reality, need to be in basic alignment. When differences arise, dialogue is needful for deeper double-loop learning to occur. Thomas Kuhn discovered that we don't see something until we have the right metaphor (paradigm) to let us perceive it. Therefore, as a learning organization, we need to continually examine the mental models, assumptions, and beliefs that determine the system structures we build and the behavior patterns we observe. The mental models that create your context can either facilitate or block your ability to see opportunities that may become leverage points.

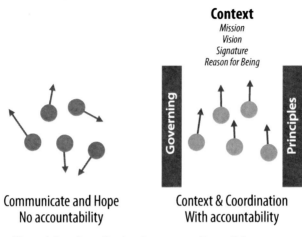

Context
Mission
Vision
Signature
Reason for Being

Communicate and Hope
No accountability

Context & Coordination
With accountability

Figure A.E.3 - Co-ordinating Outcomes to Create Coherence

7. Co-ordination

One of the key roles of leadership in an iCubed Organization is the co-ordination of commitments and activities toward agreed-upon outcomes. This involves designing an appropriate structure for communication and accountability.

Many schools have adopted a Management By Objective (MBO) approach with their faculty. Faculty are encouraged to set annual goals, and their performance is measured against them. Unfortunately, the MBO approach does not lead to breakthroughs, rather it reinforces the status quo and incrementalism. Establishing breakthrough goals requires an entirely different approach, since one of the primary goals of pursuing breakthroughs is the learning that takes place along the way. You gain a much better understanding of the system dynamics when you begin to push the system to perform in a different way. As you gain greater understanding of the system dynamics, you begin to explore possible leverage points for breakthroughs.

Protocol for a Breakthrough Outcome Management (BOM) system is a set of common terms and ground rules that allow two different parties to negotiate an agreement to pursue a breakthrough outcome, which is quite different than an MBO approach. The governing principles provide very clear boundaries for effective empowerment to occur and the

Reason-for-Being pulls everyone in the same direction. Teachers are encouraged to pursue areas of breakthroughs that align with an area of passion. It must be understood that achieving a breakthrough outcome is difficult, and will need to be modified constantly as the process of discovery and innovation unfolds.

Reporting and accountability are important system structures that will facilitate greater understanding of the challenges involved as we pursue breakthroughs in learning. As new understanding is gained, the breakthrough outcome is modified to take into account the knowledge that has been learned. Therefore, one is not managing toward an outcome, but rather pursuing a breakthrough outcome that requires constant revision of the target or end state.

Breakthrough Outcome Management Protocol

Figure A.E.4 - Breakthrough Outcome Management Prototype

This is an early prototype of a breakthrough outcome management system designed to encourage breakthrough thinking and the exploration of possibilities that otherwise would never be considered. To engage in a Breakthrough Outcome Management process, the following steps are recommended:

1. Define a desired outcome, by either offering or requesting one.
2. Negotiate, and agree to the outcome with specific conditions of satisfaction.
3. Perform following tasks:
   - Report its status or completion.
   - Agree to the frequency and nature of reporting.
   - Renegotiate outcome based on new emerging information.
4. Assess the outcome against the conditions of satisfaction:
   - Accept or reject it.
   - And withdraw which can happen at any time.

8. Competence

Credibility is an essential characteristic of a successful organization, which is earned by displaying a high level of character and competency for the role we occupy in the organization. By increasing our competency we also increase our capacity for change.

Figure A.E.5 - Competence

Faculty must have a demonstrable passion for learning and improving personal skills in various areas. A great teacher will never stop learning. Lacking competency or skill is not the issue—doing nothing about is. A person gains credibility by recognizing areas of weakness and developing a personal improvement strategy to gain competency in these areas.

The underlying principle of the Profound Learning model is empowering students through ownership of their learning. This learning needs to be personalized to maximize learning success and engagement of the student. Similarly, the professional development of teachers needs to be personalized using the very same principles and system that supports student learning.

9. Continuous Improvement

The foundation principles of the quality philosophy are summarized in Figure A.E.6. Quality Learning incorporates many of the same tools and processes as used by TQM (Total Quality Management).

It is important to recognize the limitations of using quality improvement methods. First, you must understand how observation may impact your results, which is called the *Heisenberg Principle.* Physicist, Walter Heisenberg, discovered that what we observe is not nature itself, but nature exposed to our methods of questioning. The very act of measuring alters what we are observing. Years ago a teacher at Master's was conducting a PDSA for on-time class arrival. The current condition had an unacceptable level of lates, and the idea was to collect data to help determine some of the root causes for the late condition. The teacher started to collect data by standing at the doorway entrance of her classroom with a stopwatch. She noticed that her late problem seemed to disappear. What happened? Her method of measurement altered the behavior of those she was measuring, hence her data collection became skewed.

Second, organizations do not behave like machines; they behave more like living organisms, hence they are subject to more complexity and non-linearity (causes do not always produce the same magnitude of effect). Therefore, it is essential when using the structured problem solving approach that we are continuously thinking about the whole system and how things are interconnected.

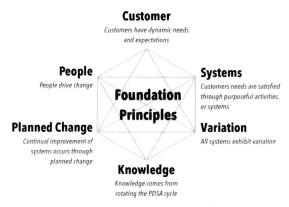

Figure A.E.6 - Foundation Principles of Quality

Starting the problem-solving or improvement process with a structured plan (PDSA) is helpful, and in most cases will reveal information about the system that is very useful in bringing about improvement.

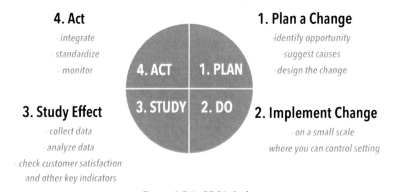

Figure A.E.7 - PDSA Cycle

A. Plan your improvements

Who will handle the improvements? When will they take place? How will you check your progress?

B. Do it

Try out your improvements on a small scale to make sure they work.

C. Study what you did

Compare the Plan and the Do. Did you meet your objectives? What did you do well, and what could be improved? What did you learn?

D. Act to further improve what you did

Document and standardize the improvements that worked. Apply these improvements wherever they would be helpful.

PDSA can be a fast, ongoing way to ensure your processes are constantly improving. Langford International is an excellent source for tools to help facilitate system improvement initiatives.

10. Courage

The final element that makes all of this work is courage. Courageous people are people of destiny. They believe that their life has a higher purpose or calling other than to just make it through life. Courageous people want to make a difference.

The following are attributes of courageous people:

1. They possess a strong faith in what they are doing. Courageous people do not believe that they are going to fail; failure is not an option they dwell on.
2. They posses a deep level of confidence and strength.
3. Setbacks, or apparent failures, are viewed as part of the learning process—a needful thing that keeps them humble.
4. They are willing to admit mistakes and move forward.
5. They are vision-focused, and press on toward the mark.
6. They are purpose-driven. Their lives are committed to a cause that is bigger than they are.
7. They are able to handle criticism. Courageous people have thick skins; they are not negative or small-minded people.
8. They are comfortable with being uncomfortable. The discomforts of facing change are viewed as a necessary part of moving forward. Courageous people are seldom comfortable with the status quo.
9. They are risk takers, willing to try new ideas.
10. They are inventors and creators of new ideas and things.

Appendix F: Teacher Anxiety Audit

2001 Faculty Survey

Please circle your answers

To gain the maximum benefit from a survey one must be able to segment the responses in meaningful groups.   No attempt is being made to identify individuals.

1. How long have you been in teaching?   a. Less than 5 years   b. More than 5 years
2. How long have you been at Master's? a. Since the beginning   b. Hired in the last 2 years
3. Majority of my teaching is in the   a. Elementary grades   b. Middle and high school
4. In which environment do you function best?   a. Structured   b. Unstructured
5. Rate your overall skill level using technology   a. Weak   b. Adequate c. Good
6. Your extra-curricular (teams or clubs) involvement was   a. None b. limited   c. very consuming

Please note:
- 7 on an anxiety questions indicates high anxiety and a 1 indicates a low level of anxiety
- 7 on a discomfort question indicates high level of discomfort whereas a 1 indicates low discomfort or a high level of comfort

Part A: Anxiety and Discomfort

1. Rate your discomfort with the level of clarity surrounding the vision of Master's.
2. Rate your level of anxiety caused by expectations from administration.
3. Rate your discomfort with the pace of presentation of the vision.
4. Rate your discomfort with implementing facets of the vision in your classroom.
5. Rate your level of anxiety with approaching Tom.
6. Rate your level of anxiety with approaching Academy Principal.
7. Rate your level of anxiety with approaching College Principal.
8. Rate your level of anxiety due to attending meetings.
9. Rate your level of anxiety regarding support for at-risk students (academic, be-havioral, emotional, etc)
10. Rate your level of anxiety regarding student behavior in your classroom.
11. Rate your level of anxiety regarding student behavior during non-instructional time.
12. Rate your level of anxiety in implementing the ongoing rework of assignments into your program.
13. Rate your level of anxiety in meeting the variable skill sets in your class.
14. Of the total anxiety you carry rate the proportionate amount caused by parents who challenge your professional decision.

15. Rate your level of anxiety regarding parents in the classroom during the school day.
16. Rate your level of anxiety in teaching staff / servant council children.
17. Rate your level of anxiety when having to confront a colleague.
18. Rate your level of anxiety concerning school-related extra-curricular commitments.
19. Rate your level of anxiety in report card preparation.
20. Rate your level of anxiety in implementing technology into your curriculum.
21. Rate your level of anxiety with regards to the stability of the network.
22. Rate your level of anxiety regarding the use of your classroom by ESSP or by rental groups.

Part B – Satisfaction

23. How satisfied are you with the clarity of communication from Tom?
24. How satisfied are you with the clarity of communication from Academy Principal?
25. How satisfied are you with the clarity of communication from College Principal?
26. How satisfied are you with the level of involvement of the administration with your program?
27. How satisfied are you that your concerns are being heard by administration.
28. How satisfied are you with the level of support you receive when student/parent issues arise?
29. Rank your satisfaction with monthly staff meeting effectiveness (i.e. productivity, time/length, content).
30. Rank your satisfaction with divisional staff meeting effectiveness (i.e. productivity, time/length, content).
31. How satisfied are you with student discipline procedures and guidelines?
32. How satisfied are you with the amount of time spent communicating with parents.
33. How satisfied are you with the amount of time you have to establish social relationships with colleagues?
34. How satisfied are you with the support and inclusion that you feel from your colleagues?
35. How satisfied are you with the effectiveness of your grade teaming partnership?
36. How satisfied are you with the variation in teacher workload?
37. How satisfied are you with the amount of time you spend on lesson planning?
38. How satisfied are you with the amount of time you spend on marking & recording grades?
39. How satisfied are you with your ability to incorporate special events with the delivery of curriculum?
40. How satisfied are you with the compatibility of your job description to your wants and needs?
41. How satisfied are you with the balance between your workload and your personal life?
42. How satisfied are you with the extent to which you feel the Master's vision is being reached on a daily basis?

43. How satisfied are you with the level of understanding of the vision at Master's Academy.
44. How satisfied are you with the technological support / training provided?
45. How satisfied are you with the speed and efficiency at which your technological concerns are being responded to?

Other

46. How frequently have you used your preps to cover other teachers' classes?
47. How frequently have scheduling changes affected your program?
48. How frequently have parents challenged your professional decisions?
49. How many different parents have challenged your authority as a teacher?
50. Rate the level of emotional energy expended in managing behavioral issues.
51. How many students consistently cause disruptive behavior?
52. Rate the frequency of upsetting colleague confrontations.
53. Rate your level of understanding of the philosophy behind the rework of assignments
54. Rate your level of support for allowing rework of assignments

Appendix G: More on Becoming Imaginal and Profound Learning

Becoming Imaginal

We invite you to visit our website and explore various options on how you can take Becoming *Imaginal* to the next level in your life or organization. You will find more information regarding specialized online training programs, keynote addresses, Imaginal Transformation Workshops and consulting services.

Website: www.becomingimaginal.com

Contact: info@plinstitute.com

Profound Learning Institute (PLi)

PLi's vision is to support the transformation of education around the world with its extensive ecosystem of solutions and services. Solutions include the groundbreaking Learning Orchestration System enabling schools to shift the learning from the factory model to personalized learning

Website: www.plinstitute.com

Contact: info@plinstitute.com

Master's Academy and College

Located in Calgary, Alberta, Canada, Master's is the prototype school for Profound Learning founded by Tom Rudmik in 1997.

Website: www.masters.ab.ca

Langford International

David P. Langford pioneered the Quality Learning movement about 25 years ago, and has trained over 40,000 teachers worldwide. The foundation layer of student ownership is achieved by implementing Quality Learning principles.

Website: www.langfordlearning.com

Advance Learning Institute

J.W. Wilson, executive director of the Advanced Learning Institute, has discovered the "Learning Code" after over 25 years of research in the fields of neuroscience, genetics, molecular biology, quantum physics, complexity science, and chaos theory.

- www.crackingthelearningcode.com

Notes

1   Harriet Zuckerman, *Scientific Elite: Nobel Laureates in the United States* (New York: Free Press, 1977).

2   J.W. Wilson, "Cracking the Learning Code" (unpublished manuscript, 2011), Microsoft World file.

3   Michael Fullan, *Change Forces: The Sequel, 1st Edition* (Taylor & Francis, 1999).

4   Ibid.

5   Rachel Redfern, "Are Personality Tests Actually Hurting the Way We Plan Our Futures?" http://www.policymic.com/articles/45551/are-personality-tests- actually-hurting-the- way-we-plan-our-futures/597017.

6   Robert Fritz, *Path of Least Resistance: Learning to Become the Creative Force in Your Own Life* (New York: Random House, 1989).

7   Richard Leider and David Shapiro, *Repacking Your Bags: Lighten Your Load for the Rest of Your Life* (Berkeley: Berrett-Koehler Publishers, 1996).

8   Ben Zander and Rosamund Zander, *The Art of Possibility: Transforming Professional and Personal Life* (Boston: Harvard Business School Press, 2000).

9   T.S.Kuhn, *The Structure of Scientific Revolutions*, 50th Anniversary Edition (Chicago: University of Chicago Press, 2012).

10 Ibid.

11 Ibid.

12 Walter Isaacson, *Steve Jobs* (New York: Simon & Schuster, 2011).

13 Peter Senge, *The Fifth Discipline: The Art and Practice of the Learning Organization* (New York: Doubleday, 1990).

14 Michael Ray, *The Highest Goal: The Secret that Sustains You at Every Moment*, (San Francisco: Berrett-Koehler, 2004).

15 Ben Zander and Rosamund Zander, *The Art of Possibility: Transforming Professional and Personal Life* (Boston: Harvard Business School Press, 2000).

16 Ibid.

17 James Canton, *The Extreme Future: The Top Trends that Will Reshape the World in the Next 20 Years* (New York: The Penguin Group, 2006).

18 C. Otto Sharmer, *Theory U: Leading from the Future as it Emerges* (Cambridge, MA: S.O.L., 2007).

19 Robert Fritz, *Creating* (New York: Fawcett Columbine, 1991).

20 Tim Brown, *Change by Design: How Design Thinking Transforms Organizations and Inspires Innovation* (New York: Harper Business, 2009).

21 Ibid.

22 Tony Fry, *A New Design Philosophy: An Introduction to Defuturing* (Sydney: U of South Wales Press, 1999), 6-7.

23 Diane Jermyn, "Bruce Mau Uses Design to Create Positive Change," *The Globe and Mail*, April 15, 2010.

24 Tony Fry, *Design as Politics* (New York: Berg, 2011).

25 Warren Berger, *Glimmer: How Design Can Transform Your Life, Your Business, and Maybe Even the World* (Toronto: Random House, 2009).

26 Tim Brown, *Change by Design: How Design Thinking Transforms Organizations and Inspires Innovation* (New York: Harper Business, 2009).

27 Richard Leider and David Shapiro, *Repacking Your Bags: Lighten Your Load for the Rest of Your Life* (Berkeley: Berrett-Koehler Publishers, 1996).

28 Ibid.

29 Stephan H. Haeckel, *The Adaptive Enterprise: Creating and Leading Sense-and-Respond Organizations* (Boston: Harvard Business School Press, 1999).

30 Everett Rogers, *Diffusion of Innovations* (Free Press, 1962).

31 King, Martin Luther, *I have a Dream Speech*, Aug 28, 1963, Lincoln Memorial, Washington DC.

32 Ibid.

33 "The mobile web in numbers" December 7, 2011 http://royal.pingdom.com/ 2011/ 12/07/the-mobile-web-in-numbers/.

34 Szymanski, Sreenivasan, Korniss, Chjan Lim, Jierui Xie and Weituo Zhang, "Minority Rules: Scientists Discover Tipping Point for the Spread of Ideas," July 25, 2011, http://news.rpi.edu/luwakkey/2902?destination=node/38887.